THE OCCUPATION OF JAPAN:

THE GRASS ROOTS

The Proceedings of the Eighth Symposium Sponsored by
The General Douglas MacArthur Foundation
Old Dominion University
The MacArthur Memorial

7-8 November 1991

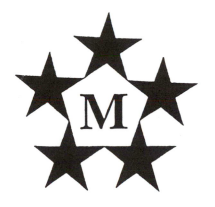

Edited by
William F. Nimmo
Old Dominion University

Copies may be purchased from the
General Douglas MacArthur Foundation
MacArthur Square, Norfolk, Virginia 23510

Printed by: BookCrafters, Falls Church, Virginia

ISBN: 0-9606418-7-4

Front Cover - GIs giving frozen treats to children.

TABLE OF CONTENTS

PREFACE

In November 1975, the MacArthur Memorial conducted a symposium, *The Occupation of Japan and its Legacy to the Postwar World*. This symposium was the first of a trio to be held by the MacArthur Memorial, the George C. Marshall Research Foundation, and the Dwight D. Eisenhower Institute of the Smithsonian Institution. The success of this first symposium and its necessarily broad scope encouraged the continuation of conferences, under the Memorial's sponsorship, which would treat more specific aspects of the Allied Occupation of Japan. Since this beginning, seven additional symposia have been conducted.

The General Douglas MacArthur Foundation, an organization dedicated to perpetuate the memory of General MacArthur and the ideals by which he lived--"duty, honor, country"--and Old Dominion University, a state-supported institution in Norfolk, have been added as co-sponsors.

Symposia have been:

"The Occupation of Japan and Its Legacy to the Postwar World" (1975)
"The Occupation of Japan: Impact of Legal Reform" (1977)
"The Occupation of Japan: Economic Policy and Reform" (1978)
"The Occupation of Japan: Educational and Social Reform" (1980)
"The Occupation of Japan: The International Context" (1982)
"The Occupation of Japan: Arts and Culture" (1984)
"The Occupation of Japan: The Impact of the Korean War" (1986)
"The Occupation of Japan: The Grass Roots" (1991)

The purpose of these symposia is to further the knowledge of this important period of history and record the personal observations of those persons who participated in the Occupation. An attempt is made to obtain participants from various countries and with differing viewpoints so that a balanced picture results.

The proceedings of the symposia are published in book form and distributed to selected colleges and universities throughout the United States, Japan, and other countries. Copies are available for purchase through the MacArthur Gift Shop. Those proceedings no longer in print have been microfilmed, a copy of which can be obtained from the MacArthur Memorial Archives.

The following individuals and groups are due considerable praise for their efforts in making this symposium a success. Edward M. Condra, III, director of the MacArthur Memorial, and his staff organized the symposium, performed the many tasks inherent in an undertaking of this magnitude and made the speakers and attendees welcome. Professors Craig Cameron and Chris Szpilman of Old Dominion University were part of the organizing committee, they moderated sessions and in the case of Chris Szpilman, he read the paper of a speaker who was unable to attend. William F. Nimmo not only presented a paper, but was on the organizing committee and edited these proceedings. Susan Wood, administrative assistant of the MacArthur Foundation, prepared these proceedings for printing.

Readers desiring information on the archives may obtain the same by writing the MacArthur Memorial, MacArthur Square, Norfolk, Virginia 23510.

Lyman H. Hammond, Jr.
Executive Director
General Douglas MacArthur Foundation

INTRODUCTION

Much of the recording and analysis of history is aimed at epochal events, centering on persons in leadership positions who were of exceptional importance, ability, or merit. The Allied Occupation of Japan certainly is no exception to this form of historiography. The efforts to reform Japan, with special emphasis on the leadership of General Douglas MacArthur, his lieutenants, experts brought in from Washington and other centers of power, and high-level Japanese officials, have been documented extensively. In all major undertakings, however, it is the people, whether soldiers in the ranks or average civilians in the provinces, who determine the success of the endeavor, especially when implemented in democratic form.

It is for this reason that the eighth and final symposium of the MacArthur series deals with the conduct of the Occupation at the *grass roots* level in the prefectures of Japan. While the previous seven symposia concentrated on the policy issues of Allied and Japanese officials at the highest levels, participants in this symposium focused on the implementation, conduct, local initiatives, and the efficacy of the attempted reforms.

One of the major objectives of this symposium was to learn how SCAP (Supreme Commander for the Allied Powers) policy instructions from Tokyo were carried out at the local level. Allegations have been made in the past that SCAP "did not care to know the results." Harry Emerson Wildes, in *Typhoon in Tokyo*, published in 1954, took the contemptuous view that "Occupationnaires operated on the militarist theory that orders alone were sufficient. Since by definition, MacArthur's directives were invariably wise and disobedience was unthinkable, results could never fail of astonishing success." Wildes even went so far as to draw a "parallel to the satire of Gilbert and Sullivan's *Mikado*: When SCAP said, 'Let a thing be done; it was as good as done and, if it were as good as done, it was done. And why not say so?'"

Other observers have been far more positive in analyzing the Occupation and its results, ranging from "one of, if not the proudest, achievements of postwar American policy" (Herbert Passin) to Kazuo Kawai's conclusion that "the Occupation, for all its shortcomings, must be judged on balance as a magnificent success."

As in the case of earlier symposia, presentations include both scholarly analyses as well as views based on personal experiences. In the case of this last symposium on the Occupation, a larger proportion of the presenters spoke from a personal viewpoint in order to provide insight into conditions at the local level as distinguished from the centers of political leadership. For this reason, some of the speakers represent "a particular view" of the experiences at the grass roots level--not necessarily a scholarly, objective view--which may be at variance with other observations.

As the semicentennial of the inauguration of the Allied Occupation of Japan draws near, it is of keen interest to note the impact of Occupation reforms on the stunning postwar achievements of Japan. Has Japan's success been due to those efforts, or in spite of them? How do the Japanese view the results? What do the American participants think nearly half a century later? Is it possible that, as the years go by, the Occupation is being seen more and more as simply, "Japan's American Interlude," with the long view of history showing a progression of Japanese adaptation to change going back for centuries? All these questions, and many other issues, are explored in the proceedings of the Eighth Symposium of the MacArthur series on the Allied Occupation of Japan.

William F. Nimmo
Old Dominion University

NOTE: At the request of Japanese participants, all names in these proceedings are written in accordance with Western usage: that is, given name followed by family name.

THE OCCUPIER AND THE OCCUPIED

Rinjiro Sodei

RINJIRO SODEI is Professor of Politics and History, Faculty of Law, Hosei University, Tokyo. He holds undergraduate and graduate degrees from Waseda University and received a masters degree from UCLA in 1965. He has conducted extensive research into the Allied Occupation of Japan. Professor Sodei has also served in visiting scholar positions in Mexico and the United States. He was Chairman, Japanese Association for Studying History of the Occupation. Rinjiro Sodei is the author of: *Two Thousand Days of MacArthur*, Chuo Koron-sha, 1974; *They Called us the Enemy: Hiroshima Survivors in America*, Ushio Shuppan-sha, 1978; and, *My Dear General: Letters Written by the Japanese During the Occupation*, Ohtsuki Shoten, 1985. (All in Japanese; the last work also translated into English.)

Let me start with an anecdote. An old lady got on a train at Pennsylvania Station in New York City. A little while later, a conductor came to examine her ticket and he said,

"Madam, your ticket is for Boston, but this train is bound to Philadelphia."

The lady responded rather philosophically,

"Oh, is that so? But does the engineer of this train know the train is heading in the wrong direction?"

We gather here today, not merely to engage in praise and self-congratulation concerning the achievements made at the grass roots level during the Occupation of Japan--although I believe there is much to be praised. Rather we are here, as I understand it, to examine: what took place then and there; what it means to the occupier as well as the occupied; and what both can learn from it. So even if this conference train may be headed toward Philadelphia, I am nevertheless going to Boston.

I am one of the Japanese who were on the receiving end of the Occupation as a mid-teenager growing up in a rural area. Not only did I witness what was going on, but I also have been studying this fascinating subject for some years. However, I am afraid that the current and entire picture of the Occupation of Japan at the grass roots level will never be drawn. Our task here seems like trying to compose a gigantic jigsaw puzzle by assembling each available piece without having the whole picture at hand.

What are these pieces and how do they look? As far as the Japanese side is concerned, they are academic studies, official local histories, journalistic histories, personal accounts, memoirs, and so on. Academic studies of the Occupation on the local level are few in number. Official local histories--like those published by towns, cities, prefectural governments, with some exceptions, tend to treat the Occupation period as no more than a passing episode, rather abnormal and better forgotten. Historical journalism that treats the Occupation does exist but only for a handful of the 46 prefectures which had a Military Government (MG) team--prefectures such as Kanagawa, Chiba, Yamanashi, and Hokkaido. Personal accounts and memoirs by those who were involved with the Occupation are, as a rule, sketchy, shallow, biased, and charged with emotion. Overall, these historical materials on the Occupation of Japan at the grass roots do not make very enjoyable reading.

Why is this so? We all agree the Allied--in fact, American--Occupation of Japan is one of the most successful--perhaps the most successful--military occupations in history. Through the Occupation, Japan was transformed from a semi-feudal and militaristic nation to a modern, peace loving country. The seed for the tremendous economic progress was sown during the Occupation period through various reforms. And the former enemy country is now America's strongest ally in Asia. Still, it seems to me, the Occupation stands in the historical memory of the Japanese people as something of an ambiguous and even awkward experience.

I have come here in search of an answer to this perplexing question. My tentative proposal is try to look at the Occupation of Japan by reexamining each side's image of its counterpart. That is, the view held by the occupier vis-a-vis the occupied should be reviewed by the latter and vice versa. The grass roots level is a wonderful vantage point to do this, because that is where the West and the East really came together. Let me dwell on my side of the story.

Professor Sukehiro Hirakawa of Tokyo University, while a visiting scholar at the Woodrow Wilson Center, happened to attend one of our symposia. Later he had this to say: "The former Occupationnaires gather once every year or so in Norfolk, where the MacArthur Memorial is, and tell the attending scholars about their good old days. I attended the meeting once and, frankly, felt very strange. Why? Because the atmosphere of the meeting was very similar to one of the reunions in Japan of those who were involved with [the creation and management of] Manchukuo."[1]

2

Of course, Professor Hirakawa's analogy is misleading. Although the Empire of Japan claimed that Manchukuo was "A Paradise Based on Just Cause" (*odo rakudo*), in actuality it was nothing but Japan's puppet regime. This illegitimate state was a disguise for Japan's imperial adventure in northern China. The Japanese were invaders and puppeteers there. By contrast, the American Occupation of Japan was an endeavor to reform and democratize the defeated foe. The Americans had no plan to colonize the Japanese archipelago. They were liberators.

I dare say, however, that Professor Hirakawa still has a point. When people believe in their cause and spend their prime time and energy in that endeavor, they can look back happily and congratulate themselves on the wonderful achievement that was made--whether the "cause" was the creation of Manchukuo or the Occupation of Japan. What counts here is one's zeal and devotion.

ZEAL AND QUALIFICATION

Nobody has any doubt about the zeal held by the American Occupationnaires for the task of democratizing Japan. From General MacArthur down to an education officer at the far corner of Japan, they were all charged with a strong sense of mission. Here is an anecdote: There was a lady who rang up her opposite number to inquire: "How many women's organizations have you democratized this month? I've democratized nine so far."[2] This sounds like a cynical story, and perhaps it is. It was told by an English lady journalist who was not quite sympathetic with American efforts in Japan.

Nevertheless, compared to this eager reformer, I am more appreciative of the modesty of Ms. Carmen Johnson, who was in charge of women's issues down in the Shikoku region. She asks herself, "Is it too much to say that a member of Military Government team made an effort to help people at the grass roots achieve democracy?...I do not think so."[3] In a moment we will be hearing from Ms. Johnson herself how her strenuous efforts were rewarded. With her firm, quiet devotion to her mission, I believe Johnson-san was well qualified for her job. However, in the eyes of the occupied people, not every person who served in the Military Government teams was well qualified. Here is an episode.

In Mie Prefecture, a certain Sergeant P was the only education officer in the entire Mie MG team. The following account[4] was written much later by Mr. Sasaki, who was his counterpart, namely, Head of the education section of Mie prefectural government. Mr. Sasaki was a prewar elite insofar as education was concerned, being a graduate of the prestigious Tokyo Higher Normal School. Besides, he had little enthusiasm for the Occupation's efforts for educational reform. According to Sasaki, Sergeant P was a 22-year old high school dropout turned Occupationnaire who was very zealous and demanding and did not mind summoning Sasaki to his MG office several times a day. One day the following exchange took place.

Sergeant P: "Mr. Sasaki, do you know the meaning of democracy?"

Sasaki: "Why, at college my major was educational psychology. Since my student days, John Dewey's *Democracy and Education* has been my favorite reading. Have you ever read it?"

"There was no answer," says Sasaki.

Of course, one could manage the job of education officer without ever having read John Dewey. But it would have been far better for the Occupation and the Japanese people as well if the sergeant had read *Democracy and Education*. I am not saying that there were many mediocre personnel in the MG teams. My only point is that there must have been much variance in the individual capacities of Occupationnaires and the whole thrust of each MG team. And that variance must have made a difference in the achievement and impression of each team.

Now, for fairness, I am going to present an opposite example in the case of the Yamanashi MG team. Captain Ralph Braibanti was in charge of education there for one year and a half. He earned a high reputation among the Japanese bureaucrats. Furthermore, his observations bore fruit in his classic study, made at Syracuse

University, of the administrative aspects of the local Occupation.[5] His scholarship is so well known that it needs no more elaboration here.

Along with Captain Braibanti, Yamanashi praises to this day the name of Ms. Hewlett, who was in charge of welfare on the MG team. Long after the Occupation was over, she was made an honorary citizen of Yamanashi prefecture.[6] Indeed, there still is a saying among the former members of Yamanashi prefectural government that "Yamanashi was lucky, for it had good Occupationnaires."[7] I wonder if Yamanashi was merely lucky, or if there could have been a conscious effort made at the top of the Eighth Army to make the Yamanashi MG team a model one. Perhaps Mr. Jacob Van Staaveren can tell us something about this.

Well, Yamanashi had an excellent welfare officer, but not every MG team had a Ms. Hewlett. In Chiba prefecture, a lady Occupationnaire is remembered not by her achievement but rather by her overzealousness. She demanded that each health center should have hot and cold running water.[8] Her request, or demand, must have been a reasonable one in America. In Japan of 1947, however, it was an impossible dream.

MANY BATTLES TO BE FOUGHT

An Occupation is an extension of war, an operation in which the conqueror, after winning the war, must next win the peace. And in the particular case of the American Occupation of Japan, it must win the battle for democracy. Therefore, the Occupation had to fight many different kinds of peacetime battles--not only the battle for various reforms, but also more prosaic battles for maintaining sanitation and preventing starvation among the occupied people. Helping local governments collect rice and crush black market activities were indeed crucial battles. Each MG team was "the front line" unit in those battles. In order to be effective, MG teams had to resort to the show of force if not actual use of it. They were supposed to be what General MacArthur termed "ambassadors of good will,"[9] but at the same time they had to be tough.

The official history of the Occupation's military phase praises its own accomplishments in the following manner: "The smoothness with which the complicated machinery of the Occupation worked in Japan surprised competent observers all over the world."[10] It enumerates four main factors to be credited for its success. First, "the foresight of Allied high level planning in utilizing the existing Japanese Government and the authority of the Emperor institution."[11] I would not argue about this point.

Second, "the wisdom of the Supreme Commander in solving the complex problems arising from a program designed to transform a totalitarian country into a democracy, by tolerant and humane treatment of a vanquished foe, rather than by punitive measures for past crimes."[12] I would not argue about this point either, except to mention the fact that almost a half million letters, mostly favorable, were written by the Japanese people during the Occupation to General MacArthur and his GHQ--thus proving his utterance that "a unique bond of mutual faith developed between the Japanese people and the supreme commander."[13]

Now, the third factor: "the patience and tact with which Occupation agencies handled a humiliated and defeated people whose national psychology differed radically from that of any western peoples."[14] Here I would like to pose a question: how was this "patience and tact" exercised at the grass roots level? I maintain that the show of force is an ingredient in any military occupation, even that of Japan. One of the threats frequently used by MG teams was this: "Any offender against Occupation policy will be sent to Okinawa for forced labor."[15] We still do not know how many Japanese who were charged with violation of the Occupation policy were actually sent for forced labor in Okinawa. But the sentence was uttered everywhere--and so frequently that if all the offenders actually had been sent to Okinawa, the island would have sunk into the ocean. Nevertheless, the fear was real. To many Japanese people, the Occupation seemed to be an exercise in the application or at least threat--of force.

Of course, MG teams' force was backed up by the legitimate power which derived from the Potsdam Declaration. The Americans were the righteous victors of the "Good

War," and they were carrying out just reforms for the good of everybody, or so it seemed. But didn't the exercise of power beget arrogance? In at least one case, what General MacArthur called the "disease of power"[16] consumed the first commander of Chiba MG team. He was charged with embezzlement, court-marshalled, found guilty, stripped of his rank, and sent home.[17]

The second commander of the Chiba MG, Lieutenant Colonel Calley, was a man of integrity--and very strict. When he found out that Chiba prefecture's achievement of collecting rice in 1946 was the worst in the nation, he blew up. Hurriedly summoning the elderly Governor and his lieutenant, he reprimanded them in these terms: "It's all your fault. You carry rucksacks and collect rice yourself. If you cannot keep up with the Occupation policy, Governor, you will be hanged!"[18] Of course, rice had to be collected. It was needed to feed the Japanese, and the Occupationnaires were helping them. After all, you cannot teach democracy to starving people. But the humiliation felt by the poor old governor was another aspect of the Occupation at the grass roots.

Military Government teams were particularly visible when they were engaged in the campaign of collecting rice, which was called *kyomai*. They always came by jeep. Hence the term *"jeep kyomai"* came into the lexicon of post-war Japan.[19] Similar was *"jeep chozei,"* collection of back taxes by the MG team. For Americans, not paying one's tax is a sign of disloyalty to the country, whereas to the Japanese, particularly in the immediate post-war period where the government had lost most of its credibility, taxes were nothing but a nuisance. Thus, there were skirmishes over tax collection everywhere. A familiar scene involved Japanese tax collectors and MG patrol teams who arrived in a jeep, rushed into the house of suspected tax-evader, and looked into closets or *tansu* (cabinet) for hidden cash or precious items.

The jeep was not only a symbol of America's technology, speed and ingenuity, but also a symbol of the power of the Occupation. And jeeps were everywhere in Japan at the grass roots. Perhaps the Japanese people saw in MG's activity, symbolized by the

"Jeep Chozei," the symbol of power.

5

jeep, more coercion than good intentions or strategic necessity on the part of the occupier. A case in point is the conqueror's maintenance of sanitation.

Maintaining sanitation seemed to be a big concern for MG teams. In the case of Chiba again, the commander kept pushing to set up a Health Section in the prefectual government. But the budget was inadequate for his request. Irritated, the commander uttered the following: "If the Governor cannot set up a Health Section, he should resign." Instead of the Governor, however, somebody's head had to roll.[20]

I still remember a scene in my early high school days during the Occupation. One sergeant used to always visit our school without prior notice. We somehow knew his name was Austin. Sergeant Austin appeared from nowhere, jumped out of his jeep, and rushed to the rest rooms, not to relieve himself but to investigate if the toilets were clean. He never took off his shoes before coming in. That offended us students very much, because we had to work hard every day to clean and even polish the wooden floor. Every time the sergeant made his investigating trip, he left his footprints on the floor to our dismay. But what could we do? Finally, in a way of small revenge, we gave him a nickname: "Benjomin Austin." "Benjo," as many of you know, stands for toilet, and "min" for "let me see."

But, looking back, we should not have given him such a derogatory nickname. Sergeant Austin must have been one of those hard-working, duty-bound, serious, and slightly overzealous Occupationnaires. Because of the efforts made by Occupationnaires like Sergeant Austin, the Japanese people under the Occupation were saved from epidemic diseases which could have consumed them any time. Likewise, one of the experiences that still remains in our memory is being showered by powdered DDT. This was mandatory at railroad stations or large gathering places. We were told that DDT would kill filthy lice instantly, thereby saving us from contacting eruptive typhus. We should be thankful for DDT, but taking its shower was at best an awkward experience.

De-licing

6

INVISIBLE OCCUPATION AND COLLABORATION

These were visible and tangible aspects of the Occupation. At the same time, there was one aspect of the Occupation which was invisible. This was the activities of CIC, or Counter Intelligence Corps. CIC was always there on the back of the Occupation's jigsaw puzzle. According to the official history of the Occupation, *Reports of General MacArthur*, "The Counter Intelligence Service maintained field stations in every prefecture, paralleling MG field stations but concentrating on ultra-nationalist movements, subversion, sabotage, espionage, operations of Japanese or foreign agents, social unrest and agitation, the development of Communism, etc."[21]

By nature, CIC's activities were kept secret or confidential. All its members are bound by law to keep their mouths shut forever. Granted that intelligence is a necessary part of war, one earnestly hopes that someday CIC's activities will be open, so that we will know the Occupation of Japan in its entire picture--its shady as well as open aspects. After all, today we are witnessing the hitherto unthinkable phenomenon that even the notorious KGB files are being made open. Should we demand less from the United States?

Incidentally, the term "foreign agents," as used above, implies agents who acted against the interest of the Occupation. But it was an open secret that each CIC unit employed a certain number of agents among the Japanese. In the case of Chiba, we are told, those agents were "journalists, bureaucrats of the prefectural government, and members of political parties. Their number was around ten or so at one time and they kept sending bits of intelligence information to CIC."[22] It is important to know how these Japanese agents were recruited, and how they served the Occupation regime. We need to know a great deal more about the nature of collaboration at the grass roots level.

When an Occupation is good and just, collaboration is an honorable act and carried no stigma. Because the American Occupation of Japan had such an honorable aim, many Japanese wanted to help, even in the form of volunteering to become agents. Here are two excerpts from typical letters written to SCAP. One is from a lady living in Fukushima prefecture: "Because I am fluent in English, please hire me as America's spy. The world is at peace now, but you never know when people may change their minds. Please utilize me as a hired-hand of America. Beggingly yours."[23] Another example came from a man living in Tokyo: "If you hire me as your agent, I will abandon my mother country Japan, my home, everything. No matter what my friends might say about me, I would not mind at all selling Japan and my fellow Japanese in order to work for the benefit of *shinchugun* (the Occupation troops). Please, by any means, hire me."[24]

With such strong, almost blind, support among ordinary people, it is a small wonder why the Occupation of Japan achieved such a success. In fact, *Reports of General MacArthur* attributes the fourth and final factor for the successful Occupation of Japan to: "the unexpected cooperation of Japanese officials and population, in response to tolerant and intelligent guidance."[25]

Well, since I have already acknowledged such "tolerant and intelligent guidance" in the case of Chiba and Mie, let me say something more about the Japanese populace and officials. Captain Braibanti of the Yamanashi MG team persuaded one able teacher, Mr. Nara, to join their team by arguing that "military government would continue for the next ten years." Two years after Nara joined the team, the MG system was disbanded and he lost his job. In complaining, Nara wrote to Mr. Braibanti who was already back in America fast becoming Dr. Braibanti. His reply was: "Such speedy end of the MG is attributable to the fact that the Japanese are smart and quick to learn democracy. But, sorry for you losing job."[26]

It may be true that the Japanese are smart. They learned democracy very fast, or so it seemed. But in point of fact, it might be that most of the people pretended to accept reforms willingly in order to shorten the Occupation or make their encounter with the Americans easier. Prime Minister Yoshida used to say, "GHQ stands for Go

Home Quickly." To terminate the Occupation as quickly as possible, Yoshida maintains, he followed SCAP's directives as much as possible.[27]

Likewise, on every grass roots level, the Military Government team, a little GHQ, might have been seen by the Japanese people as "Go Home Quickly." This may be particularly true on the part of local officials. In Yamanashi, they say that the Military Government made the prefectural government a bunch of "Yes Men."[28] This was because the people, whenever they felt hard pressed, turned to or wrote to MG team directly and got much quicker results than going through the prefectural government. In this form of duality, power resided with the Americans. Although the official history written by the Occupation maintains that "team commanders were in no sense military governors,"[29] sometimes a commander "behaved like a feudal lord or little king."[30] His MG team acted like a government in power, leaving the prefectural government a matter of form only. Whether the Japanese officials willingly cooperated or just felt compelled to accommodate the occupier is a debatable point and the picture varies in every case. In the case of Mie, a stubborn official named Sasaki seems to have never understood the spirit of the new 6-3-3 school system in which old elitist middle schools were abolished and in their place compulsory, i.e., democratic, junior high schools were introduced. Sasaki was never convinced by the reform, saw all the orders from MG team as "interference," and felt liberated from heavy burdens when the Americans finally left Mie in 1950.[31]

CONCLUSION

There cannot be a good military occupation as such. As General MacArthur acknowledged, "history clearly showed that no modern military occupation of a conquered nation had been a success."[32] In that sense, the American Occupation of Japan was a rare exception. The Americans did not become master and the Japanese became no slaves. But the whole process was not as smooth as the official history claims to be. No matter how righteous the Occupier's cause is, it is human nature to resist what is forced upon one. No matter how the occupier tries to bring something good to the occupied people, more often than not, the latter cannot comprehend it. If it is accomplished with a show of force, people resent it. They don't like to be forced even to be "democratic," for instance. Mr. Charles Kades, the powerful deputy chief of Government Section at GHQ/SCAP, once told me that he objected to this expression of "being forced." He said, "the Japanese were induced to democracy."[33] Mr. Kades may be right, but sometimes, inducement to reforms was conducted in forceful manner in which the potential beneficiary did not really understand.

Besides, democracy is a loose word that can be interpreted in various ways. It may differ between the Japanese specialist in education who was an avid reader of John Dewey and the 22-year old education officer in the Mie MG team. The victor might not interpret freedom as the vanquished did. When the both sides cannot agree, those who have the power have the final say. This is what a military occupation is all about. In such an endeavor as the American Occupation of Japan, the Occupier monopolized power, but they did not have enough time and human resources to realize all its high ideals. Perhaps again Ms. Johnson could tell us about the acute shortage of MG personnel in her vast area of Shikoku region.[34]

But being mighty and righteous, the American tried to accomplish which was rare in modern history: a successful military occupation. History must judge that they almost made it. Nearly forty years after the Occupation ended, many basic reforms have taken root--land reform, labor reform, emancipation of women, a good health care and social welfare system, and, above all, a peace constitution based on fundamental human rights. Looking back, the hardship the Japanese had, or felt they had, to go through during the Occupation was, after all, a small price to be paid for those great benefits.

There has been a new tendency to underestimate the achievements made in Japan by the Occupation. Some say that in that task, "the United States had superficially accomplished its goals,"[35] or that reforms were left unfinished.[36] Of course, the American

Occupation of Japan was far from perfect. There are so many could-have-been-dones and should-have-been-dones in this historic enterprise. But I for one am inclined to appreciate what has been accomplished rather than lament what was not achieved. The bottle is at least half full, and that's enough to make a toast to all those who were involved. Thank you.

NOTES

1.   Sukehiro Hirakawa, *Heiwa no Umi to Tatakai no Umi* (Sea of Peace, Sea of War) (Shinchosha, 1983), p. 227.

2.   Honor Tracy, *KAKEMONO, A Sketch Book of Post-War Japan* (New York: Coward-MaCann, 1950), p. 18.

3.   Karumen Jonson [Carmen Johnson], *Senryo Nisshi: Kusa no Ne no Onnatachi* (The Phoenix Stirs--Japan: 1946 to 1951) (Tokyo: Domesu Shuppan, 1986), p. 226.

4.   Nisaburo Sasaki, *Mie-ken Shusen Hiroku* (Private Accounts Over the Termination of World War II) (Mie City: Mie-ken Kyodo Shiryo Kankoka, 1970), pp. 98-99.

5.   Ralph J.D. Braibanti, "Administration of Military Government in Japan at the Prefectual Level," *American Political Science Review*, 43 (April 1949): pp. 250-275.

6.   Yoshichi Amemiya, *Fusetsu Nijunen: Yamanashi no Sengoshi* (The Stormy Twenty Years: Post-World War History of Yamanashi Prefecture) (Tokyo: Showa Shoin, 1969), pp. 73-77.

7.   Ibid., p. 72.

8.   Hiroshi Yuasa, *Shogen: Chiba-ken Sengoshi* (Post World War II History of Chiba Prefecture: Testimonies) (Tokyo: Ron Shobo, 1983), pp. 109-110.

9.   Douglas MacArthur, *Reminiscences* (New York: McGraw-Hill, 1964), p. 283.

10.   Supreme Commander for the Allied Powers, *Reports of General MacArthur*, vol. I supplement, *MacArthur in Japan: The Occupation: Military Phase* (Washington, D.C.: U.S. Government Printing Office, 1966), p. 230.

11.   Ibid.

12.   Ibid.

13.   MacArthur, *Reminiscences*, p. 283.

14.   *Reports of General MacArthur*, p. 230.

15.   Yuasa, *Shogen*, p. 104.

16.   MacArthur, *Reminiscences*, p. 282.

17.   Yuasa, *Shogen*, p. 106.

18.   Ibid., p. 105.

19.   Ibid., p. 105.

20.   Ibid., p. 110.

21.   *Reports of General MacArthur*, p. 230, footnote 3.

22.   Yuasa, *Shogen*, p. 34.

23.   Rinjiro Sodei, ed., *Haikei Makkasa Gensui sama: Senryoka no Nihonjin no Tegami* (My Dear General: Letters Written by the Japanese to General MacArthur and his GHQ) (Tokyo: Ohtsuki Shoten, 1985), p. 360.

24.   Ibid., pp. 359-360.

25.   *Reports of General MacArthur*, p. 230.

26.   Amemiya, *Fusetsu Nijunen* (The Stormy Twenty Years), p. 76.

27.   Shigeru Yoshida, *Kaiso Junen* (Yoshida Memoir) (Tokyo: Shinchosha, 1957), 1:117.

28.   Amemiya, *Fusetsu Nijunen* (The Stormy Twenty Years), p. 68.

29.   *Reports of General MacArthur*, p. 203.

30.   Yuasa, *Shogen*, p. 97.

31.   Sasaki, *Mie-ken Shusen Hiroku* (Private Accounts), pp. 195-196.

32.   MacArthur, *Reminiscences*, p. 282.

33.   Kades interview in Sodei, *Senryo Shitamono Saretamono* (The Occupier and the Occupied) (Tokyo: Saimaru Shuppankai, 1986), p. 34.

34.   Jonson, *Senryo Nisshi*, p. 221.

35.   Howard B. Schonberger, *Aftermath of War: Americans and the Remaking of Japan, 1945-1952* (Kent, Ohio: Kent University Press, 1989), p. 279.

36.   Daizaburo Yui, *Mikan no Senryo Kakumei: Amerika Chishikijin to Suterareta Nihon Minshuka Koso* (Unfinished Occupation Reforms: American Intellectuals and the Abandoned Idea for Democratization of Japan) (Tokyo: Tokyo University Press, 1989), passim.

WOMEN'S RIGHTFUL EQUALITY: AN OBJECTIVE OF SHIKOKU MILITARY GOVERNMENT REGION

Carmen Johnson

CARMEN JOHNSON served as Women's Affairs Adviser in the Shikoku Military Government Region from 1947 to 1951. She graduated from Northern Illinois University in 1936 and completed her M.A. degree in Adult Education at the University of Chicago in 1952. In addition to her service in the Allied Occupation of Japan, Miss Johnson has been a teacher, Girl Scout Executive, a member of the Women's Army Corps during World War II, executive director of Pi Lambda Theta, and a writer and editor for the federal government. She has published *Senryo Nikki: Kusanone no Onna Tachi* [Occupation Journal: Women at the Grass Roots], Domes Publishing, Tokyo, 1986. Miss Johnson was featured in a 1991 Japanese TV documentary on the history of women's rights in Japan (a videotape was shown during the symposium).

In the familiar fable, five blind men, each feeling a different part of an elephant, could not agree on what the beast looked like. Change the analogy to twenty-five American women's affairs officers trying to explain how they assisted Japanese women understand and begin to attain equal rights given to them by the new constitution. Now listen as one of those women, with help from her journal, describes her elephant.

While a member of the Women's Army Corps, I learned that part of the Occupation force in Japan was called military government and that its members were in direct contact with people in the prefectures. When on terminal leave and still interested in such a position, I wandered the halls of the Pentagon in uniform in April 1946 but found no one knowledgeable about this branch. So a year's contract was accepted as a civilian clerk-typist in Nagoya with the Fifth Air Force. Then behold. When unknowingly I did not first obtain permission from military government to speak to college students, the military government found me.

After my year's contract was fulfilled, I became part of Eighth Army, assigned as combined regional and prefectural women's affairs officer in civil education for the four prefectures of Shikoku Military Government Region. Although the term *military government* appropriately was changed to *civil affairs* in mid-1949, this paper will use the original designation.

Shikoku held a unique place in the Occupation of greatest import to those living there. The British Commonwealth Occupation Force (BCOF) shared the Occupation of Japan with the Eighth Army of the United States. BCOF was responsible for two regions bordering the Inland Sea. Chugoku on Honshu Island held forces from Australia and New Zealand; Shikoku, from Britain and India, most of whom had left before my arrival. Two men from BCOF, whom I knew well, however, remained assigned to American prefectural teams--an Australian warrant officer in Tokushima and an English lieutenant in Kagawa. Simply put, the island, directly under Eighth Army, was unoccupied by troops of the allied forces while I was there. Disadvantages and advantages resulted from this isolation: disadvantages such as lack of information and material from higher headquarters and advantages such as independence to plan programs that needed approval of only the regional commanding officer. Only once was a question raised by SCAP about what was reported through channels of activities of the women's affairs officer.

Shikoku, with prefectures of Ehime, Kagawa, Kochi, and Tokushima, is about the size of Massachusetts and, in 1950, had approximately the same population of four and a half million. Generally speaking, Shikoku in 1947 could be called a small, rural area of great natural beauty, with a conservative air because of its isolated position and resultant limited contacts with the rest of Japan and the world.

I was assigned to the Shikoku Military Government Region headquarters in Takamatsu in August 1947. Apparently they were not expecting me as no housing was available for the lone American woman on the staff. Fortuitously, housing was available in Tokushima, where a team was located, and I was assigned there. The next ten weeks, like the year in Nagoya, allowed me to become familiar with how a team operated before becoming a full member of the regional staff. I participated in activities with the Tokushima civil education officer, a major, and spoke at many meetings we attended. I was invited to speak to thirteen *fujinkai* (women's organizations) to an estimated total of twenty-five hundred--not counting babies. Also, I became aware of many situations apparently common to *fujinkai*, such as the fact that men served as presidents. [MG team members stressed the point that women should serve as presidents, but this change was slow in materializing.]

Three steps were taken soon after my move to Takamatsu on 4 November 1947. I was convinced by then that women and men had little conception of what constituted democratic principles as we knew them and that equality did not exist between sexes. First, a regional press release to Shikoku newspapers explained my position "with Shikoku women to teach them their rights and how to exercise those rights." Second, we requested each *fujinkai,* through prefectural social education sections, to complete a questionnaire we had prepared by 31 December 1947.

12

A third undertaking was attendance at an all-Japan conference of women's affairs officers at Eighth Army Headquarters in Yokohama. Some twenty-five American women gathered on 1 December 1947--a few just arrived in the country and others with months of experience. All knew, of course, that equal rights were clearly enunciated in Article 14 of the national constitution that went into effect in May 1947, a guarantee still sought by women in the United States. "All of the people are equal under the law and there shall be no discrimination in political, economic or social relations because of race, creed, sex, social status or family origin."

During the three days of the meeting, the scope of women's affairs was discussed by women officials from SCAP concerned with activities in which women were involved. Several prominent Japanese spoke, including Mrs. Kikue Yamakawa, head of the Women's and Minors' Bureau, and Mrs. Shizue Kato (former Baroness Ishimoto), elected to the Diet. Two major suggestions were presented by SCAP officials. One: begin to work with women in *fujinkai*, already in existence. Two: encourage associations to be independent of governmental control that, until the end of World War II, operated through federations at every level from the national to the village, directed from the top.

FUJINKAI (WOMEN'S ASSOCIATIONS)

Introductory field trips were taken to all prefectures in December 1947 and January 1948 because, with the exception of Tokushima, American and Japanese personnel and settings were unknown. The subject appropriately was election of officers, as I was already aware that men were presidents of most *fujinkai* and thought they should be replaced by women as soon as possible. The artist on the regional staff produced six large posters that could be seen throughout a meeting room to illustrate the process. This use of appropriate, large posters continued based on whatever subject was being addressed.

How could one American reach perhaps a million women? Experience in Tokushima had shown the futility of meeting with any group that issued an invitation. My work in the United States as a professional with a volunteer organization was the foundation for plans that evolved. At prefectural meetings, the women's affairs officer could explain a process to a group of *fujinkai* presidents, each of whom could, in turn, reach more women--scores, perhaps hundreds. The American could discuss, for example, how necessary for an association was a good constitution. Each president, in turn, could report back to her *fujinkai* and a constitution could be written based on a sample available from the regional office.

Preparatory to prefectural meetings with presidents planned for February 1948, a second press release was issued by the region. In relation to *fujinkai*, "two trends have been noticed that are not in keeping with democratic principles...Federation of women's organizations under the sponsorship of the prefectural officials is premature and unwise...There should be no government interference or connection with women's associations...Two great needs are...the reorganization of women's organizations along democratic lines and the education of women leaders in the ways this may be accomplished." Only almost two years later did my assistant tell me on 21 December 1949 that this press release was known as "Jonson-san's *Sengen*" (Declaration). Although no edict was intended, perhaps some credit should be given to the press release for any positive results toward discouragement of federations and government control.

Plans were then readied for the prefectural meetings at which making motions and voting were explained. Could concepts so foreign to Japanese culture and practice be made understandable and meaningful? Certainly not by just a description. Consequently, a skit was written that used fifteen participants to be picked at random. The little play was then translated and duplicated so each actress had a copy. Parts were then read to illustrate how a motion was made and a vote taken. This highly-successful device, as well as large posters, was used repeatedly to explain principles of democracy.

A second questionnaire given *fujinkai* in December 1948 revealed little change.

Moreover, other problems appeared; two noteworthy. Regular, planned meetings were not customary. Some groups met once a year and some not at all. And because the amount of dues was almost infinitesimal, little money was available for association business or programs. The average, yearly dues for Shikoku were approximately twenty-four yen or seven cents. A disturbing discovery made verbally after questionnaires were tabulated was that "the treasurer is usually a wealthy person. Then if money is needed or there is no money or the money is a little short, the treasurer puts some in."

Obviously, *fujinkai* should be encouraged to meet more frequently and to offer regular programs. The pamphlet I wrote and that my interpreter translated was offered to prefectural social education sections for reproduction and distribution, with the English title of *Planning a Year's Program for an Organization* (and Japanese as *Dantai no Ichinenkan no Puroguramu Keikaku ni Tsuite*). Suggested programs were included for *fujin dantai* (women's organizations in general), parent-teacher associations, and *seinendan* (youth groups).

Another shorter pamphlet, *Discussion - A Technique of Democracy*, was produced soon after because of the lack of organization funds revealed by the 1948 questionnaires. The booklet described the uses of various kinds of discussion groups such as panels that could provide programs with little or no cost.

In August 1948, title and responsibilities were changed when women's affairs officers became assistant civil education officers with added duties. Regular meetings continued, however, with leaders of *fujinkai*. Discussions were based on democratic principles, with a different concept added for each series.

"Some little progress" was noted in my journal when *fujinkai* questionnaires were tabulated for 1949. Plans were being made for meetings, with chosen subjects. In 1949, of the some eight hundred responses, sixty-one percent had a planned program for at least four meetings during the year. Common sense in 1991 suggests this more-than-a-little progress resulted from availability of pamphlets prepared in the regional office.

OTHER GROUPS

Education, labor, agriculture, public welfare, public health, leaders for an association of girls, elected government officials--the women's affairs officer was involved in the activities of all of these groups. While early efforts were with *fujinkai*, other fields were added until relations--albeit some only slight--existed with all. No one could be expert in every field, but assistance could be offered to help women understand their new rights under the law.

Prefectural meetings were held with nurses' associations until an American woman joined the public health staff for the region. Midwives were conspicuous for their relative aggressiveness over clinic and public health nurses.

Conflicting comments were recorded about two prefectural conferences with women members of labor unions.

In the afternoon had sixty-five women from labor unions. They were young, alert, and interested. [March 1949]

My, but it's hard to get a reaction from them! We acted like silly fools but could hardly get a glimmer. I finally experimented and asked a direct question of the women. One just simply refused to even lift her head to look at me. How in the world can we get around that! [July 1949]

Why were descriptions of meetings held within a few months of each other so diverse? Simply because some women took an activist viewpoint while others wanted to get along with the group.

During the 1930s, as totalitarianism replaced any tendencies toward democracy, labor unions were suppressed. After World War II, the labor union movement was encouraged by the Occupation forces; laws were revised so unions became powerful. At

14

the same time, leaders with leftist inclinations began to gain control of some unions. Consequently, the women noted in my March notes may have been of the energetic, aggressive group. On the other hand, many women like those met in July were not active even in unions where most of the members were women, taking little part in labor activities for several reasons. Many expected to work only until marriage; all were brought up to be shy and modest; and chances of a good marriage were materially diminished if they were assertive. Women's sections in labor unions, therefore, were not uncommon, where women devoted time to activities such as the tea ceremony and flower arrangement rather than labor business.

The field of public welfare presented the most problems over the years. Frustrations of the women's affairs officer were due in great part to the policy that only SCAP at the national level could take action with the Japanese to correct violations of their own laws and regulations. Military government officers could call such infractions to the attention of SCAP, through channels. In my experience, no evidence appeared that anything was done to remedy such breaches.

In November 1948, "General MacArthur had ordered the women to join" was the startling reason given by *fujinkai* (women's organizations) leaders for the "compulsory joining of the Red Cross Volunteer Service." But when I tried to pin down the people who complained the loudest, they wouldn't even give their village names. *Fujinkai* leaders were understandably confused because compulsory membership was opposed to what they were told about *fujinkai*. The *sengen* (directive) nine months earlier stated that women "are not compelled to belong to any organization."

Reports to SCAP brought no change in the compulsory joining of a volunteer service "done by order of GHQ" (general headquarters). In November 1949, my journal notes state "women of *fujinkai* also in Red Cross volunteer service here. Same members and same officers. What a mess."

A similar story revolved about *haha no kai* (mothers' clubs). But in this case, information was obtained that enabled us to put together what actually took place, with the Ministry of Welfare the culprit.

Only eight months after our regional directive that women's groups should be voluntary, the ministry, on 13 October 1948, in an instruction addressed to prefectural governors, directed that

> It is desired that *haha no kai* and child guidance groups be formed in your prefecture...In order to conduct a sound guidance of child life, first of all mothers must be informed correctly on how to guide the child's leisure hours, health, nutrition, way of living, and the like. *Haha no kai* will, therefore, be formed geographically. [Instruction No. 693].

The contents of this Ministry of Welfare directive were then included in documents sent by prefectural governors to mayors, town and village headmen, principals of primary and secondary schools, and chiefs of child welfare institutions.

A special report of the women's affairs officer based on this evidence was then forwarded to Eighth Army by the regional commanding officer. The Ministry of Welfare's directive for geographical formation of women's groups by prefectural welfare sections was directly opposed to what women's affairs officers were encouraging.

My assistant gathered evidence about consequences of this directive on a field trip she made by herself in March 1949 to a *fujinkai*. Also to the meeting went "a man from the village office" to establish a *haha no kai*. Her written report told what happened.

> A man from the village office told the members about the aim of the movement. He said, "Women should be mothers not only of their own but also of children in the whole country. From this point of view, you, women in a *fujinkai*, should agree to join the movement."

"It sounds very good, I think," whispered someone.
"Do you agree with it everybody?" asked the chairman.
"How about people in other places?"
"Several organizations have already started."

After a little discussion was held, the constitutions which he had made were distributed, in full speed, the president and other officers were appointed, while all the members were wondering in a dense fog.

Nothing was heard about a change in policy of the Ministry of Welfare relative to *haha no kai*.

WOMEN OFFICIALS

Words of tribute must be paid women officials in many positions who were of inestimable assistance. Handicapped by education inferior to that of men; limited by social pressures to modest behavior; paid inadequate salaries less than to men; ill-equipped or lacking in administrative training and experience; circumscribed by culture and tradition reaching back thousands of years--yet they persevered and achieved while retaining the admirable qualities of Japanese women. To them, after more than forty years, esteem and respect are proffered.

We first met appointed governmental officials in social education sections because beginning efforts were with *fujinkai* whose members were almost all housewives. In time, efforts were extended to include those responsible for guidance of working women--heads of Women's and Minor's Bureaus (W&MB) and home demonstration agents.

As early as January 1948, an all-Shikoku meeting of prefectural officials in social education was held in Takamatsu. At the close, "they expressed a wish to repeat this kind of conference. Feel very pleased from my point of view." Judgment of a later gathering was that "it was very successful. Discussion by them is now extensive and encouraging." As they met for the last time in January 1950, "they said they felt women had changed since I have been here. I wonder if that's really [so]."

The W&MB of the Ministry of Labor was established early in the Occupation. The ministry announced at least three times that the bureau was to be abolished, later changing its mind in large part due to vigorous protests by women's groups. By July 1948, all prefectures had heads. Regular visits were made to their offices and all-Shikoku conferences held in Takamatsu beginning in August 1948. When talking about principles of democracy, one woman "told of a labor union where eighty percent of the ballots cast were blank. She said the Japanese cannot make up their minds how to vote."

The chiefs expressed special concern about young women employed in factories who lived in dormitories where they worked. In the Meiji Period (1868-1912) when young women became factory workers, daughters showed filial piety by allowing their fathers to sell their services as little more than indentured servants.

A basic labor law passed by the Diet after World War II ostensibly corrected one great abuse of the past--the borrowing of money in advance by a farmer for the employment of his daughter in a factory. The story was told that a girl might be "bought" for factory work for possibly Y2,000 (a little more than $5). A young woman on the staff of the region reported that she gave her entire salary to her father, saying "I am one of the possessions of my family."

When the chiefs asked us to include factories in field trips, visits in one prefecture included a match factory that "looks pretty horrible" and two spinning factories. "Particularly interested in the dormitories...Supper at one--sweet potatoes. The menu posted, however, looks fine." Two months later, "our visits to factory dormitories have resulted in activity by Japanese officials...Isn't it regrettable that the visit of Occupation personnel seems to make the Japanese jump when they [already] know something is wrong."

16

During two years beginning in September 1949, conferences on regular field trips were held with home demonstration agents, whose positions were similar to those in the United States with the Department of Agriculture. Both men and women agents were met in one prefecture that month. A man commented that "Japanese women like to work in the fields" so how "can we raise the culture of Japan for farm women?" Later, in personal conversation, the agent said, "Two things are important. 1--lessen the burdens of the farm women and 2--democratize the home. She wants material on the latter about American homes. If the women know that homes are democratic somewhere, they think it is possible, too, in Japan."

Officially, I was the only woman of the Occupation working with women of Shikoku; unofficially, each team eventually included one English-speaking woman to assist the team civil education officer. Experiences of these women were shared on regular field trips and at conferences. Bits of information discussed at these informal meetings were especially helpful--and precious. Two women on the regional staff--assistant and interpreter--were held in highest regard, with gratitude and admiration.

ELECTED OFFICIALS

Meetings with women voted into office were limited and brief. Prefectural boards of education were elected in October 1948, and military government officers actively encouraged people to vote. At one of many *fujinkai* meetings attended, "a woman arrived with a banner across her front and back, complete with a blue rosette at her shoulder. The banner said she was a candidate for the Board of Education and gave her name." Women were elected in Ehime, Kochi, and Tokushima.

Soon after the election on a regular field trip, "I dropped in on the prefectural board of education. One woman's appearance did not impress me. She is an old *fujinkai* leader. [Another leader who regularly attended training meetings] had told me to be sure to tell her to be democratic."

"I was surprised" at the women who attended meetings held in May 1948 for elective officials. "All [were] women in city and village assemblies. They were older. Believe most of them can hold their own with the men any time...Find the women elected a very energetic, talkative group...Those elected to assemblies were vocal and aggressive."

Four diverse quotations from my manuscript, *The Phoenix Stirs--Japan: 1946 to 1951*, conclude this paper.

Although there may still be some skepticism abroad, there can no longer be anyone in close touch with Japanese conditions who has the slightest doubt about the sincere desire of the Japanese to embrace democracy. [Opening sentence of an editorial, "The Technique of Democracy," *Nippon Times*, 13 November 1947]

But some Japanese forms and customs seemed to an American to present obstacles for achievement of the democracy promised in the new constitution. What--if anything--was to be done about: subordination of the individual; the traditional concept that women were inferior to men; hierarchy that put people into positions as inferior, equal, or superior in comparison with others; filial piety that taught duty and obedience to parents and ancestors, and, for wives, to mothers-in-law in particular; the family system; the complex categories into which fell *on* or obligations; and decision making. [From the chapter titled "Unfamiliar Concepts," in my book.]

It takes time to democratize Japan. The way toward democracy lies in awakening our moral sense and by the election of good representatives...But I believe, in some time in the future, wave-rings in the water made by a stone of justice thrown by us will reach the banks. [Letters from a *fujinkai* president in "The Way Toward Democracy"]

Curiosity may have led me to Japan, but desire to assist women in particular was the reason for my long stay. The goal for them was never in doubt--equality guaranteed by law. ["Epilogue"]

National Japanese Women's Week is celebrated by *Fujinkai* (Women's Association) members in Utsunomiga.

SESSION II

THE CONTRIBUTION OF
WOMEN'S ORGANIZATIONS TO THE
GOAL OF THE OCCUPATION:
DEMOCRATIZATION

Helen Hosp Seamans

HELEN HOSP SEAMANS served as an adviser for Women's Higher Education in GHQ, SCAP. She was instrumental in the preparation of long-range policies leading toward equal education opportunities for Japanese women, and organized and conducted the first training course in Japan for Deans and Advisers of Women. Mrs. Seamans graduated from Goucher College in 1923 and received an M.A. from New York University in 1929. In 1950, she was awarded the LHD (Doctor of Humanities) from Goucher College. Helen Hosp Seamans served in numerous posts in higher education in the United States, including Dean of Women at the University of Nebraska; Dean of Women at Bethany College; and, on the headquarters staff of the American Association of University Women. She has published numerous journal articles including, *An Occupationnaire Observes: The Progress of Japanese Women.*

Of all that has been said and written about the Occupation objective in Japan--the democratization of that country--relatively little has been focused exclusively upon the Japanese women during that period. Yet their personal hopes, endeavors and accomplishments held the greatest promise for the creation of the new society that democratization implied for Japan.

Observation of this fact commenced for me, at the very outset of being in Japan, during attendance at a several day Women's Leadership Training Conference, held in Saitama, through the cooperation of SCAP and the local military government. About ninety Japanese women were present. Their purpose in attending was to gain experience in working on a committee and in program planning. The outlining of their problems led into the day's consideration of methods and techniques of leadership, of round table discussion, and committee organization which then were applied by the Japanese women in practice groups.

Some of these practice groups, calling themselves committees, came out with very revealing statements, such as the Education Committee's incontrovertible conclusion: "Fathers should not scold Mothers in front of children." In all its frank simplicity, this statement disclosed, I felt, the desire for new family relationships wherein the wife would have "dignity of person."

The "Agriculture Committee" presented as its recommendation: "Changes in patterns of living." Perhaps no comment is needed except one of sympathetic understanding, for farm women worked longer hours than men, according to the Ministry of Agriculture. Furthermore, the universal custom that young wives are the first in the family to get up in the morning and the last to go to bed at night had a bad effect upon their health, especially during pregnancy and the birth of a child, the Chief of the Women's and Minors' Bureau reported. Also, the feudalistic custom that required women to eat privately after the men had finished meant that many women existed on a meager fare, insufficient for good health.

The "Better Homes and Home Life" committee offered that "Discussion groups be held between mothers-in-law and parents and brides especially." (This was not the only time in Japan I was to hear dissatisfaction with the traditional dominating role of the mother-in-law in the Japanese family system.) The committee's other recommendation dealt with the simplification of weddings and funerals.

The recommendation for the simplification of funerals was spelled out for me sometime later at a similar Women's Leadership Training Conference held in Sendai. There, the Conference members proposed that "all families agree not to pay more than 10 yen per person for attendance at a funeral."

"Do you pay people to attend a funeral?" I later queried. Not exactly, I learned, but the rigid Japanese custom of "always giving something in return"--in this instance to the mourner who had come with some token--"often laid a heavy burden on the bereaved."

Here then, too, in Sendai, as in Saitama, as everywhere in Japan, women were courageously trying to break away from the rigid feudalistic customs.

Of greatest help to them in all their endeavors, I feel, were the Women's Affairs Officers of the local Military Government teams. It was these women officers who worked, from the outset of the Occupation, locally and directly, with the women in the farm areas, the fishing villages, and in the cities. They worked with the women towards a practical meeting of daily needs in their lives as expressed by the Japanese women themselves.

As one woman in 1948 put it, "We Japanese women work under top. So we are always waiting." That is what the Women's Affairs Officers helped them to outgrow. They encouraged them to use initiative and to work together towards their desired goals.

So, Women's Institutes, a development from the Women's Leadership Training Conferences, were held throughout Japan and attracted an attendance often beyond the capacity of the meeting hall. In Yamagata Prefecture, for instance, of the 1300 women who came, only 700 could be seated. The overflow stood throughout the two day session. And often, to attend these meetings, women had to ride in incredibly crowded trains for as long as 12 to 14 hours, after a preliminary 3 or 4 hour walk to the stations.

"Women's Week," related in general purpose to the Institutes, was first observed in 1949. It became an annual event sponsored by the Women's and Minors' Bureau of the Labor Ministry. The April 1951 theme: "An informed participation in local elections" helped to effect a new high in the development of a democratic Japan. Ninety-one and one-tenth percent of the eligible voters went to the polls. And, be it noted, women outstripped men in casting their ballots.

In any discussion of voting by the women of Japan, one can hardly forego the picture given by a Japanese of his wife and mother on the first election day in April 1946. Toru Matsumoto, in his book, *The Seven Stars*, published in 1949 by the Friendship Press of New York, said:

> Another big directive came. This one gave equality to women. They were granted universal suffrage, and all the legal rights of women were now on the same basis as those of men.--What would equality do to women? How were we men to become accustomed to this changed status of our women? My wife would be a legal equal with me. That was all right with me, but my wife who would not even talk with me unless she was answering my questions or saying 'yes'-- how would she vote? What did she know about elections? The more I thought about the freedom of women, the more strange it all seemed.

Mr. Matsumoto then commented that the draft of the Constitution did not arouse much debate among the people but with the election it was different. It was really a major national event; a new day in his home, too.

His wife, Soyoko, and his Mother acted differently, almost queerly. They were seated at the breakfast table waiting to eat with him, as they did only on Sundays! Upon enquiring what was the matter with them, his wife responded, "Don't you know?"

Flabbergasted upon learning that they had registered to vote, he nevertheless acceded to Soyoko's plea to take them with him to the polls. "Except during the war," he later recalled, "when we were driven out of the house by the siren or an air raid, we had never been out together."

"Soyoko," he noted, "was a picture of happiness, even of triumph, as she came out of the voting place with Mother."

Indeed, as Japanese women came to feel a necessity of participating in activities outside the home, innumerable women's groups were organized, on women's own initiative, commencing 1946.

In connection with my position, as Adviser for Women's Higher Education, SCAP, it was my privilege to work directly with three groups of Japanese women who organized specifically for educational objectives. One of these was The National Conference of Women Students. This organization developed from small group meetings held in Tokyo, commencing November 1947, and was organized nationally in May 1949 at Nara Women's University.

The leadership quality of these women students was singularly high. I judge this quality from my experience in the United States where I had been the Dean of Women in a co-educational college and also in a large State university.

In a later conference at Nippon Women's University, the women students asked me so many questions regarding new professional opportunities for women, the new civic obligations of women, marriage outlook, women's place in the home and in society in a democratic country, that the college president and the dean who also attended the conference said, "We now see clearly the special guidance needs of women students."

The comprehensive field of Guidance had been explored and developed with the Japanese on every educational level from the very beginning of the Occupation. Even so, my proposal in August 1949, submitted to the Japanese Ministry of Education to conduct a Training Course for Women as Deans and Advisers of Women, met with consternation of which "Women are not capable" was the essence. And it required protracted sessions with the Ministry to secure its sponsorship of the course.

When sponsorship finally was attained, the Ministry delayed in extending invitations to the institutions to send a woman representative to the training course. By telegram, only the day before the course was scheduled to begin, were the women specifically notified of their appointment.

Nevertheless, they came! Seventeen of them and from a wide geographical distribution. How these women were able to come away from home for a three-month period on a one day's notice was difficult to understand. Only their eagerness to attend the course accounted for it.

The course was held at the Takehaya Branch of Tokyo Gakugei. As the practical laboratory part of the course, it was arranged that each member serve as a counsellor to a group of the Gakugei students. She was to work with them both individually and as a group.

Daily in class the women exchanged reports of their conferences with their respective counsellees, seeking suggestions from others in the training group that might provide better understanding of a given student. Thus they learned to work together, to share problems, to modify ideas, in democratic fashion.

In response to my request for suggestions of topics to be included in the course, co-education out-numbered all others. Co-education, by now, had been in practice some eighteen months in the lower secondary school, and there was a readiness by educators to admit, even to put in print, their great surprise, that girls do possess ability equal to that of boys. And on the university level, professors were attesting, "Any cultural work can be done by a woman if it can be done by a man."

Yet, in the training course for women deans and advisers, co-education had to be considered lengthily, as there still was fear, particularly in rural areas, that co-education was an inevitable breaking away from all moral standards. When I learned "we have men bamboo poles and women bamboo poles to hang the washed clothes...we have different washing tubs for men and women's clothes"--you see, separation of the sexes even in these matters--I could appreciate why these class members, especially from rural areas, wanted to be well prepared about co-education in order to help in their own schools and with public opinion.

The subject of marriage was also to be included in the course, from the angle of counselling students, but the subject came up sooner than planned when one of the women confided that on her wedding day, her husband had called her *Okusan* (honorary term for wife) which made her very happy. At this, all the class very emotionally nodded their heads "Yes," and vowed, "This is what we must teach our boys to do." It seemed that men did not usually address their own wives with this honorable term for wife.

From this agreement regarding *Okusan*, the group explored their further thinking, without any input from me, so as to compile a list of factors favorable to a good marriage.

How I wished that this list had been in existence on an earlier occasion of my visiting a private university under a foreign mission board, when an American woman faculty members and her Japanese woman associate asked me for materials on marriage. They were desirous of introducing a course on "Marriage and Family Life" but were "stumped," the American woman said, "as there are no Japanese reference materials." The *Onnadaigaku* was the sole guide for the bride. As you know, this compendium of instructions, chiefly for propitiating husband and mother-in-law, is purposed for the perpetuation of the old family system and the superiority of the male sex.

In talking originally with the Ministry of Education officials about the proposed training course, I had explained the likely duties of a dean of women or adviser of women students. When I finished, a Ministry representative said, "Ah, then, a man is the Dean of Women!"

"No!" I exclaimed, "Why do you say that?"

"Because," he replied, "no woman could do all the things you describe, especially manage a residence hall."

But the women in the training course thought differently, as they expounded in their book, *The Guidance of Women Students*. All the members of the class, without any outside assistance, had shared in the planning and writing of the book.

Duly submitted by the group to the Ministry of Education, the book was accepted, printed, and copies distributed by the Ministry to all institutions of higher education enrolling women students. And later, in speaking proudly of the training course, "Never before," they emphasized, "in the history of Japanese education had a group of women educators assembled, without their male counterparts, to discuss matters applying to women students."

Commendation also was given by the Ministry to the group's decision to organize into a permanent association to be known as *Joshi Gakusei Bucho* (The National Association of Deans of Women).

Formal graduation of the group occurred on 23 December 1949, with each member receiving twelve points of academic credit from Tokyo University. TOKYO UNIVERSITY!

The third group I worked with, *Daigaku Fujin Kyokai* (The Japanese Association of University Women) was organized in September 1946. The original leadership of the Association was a small group of Japanese women who had been educated in the United States and who patterned their Association largely upon the organization and objectives of the American Association of University Women.

The Japanese Association gave strong leadership to educational institutions in developing new patterns for women's higher education; they urged particularly the inclusion of liberal arts and the humanities.

Recognition of the accomplishments of the Japanese Association was given in Japan, in the United States, and indeed by the International Federation of University Women who in 1950 invited the Association to apply for membership in the Federation.

Though all terms of membership could be met, such as quality of program and now also numerical size, the Japanese Association decided to postpone application for membership.

Arrival at the decision was not easy. They greatly desired the prestige of that membership; however, because of financial stringencies, payment of the international dues might curtail, they felt, the number of scholarships they awarded nationally to Japanese women students.

The reason for the priority given to scholarships for women can be understood. Women comprised less than one-tenth of one percent of the graduates of universities (according to the 1946 figures) and the newly democratic Japan needed an educated leadership of both men and women in all aspects of civic, personal and professional life.

The women students, of those years, in taking the university entrance examinations, still had the handicaps of girls' "watered down" textbooks. For example, their books for instruction in English, in their earlier schooling, contained one-half the number of words that were in the textbooks for boys.

Nevertheless, in connection with the women students' consequent current difficulty in passing the university entrance examinations, it is interesting to note that the representatives of *Daigaku Fujin Kyokai*, when questioned at a meeting with the Ministry of Education, held firmly to the view that no special consideration be given women students, even temporarily, in these examinations, "as university standards must be kept high."

Branch Reports, given at the annual conventions of *Daigaku Fujin Kyokai*, demonstrated the Association injunction to help shape public opinion on matters of education.

At the 1949 convention, the Chiba branch told of sponsoring a conference on "In-service Training for Teachers." Over 600,000 teachers in Japan had been trained only in the old methods, and many administrators continued to hold the old views about the female sex and education.

Furthermore, the up-grading of professors in normal schools which were now being amalgamated into the universities, was highly necessary. In May 1949, it was reported that 49% of these professors were not university graduates. At the very least they needed in-service training, a procedure newly being introduced. Hence, Chiba and other branches worked to spread an understanding of and a willingness of programs of "In-service Training."

In Gifu, branch members taught evening classes for working girls, many of whom hoped to qualify through these classes for various career examinations, such as public health nurses.

All of the branches seemed to take especial pride in announcing either the number of their own members serving on School Boards or that they had helped in the election of a woman to the School Board.

As the objective of *Daigaku Fujin Kyokai* is to unite college women for work on both the educational and the social problems of the country, it perhaps should not be too surprising that the Association took a large measure of the initiative in the introduction of "Mother's Day" in Japan.

In the book entitled *Japan*, published in July 1951 by the Cornell University Press, several sections furnish material relevant for an inauguration of a Mother's Day in Japan.

In Chapter XII, "Way of Life," it is pointed out:

> The traditional etiquette exalts males. A woman sedately follows some three paces behind a male companion, carries his parcels and bags, opens doors, assists with his wraps, serves his meals, and does not eat until he finishes. In public conveyances, she may offer her seat to a man. Men lift their hats to other men, not to women.

Thus, the Japanese Association of University Women very probably felt that overt demonstration of respect and honor for mothers had potentialities for improvement of women's social status.

Perhaps, at this juncture, it is appropriate to quote from the Memoirs of General MacArthur, "...the transition in women's status is the most 'heart-warming' of the Occupation reforms."

A participant in the 1980 Symposium, here in Norfolk, wisely said that the Occupation did indeed change human behavior, but in a nation of 70 million people, with their own patterns, there were not radical changes immediately in the lives of all those people; the changes would show up in generations later.

During these generations later, I have been privileged to observe many of the desired changes and also tremendous developments. In 1961 some of the 1949 deans of women and I had reunions, when Japan was one of the countries I visited as a Specialist in a U.S.I.S. Program. Seven of the seventeen deans had convened in Tokyo, at Nihon Joshidai, where the once hoped for and now materialized Alumnae House was a featured item of our discussion and admiration.

And then, surprise! Several more of the deans to visit with had gathered at Ochanomizu Women's University where they could hardly wait to show me the Student Health Department and the Student Union Building. They asked if I had dreamed the dozen years ago when speaking of such services and facilities that they would be achieved within this time period. No, I had not.

Numerous other reunions too, in 1961, were very happy occasions, such as with the Japanese President of International Christian University. I quote him: "The movement towards democracy is definite and irreversible. The tide cannot be turned back to the old ways. And primarily because of the women."

This statement was glowing testimony of the changes from the 1940s. Indeed, the general prevailing psychology of the country in 1961 no longer was "Women are not capable." There still were discriminations, yes!--but not the almost universal inflexible mind set. I did once hear, in 1961, a variation of the old refrain: "Women are not capable." It was "When women are more active or prominent, a woman will be appointed to the school board."

By 1961 the Japanese Association of University Women, which had postponed, by vote at the 1949 Kobe Convention, application for its desired membership in the International Federation of University Women (I.F.U.W.), for financial reasons, had long since been able to maintain its national undergraduate scholarship program and likewise meet the membership dues of the International Federation.

In addition, the Association granted fellowships to members of the I.F.U.W. affiliate countries for graduate study in Japanese universities. The women felt an eagerness to reciprocate the generosity of foreign fellowship grants which they received and also to have the prestige of foreign students pursuing graduate study in Japanese universities.

THE XVIIITH TRIENNIAL CONFERENCE

In August of 1974 came the signal honor to the Japanese Association of hosting the XVIIIth Triennial Conference of the International Federation of University Women, the very first I.F.U.W. Conference to be held in Asia and the very first large international conference to be organized by women in Japan.

Representing 39 countries, 940 members of I.F.U.W. were in attendance. Three languages (i.e., English, Japanese, and French) were in use through a system of simultaneous translation.

The Japanese women, I know, always understood that acceptance of their country, "again into the family of nations," though greatly desired, would not be total, immediately. But in the spirit evidenced at this 1974 Convention, they saw a large measure of fulfillment.

In a major address at this 1974 Conference, the Japanese Minister of Education made a stunning announcement: "The Japanese Government is making plans to establish The National Women's Education Centre, scheduled to be completed by 1977..." And it was! It is a magnificent complex, located in Saitama, dedicated to women's studies, housing a library, research facilities--a whole array of opportunities for women's further education.

In 1980, in Vancouver, British Columbia, a Japanese woman educator was elected President of the International Federation of University Women. In the introduction of this I.F.U.W. President to the Convention of the American Association of University Women in Boston, in July 1981, the A.A.U.W. President said,

> "The Japanese women are courageous, committed. They do not want to be parochial or insular..."

To what, at this point, did my mind quickly revert? To the members of the dean's training course in 1949 earnestly extolling the Japanese artist Sesshu for his philosophy, "of looking at the whole world and seeing its relationship."

In an informal conversation with me during the Boston Convention, this Japanese I.F.U.W. President, said,

> "Yes, women had very low status in Japan, but, at the end of the War, instead of lamenting the past, we thought of the future! Our chance came to us through the Occupation."

It was women's awareness of this chance that spurred the emergence from feudalism to democracy. And women on all social levels responded! For example: I recall the keen interest of Her Majesty, the Empress of Japan, to whom, in 1950, I had the honor of being presented. In our conversation, she expressed her pleasure over women's new educational opportunities and her gratitude to the Occupation.

Another stay in Japan, in 1986, afforded me many highly satisfying experiences. There are several: I saw "the friendly partnership in marriage," as envisioned by the prospective deans in 1949.

25

Evenings, the father, in the home where I was a guest, participated in the recreational activities of the two children. And, free from the office on a national holiday, accompanied all of us in a lengthy "just looking" visit to downtown Kyoto department stores.

In response to my later comment of surprise about her husband's going with us, my hostess said, "We always go out together as a family."

How different the statement in the 1949 book: Except during the war when driven out of the house by a siren or air-raid, the husband and wife had never been out together.

At a luncheon visit to the Osaka Prefectural Center for Elderly People, I thankfully witnessed the men and women members eating together!--a long desired change, voiced that 1948 day in Saitama, at the Women's Leadership Training Conference.

From a talk by the Dean of Kobe College, I learned that the 1984 "National Survey of University Students" showed women as outstanding in scholarship and attitude as their predecessors of the late 1940s, when university education was new to them.

On a walk through a park, I was intrigued with the sight of numerous middle-aged men and women playing together, in games of croquet. My young Japanese woman companion could not comprehend why this so pleased me. She took the present social relationships for granted, being life-long accustomed to them.

Hence, in 1986, when I was interviewed on Japanese T.V. stations, in several Japanese cities, and invariably was asked what biggest change I had noted in Japan over the decades, I confidently said, "In Human Relations."

And for their part in the steady gain of monumental changes in Human Relations, the Japanese women of the Occupation Period deserve the greatest credit and recognition. So quickly comprehending democratic principles, they had zealously worked through their organizations for the attainment of the Occupation Goal: Democratization.

GENERAL DISCUSSION

Grant Goodman. I would like to go back to something that I believe was alluded to by Ms. Johnson and that is the question of language. Unfortunately, in all of the presentations we've heard there was really very little reference to the language "problem," if I can call it the language problem. That is to say, I take it from your presentation, Ms. Johnson, that you were not a native speaker or that you did not have a special training in Japanese language. Is that correct?

Carmen Johnson. No, I had none.

Grant Goodman. Okay, and I don't know if you, Ms. Seamans, were language competent or not. Did you know Japanese?

Helen Hosp Seamans. I can say this that the Japanese themselves really did, at that time, did not really encourage our learning Japanese. They were so eager to learn English. They wanted to hear you pronounce it. If I knew the floor in the hotel and I would say to the operator of the elevator the floor I wanted, he would practically just droop. He knew the word "eight," he knew it in English. He wanted to hear me say it. It was so totally different--the experience I had in Latin America in the 1930s it was--I don't know how they are today, but in the 1930s they would go into ecstasy over you if you said the simplest phrase in Spanish and--then anyhow, you see I had my excuses, my alibis. I didn't really need it because...

Grant Goodman. Excuse me, I didn't mean this at all as a criticism. It is simply a preliminary to my question. And my question very simply is: To what extent were you dependent upon Japanese interpreters, that is, native Japanese speakers who communicated these rather sophisticated concepts, which you have described, for you to other Japanese? I think that in this conference there is no paper on the role of interpreters and it occurs to me that, as someone who modestly tries to speak Japanese, that the dependence in any situation in Japan or in Norfolk, Virginia on interpreters introduces a particular element into the situation in which you find yourself.

In short, I wonder realistically what kind of dependence you experienced on interpreters or translators. For example, Ms. Johnson, you referred to a very complicated--to me it sounded complicated--title of a pamphlet which in English had a rather sophisticated and complex title that you apparently made available to Japanese in your prefecture. I inferred from your presentation that somebody had to translate that from the English into the Japanese and it occurred to me that realistically there was no way in which you could check what indeed was translated or was interpreted and that all of your impressions had to be filtered through interpreters and/or translators. I wonder if you would comment? Both of you.

Carmen Johnson. I can see your question and I'm trying to think how I can answer it the way I want to. The woman who was my interpreter went with me on all these trips. She could have given the speech; she could have said everything that needed to be said without me saying anything because we were together. We would go on trips, we would spend days together. And I trusted those people. I'm sorry, I just never questioned them at all. And I still don't. It seems to me that if you had been there and you had seen what it meant to the Japanese women that were listening to things, you would never have questioned it either. I had no, there was no way for American women to learn Japanese back when I was going to school. There were no classes taught in universities and colleges. We just went and we got it just as we got there. Women were always, to me, much better translators and interpreters than men and I know this is true, because I can say why. If my interpreter didn't understand something, she would turn and ask me and I doubt if a man would have done that. (Laughter) Now, I'm serious. It's not a joke. Because the position of women to women, especially when you got to know somebody as I did with my interpreter. We got to know each other; we knew what we thought together. And the woman who was my assistant, I would have felt the same way. I know one time, because I heard this, that a man was interpreting, a Japanese man interpreting for a man, and he said (I have forgotten now what the comment was), but he said, 'That's what he says but I don't think that's true.' (Laughter from audience) I don't think the Japanese women who were working with me would ever have said anything like that.

Helen Hosp Seamans. I'm sure there's no question but what much is lost in translation. There's no question about it, but fortunately I did have very good translators. I'm trying now to think of the one I had especially in Tokyo when I conducted a six months training course in guidance for both men and women through a lecture series held in my office. He was excellent--superb. He had been educated himself at Bates College in Maine and had been a person who had experienced guidance at Bates College so he knew the factors. So that, I can speak well for this man. Now, the women who interpreted for me <u>knew</u> what I was trying to say, these concepts that they wanted were not far into their inmost being. This was what they knew. We felt it; they understood. It was not something technical--I mean, it wasn't difficult in the sense of some scientific experiment might be in a laboratory. This was human relations and we understood each other.

Thomas Burkman. I would like to ask Carmen and anyone else who served on the military government team. You were SCAP--you were not on the military government team? Okay. For the historical record and for my own curiosity, I would like to know more about the pervasiveness, the size, the make-up, the chain of command, and so on of military government teams. In Professor Sodei's keynote address, he said that there were only a few prefectures that had military government teams, but I learned from you that there was one in each of the four Shikoku prefectures and then in a provincial regional military government team over those prefectural government teams. I'm curious to know in your Kochi prefecture team, how many personnel were there? How many native Japanese employees were on the team? And to whom did you send your reports? I have more questions, but I had better stop there. So, could you kind of fill us in on the nuts and bolts of military government teams?

Carmen Johnson. First of all, I think we'll just cancel the rest of the symposium. (Laughter) Because it's going to take me this long to try to explain. Recently, both Mrs. Seamans and I had a visitor from the National Women's Education Center--Mrs. Uemura--and she asked me about this question and I tried to make a little chart. After I spent two days, I gave up because there is no way to chart this. We were--Takamatsu--directly under 8th Army and there were four prefectures. There was a regional office which was in Takamatsu and then in each of the four prefectures there was a team. In the regional office there was one person, for example, in each of the fields. Now, I'll probably forget the most important, but they are: education, information, public health, public welfare, legal, whatever. Usually in a region there was one person. In my case, I was responsible for both the region and the teams. This is the only region, I think, where this applied.

Jacob Van Staaveren. May I answer that question more fully? I was formerly with the Yamanashi military government. Initially, 8th Army military government was composed of detachments, companies, and other units of varying strengths. On 1 July 1946, there was a major reorganization of all these units into military government teams. They were divided into four categories: minor, intermediate, major, and special. Yamanashi was an intermediate team and there were approximately 6-8 officers and 25-30 enlisted men assigned to each team depending upon their size; except for the special teams such as Tokyo and Osaka. The military government structure went from 8th Army Headquarters to IX Corps in Sendai and to I Corps in Kyoto. There were ten teams directly under 8th Army. Underneath IX Corps and I Corps was another administrative layer consisting of military government regions. I fell under the Kanto military government region. There were eight prefectures. Further north was the Tohoku military government region. Those of you who served in other parts of Japan will recall that there were also military government regions there and, of course, Ms. Johnson served in the Shikoku military government region. So, it was very well structured organizationally. (See chart on page 66).

28

THE CONQUEROR PROCLAIMED LIBERTY

Cornelius K. Iida, with Isako R. Iida

CORNELIUS K. IIDA   is Lecturer, University of Yamaguchi, Yamaguchi Prefecture, Japan.   Mr. Iida graduated from Meiji Gakuin University in 1953.   He received a Master of Theology degree from Calvin Theological Seminary, Grand Rapids, Michigan, in 1962 and completed advanced studies at Westminster Theological Seminary, New Wilmington, Pennsylvania.   Mr. Iida has published *Iesu no Toki* (Jusus' Hour), Kodansha, Tokyo, 1985, and *Naze Nihon wa "Unfair" to Iwarerunoka* (On Fairness), PHP, Tokyo, 1989.   Mr. Iida served as a diplomatic interpreter for President Carter and President Reagan from 1979 to 1988.   He was a member of the Political Section, U.S. Embassy in Tokyo, from 1980 to 1982.   Mr. Iida is an independent researcher in U.S.-Japan relations, specializing in cultural differences between the two nations, and the concept of fairness in particular.   **Mrs. Isako Iida** graduated from the Japan Women's College in 1952, and the Reformed Bible College, Grand Rapids, Michigan, in 1959.   She also attended the Japan Theological Seminary in Tokyo.   She was personal secretary to Mrs. Mike Mansfield when Mr. Mansfield was U.S. ambassador to Japan.

The title for this presentation has been inspired by the inscription found on the Liberty Bell enshrined in the Independence Hall in Philadelphia. The inscription reads,

Proclaim liberty throughout all the land
unto all the inhabitants thereof.

The words are from the Authorized King James Version of the Holy Bible, the Book of Leviticus, chapter 25, verse 10. They were the divine directives to set the slaves free, to forgive longstanding debts and to cause a nationwide celebration of freedom in the ancient Israel.

These words were quite appropriate with which to proclaim the freedom won through the struggle in the American Revolution. Thus, a nation was born that inscribes even on its coins, "In God We Trust." The government thus formed inaugurated its first chief executive by an oath pledged on a copy of the Bible. The practice is every bit as significant today, as it was more than two centuries ago.

The reality of a major paradigm shift in Japan of 1945 is no less dramatic as it was in the British colonies of the New Continent in 1776. In both cases the resulting social, political and economic changes were quite significant. In both cases, the changes were worthy of celebrations, as the year of jubilee was in the theocratic Israel of the Biblical times.

The present paper is to a large extent based on personal testimonies. It shall endeavor to present some first hand impressions of the Occupation felt at the grass roots level. It will strike a note of gratitude to that nation which not only restored, but also enhanced religious freedom in Japan. The testimonies are also testimonials, tributes offered to the memory of that one truly great man of faith, who on behalf of his beloved country, heralded the good tidings. Mrs. Iida, whose name appears as the co-presenter, will describe her encounter with an American missionary during the Occupation.

RELIGIOUS INTOLERANCE DURING THE WAR

It bears an occasional reminder, that the conqueror bestowing liberty to benefit its vanquished foe, is quite unique in the history of the world. Japan began to taste freedom in its full dosage almost immediately after the end of the war. Thus, a genuinely significant paradigm shift took place in Japan during the Allied Occupation.

Of particular importance among the many facets of human pursuits thus affected by the change, is the freedom of religious affiliation. Christianity, along with other religious faiths of the pre-war Japan with the exception of then sacrosanct Shintoism, was severely oppressed during the war. The extent of religious intolerance was such that the protestant Christian denominations were forced to merge into one entity easily controllable by the government. Leaders of that entity now called Kyodan went to pay homage to the milliard gods of Japan at the Grand Shrine of Ise. They dispatched emissaries to Korea to persuade Christian leaders there to bow at the Shinto shrines to express their allegiance to the nation that had enslaved them.

Compromises of this nature means utter departure from the faith. It would be easy to criticize the Japanese Christian leaders of those days. Yet, one should not forget that there were many Christian pastors who refused to compromise, and sealed their testimony to the faith with their blood. Such was the intolerance, the enslaving of religious conscience by the military in Japan during the War. That changed overnight as the Occupation Forces landed in Japan.

FOOD FOR THE HUNGRY SOUL

Shuuhei Fujisawa, born in 1927, is a well known Japanese novelist. A certain Japanese company recently featured in its magazine advertisement a photo of the copy of the New Testament Fujisawa cherished as he was struggling through the difficult post-war years. I was delighted to see that photo, because I also owned one like it in my youth.

In the ad, Fujisawa's New Testament was described as the very first copy of the Bible he ever owned. He is not a Christian. But, this Bible he obtained shortly after the war as a teenager, brought to him much needed solace. When thoughts arose that distressed him, or when he was incapacitated through illnesses, the young writer often found "salvation" in the power of the words of the Bible, according to the ad. It was his constant companion. It inevitably grew old and the pages became brittle, even as its owner highlighted its words with a red pencil. Eventually it left the writer's side and was assigned a corner on the bookshelf. He reminisced fondly, and said that even now he occasionally opens the Bible, concluded the ad.

The miraculous fact was that the Japanese New Testament Fujisawa obtained had been printed in New York City while mortal combats were raging in the Pacific. As I mentioned in my after-dinner talk at the symposium held at this Memorial in 1978, the production of the Japanese New Testaments was funded through the donations Americans freely gave to the American Bible Society in response to the appeal. The copies of the New Testament were available in my country soon after the hostilities ceased. They were sold for nominal sums. They were also handed out, sometimes by uniformed GIs, even as the smaller English New Testaments of the Pocket Bible League were.

Fujisawa's experience is shared undoubtedly with thousands of the Japanese, some of whom grew up to be prominent in politics, literature, science, and commerce. The truly remarkable action on the part of the American Christians must be appreciated. And the American GIs were by no means strangers to the faith.

Many a GI stood at busy Tokyo street corners not only handing out Christian literature, but also giving short messages interpreted by Japanese students whom they hired. In fact, I received many tracts as I passed by tall GIs. During my college years, I accepted invitations from some American GIs to interpret for them as they preached the Gospel in Ginza. I was properly remunerated for the services.

The copy of the same photostatic reproduction of the Japanese New Testament as the one Fujisawa cherished was very precious to me also. Through perusing it, I was drawn to the little Christian preaching station which had opened up near my home. I, who once aspired to be a Kamikaze pilot, surrendered my heart to the Savior depicted in the Book, as He was preached.

To some Japanese researchers, these deeds of the members of the Occupation forces may appear to be a part of an unwelcome proselytizing effort. There are some prominent American scholars of varying Christian persuasions, who appeared at the Memorial's earlier symposia. Some of them condemn the missionary zeal exhibited by the uniformed American personnel in Japan during the Occupation. Yet, the gift of the New Testaments provided much needed spiritual food to the starving thousands.

These negative assessments are misplaced. The fact of the matter is that the Americans who brought their faith to bear upon their relations with the Japanese were behaving at their best. By nature Christianity is compassionate. It is not to be ranked with State Shintoism. Shintoism, in the guise of the "civic religion," sent many an unpersuaded soul to their early demise. Even Buddhism was well known, as it was practiced in the pre-WW II Japan, for its general clannishness. Several of the most prominent sects of Buddhism used to refuse members of certain segments of Japanese population into their fold, even denying them decent interment in the temple cemetery. The American openness and lack of coerciveness in sharing their Christian faith should be viewed in the backdrop of the Japanese arrogance relative to Buddhism, and oppressiveness relative to Shintoism. The contrast is quite instructive.

Indeed, the gift of the faith was the greatest of the largess which the Occupation Forces showered upon the emaciated erstwhile foe. I know that the Gospel set me free. Moreover, without the sincere efforts of men and women of the Occupation Forces, I probably would not have had interest in the great freedom that the Gospel brought into my life. There was something about the Americans in general, then, that was attractive:

that made us stop to think. Thus, in my case, as in countless others, the conqueror was the liberator. I seriously doubt if I would be as happy a man as I am today, had I not been touched by the Good News in which the Commander in Chief of the Allied Occupation Forces frankly believed. I know, I could not, and perhaps would not have served Presidents Carter and Reagan as their sole Japanese official interpreter, had I not been set free to accept the faith on which they stood as they guided the course of this nation, and that of the world. For these realistic assessments, I am deeply appreciative of the missionary efforts the Occupation Forces not only condoned, but encouraged.

SAVED AND SET FREE

My wife, Isako, will now assume the podium and give a first hand account of how she found a new life during the Allied Occupation of Japan.

I was born and raised in a Buddhist family in Tokyo. My parents had five children, and I was the second youngest. My two older brothers were drafted into the Imperial Navy, but my father was with us working in an office nearby. My mother, the younger brother and I were particularly close. I often took this brother to museums and parks. However, that all changed overnight. During the severe air-raid of March 10, 1945, mother, the little brother and the elder sister perished.

I do not wish to dwell on the horrible details of the fateful night. Suffice it to say that when the morning finally came, I too was at the point of being disposed of as one of the fatal casualties. The family had fled towards a river, but we simply could not keep together because a mass of people was moving about in a great turmoil. When I found a foothold on a bridge over the river, a middle-aged Japanese man struck me with his portable safe, apparently to gain a space to put it down. I fell headlong towards the river.

Early next morning, soldiers were gathering the bodies of the victims who had drowned escaping the inferno. One of them was startled to find that I was still alive. All night long I was in the river, but my face was held just above the water. I was wearing a heavy winter coat, and it had a hole in the back caused by the sparks flying around. The hole miraculously caught the tip of a pole sticking out of the water as I fell. I was knocked unconscious, but was kept safe from both the water, and the raging fire on land.

Roaming about the once familiar neighborhood now totally destroyed, I found my father. But, mother and the little brother and the elder sister were never found. A mass funeral took place. Then two years later, father remarried, and I resolved to love and honor the stepmother in the place of the late beloved mother. In fact, I pledged this to my late mother at the cemetery. To an extent I succeeded, but it was quite difficult to mediate between the stepmother and the two older brothers, who refused to accept her. That made me feel guilty and wept, thinking that my promise to the late mother was not being kept.

Things began to change when I met an American Christian Missionary. I was then in college in Tokyo, and was actively taking part in a campaign to get one of the professors of that college elected. The campaign took me to Shizuoka, and I stood on a stage and started giving a memorized speech in support of the candidate. The audience jeered, and I became tongue-tied. I could not even move. Tears began to stream down my cheeks, and the sadistic ones in the audience loved the situation.

Suddenly I felt the touch of a large hand on my shoulder. Unbeknown to me, a tall gentleman had appeared on stage and approached me from behind to rescue me. He spoke with fluent Japanese, and uttered some light-hearted comments. The jeering audience paid attention, and laughed as the towering figure skillfully told a joke. Relaxed, I was able to trace my steps to the back stage. The man, I later learned, was one of the Americans who responded to General MacArthur's call for Christian missionaries to go and serve in Japan.

That was my very first encounter with Christianity. As my interest was kindled in what the gentleman believed in, I became aware of my sins and shortcomings even more. I started reading the Bible, and soon afterwards began attending the missionary's meetings. I realized that the only way to fulfill my pledge to mother was through the help of the Living God. I wanted to have my sins forgiven and to be set free to do good. This was a new approach. This was the good news as the gospel was driven home to me. The Bible declares in The Epistle to the Romans, chapter 8, verses 3 and 4, the following:

> For what the law could not do, in that it was weak through the flesh, God sending his own Son in the likeness of sinful flesh, and for sin, condemned sin in the flesh: That the righteousness of the law might be fulfilled in us, who walk not after the flesh, but after the Spirit.

One cold December morning, the missionary took several young Japanese to the Tamagawa River in Tokyo. He baptized them, and I was one of them. The change I underwent then must have been quite striking. Not long after, my brothers were reconciled to the stepmother, as they all confessed their sins and accepted Christ as their savior. Happiness filled the home for the first time since the war ended.

More than forty years passed since that December morning, and I am deeply grateful to God who loved me and saved me. I am grateful to the missionary who gave the best years of his life to go to war-devastated Japan, to proclaim the gospel of that sets men free from sin and hatred. And I am grateful to the American people who through General MacArthur showed deep compassion to us Japanese, and shared with us their faith in God.

THE OCCUPATION: A NEW DAY IN JAPAN'S RELIGIOUS HISTORY

James A. Cogswell

JAMES A. COGSWELL is a Presbyterian minister and was a missionary in Japan from 1948 to 1960. He was instrumental in the founding of Shikoku Christian College and served as president from 1952 to 1953. Mr. Cogswell was a professor at Kinjo College, Nagoya, from 1957 to 1960 and later served as Secretary for Asia, Board of World Missions, Presbyterian Church, U.S. He graduated from Southwestern at Memphis in 1942, received a Bachelor of Divinity degree from Union Theological Seminary, Richmond in 1945, performed graduate study at Princeton University, and completed the Ph.D. from Union Theological Seminary in 1961. Mr. Cogswell is the author of several books, including a work on the Japan mission of the Presbyterian Church, U.S. from 1885 to 1960, titled *Until the Day Dawn* (Nashville: Board of Presbyterian Missions, Presbyterian Church, U.S., 1957).

I deeply appreciate this opportunity to take a trip down memory lane and I've been especially pleased and *natsukashii,* I can't think of a good English word for that, [fond memories, ed.] to meet a fellow worker from Shikoku where we spent our first term of service and to find out that Professor Iida was a student at the seminary later after I had taught there for one year during our first year of service in Japan. So there are many memories stirring up in my own mind and heart in the midst of this occasion.

Professor Iida has quoted that very famous statement of General MacArthur at the time of the signing of the surrender documents. It was a statement that motivated many people, both within and beyond the missionary community, with a set of ideals for a new relationship between the conqueror and the conquered. It did bring forth a new breed of missionary idealists who saw service in the Christian mission in Japan as an avenue for peacemaking, for reconciliation, for rebuilding, the total life of a nation which our own nation had participated in destroying. My wife and I had made the decision to serve in Japan, actually shortly after the beginning of the Second World War, at a national youth convention as speakers challenged the youth who were there to prepare to join an army of peace in the aftermath of the terrible destruction of war.

We were ready to go as soon as the war ended, but the restrictions on entry of new missionaries delayed our departure until the latter part of 1948. We were the first of the new missionaries of our own denomination to serve in Japan. Those first few days in Japan left some very indelible impressions upon us. First of all, the warm reception on the part of all the people whom we had the privilege of meeting. We could count, really, on one hand the expressions of a spirit of anti-Americanism, or hostility toward us personally. Then, of course, the sense of the overwhelming devastation that prevailed in Japan as we travelled through large areas of bombed out factories and communities and saw the pitiful sight of disabled soldiers begging on the street corners. In spite of these dismaying circumstances, it was evident that Japan had entered a new era that would bring a more profound change in her way of life than anything she had yet experienced in all her long history.

THE WAR'S IMPACT, PHYSICAL AND SPIRITUAL

The Japan that faced this new day was a nation that had been completely crushed and devastated physically. Out of the very flower of her manhood, over one and a half million lives had been sacrificed upon the battlefield. Within the nation, the lives of almost 300,000 civilians had been snuffed out in air attacks. And there was no means of computing the millions of injured, maimed, and crippled who would bear in their bodies for the rest of their days the scars of this terrible catastrophe.

An estimated one-fourth of the national property was destroyed. Some three million houses and buildings were burned, leaving almost nine million people homeless. One hundred sixteen of her cities lay in ruin.

The vast empire which Japan's militarists had carved out as their so-called Co-prosperity Sphere, taking in half the Pacific and a large share of eastern Asia, they were now forced to disgorge, and Japan was reduced to those four islands which were her only possessions when Perry first woke the country. Into those crowded devastated islands were pushed some eight million demobilized soldiers and hundreds of thousands of Japanese repatriates from Korea, Manchuria, China, the Philippines, Malaya, and the South Seas.

How could these millions find subsistence? Japan's economy had been ruined. Her industries had been laid waste, her sources of raw materials were lost, her markets had vanished, her merchant marine had been swept from the seas. But Japan's undoing was more than physical. Spiritually, she had been shaken to her very foundations. Her military defeat brought the stark realization that all the pretense about Japan being a divine land and her people a race of supermen, destined to bring the world under the sway of their heavenly emperor--all was unfounded myth. Suddenly there was nothing to live for and nothing to live by.

The general devastation of the country was poignantly portrayed in these desperate words spoken by a Japanese to the first deputation from the churches in the United States:

> Everything in Japan is crushed, smashed, or diminished, spiritually and materially. She has surrendered completely. She has no sovereignty at present, has no diplomacy, no army, no navy, no steamers, no honor, no pride, no confidence, no houses, no clothes, no food to live on. I do not want to exaggerate the desperate condition of Japan too much and give you a misunderstanding - but I cannot give you false information.

THE OCCUPATION INTRODUCES RELIGIOUS LIBERTY

After almost two millennia of proud isolation and independence, Japan was compelled in 1945 to submit to occupation by a foreign power. In principle, the Occupation policy was to be determined by the Far Eastern Commission (FEC), established by the nations that had participated in the fighting on the Pacific front, and the Supreme Commander for the Allied Powers (SCAP) was expected to consult the representatives of the nations that constituted the Allied Council. In reality, however, the Occupation of Japan was conducted almost solely by the United States, and General Douglas MacArthur, the first Supreme Commander for the Allied Powers, almost singlehandedly directed activities of the Army of Occupation. The Occupation, under General MacArthur, had as its objective the reconstruction of every phase of Japan's life, with the aim of creating a peaceful and democratic nation.

Where to begin in the accomplishment of such a momentous task? Those in the Occupation with responsibility for religious affairs perceived that the key to the whole structure of Japan's militant nationalism was the identification of the State and the Shinto religion (*saisei-itchi*). The groundwork for change was prepared by the Basic Directive issued by General MacArthur on 4 October 1945, which ordered the Japanese government to remove all restrictions on political, civil, and religious liberties. Instantaneously, the notorious "Religious Bodies Law," enacted in 1939 and enforced to secure rigid government control over all aspects of religious life, was abrogated.

Then, with one fell stroke, the Occupation attempted to cut the Gordian knot by the Shinto Directive, issued on 15 December 1945. In its most significant provision this order read:

> The sponsorship, support, perpetuation, control, and dissemination of Shinto by Japanese national, prefectural, or local governments, or by public officials, subordinates, and employees acting in their official capacity are prohibited and will cease immediately.

The announced purpose of the Shinto Directive was "to separate religion from the state, to prevent misuse of religion for political ends, and to put all religions, faiths, and creeds upon exactly the same basis, entitled to precisely the same opportunities and protection."

Within two weeks after the Shinto Directive, on New Year's Day, 1946, the people heard from the lips of their own Emperor a rescript such as no Japanese emperor had ever issued before:

> The ties between us and our people have always stood upon mutual trust and affection. They do not depend upon mere legends and myths. They are not predicated upon the false conception that the emperor is divine and that the Japanese people are superior to other races and are fated to rule the world.

With the disestablishment of State (*Kokutai*) Shinto and the Emperor's own renunciation of any claim to divinity, the way was now open for laying the foundations

37

for a democratic way of life. As the result of a directive of 4 January 1946, those Japanese officials who were declared to be "undesirable personnel" were purged from public office (some 200,000 persons, nine out of every ten high officials, and 120 political organizations), and an International Military Tribunal for the Far East was established to prosecute "war criminals." The first postwar election was held in 1946.

The Occupation's tour de force was the new Constitution, made public in May 1946 and adopted by the Diet in May 1947. In striking contrast to the Constitution of 1889, which it replaced, the new Constitution began with this extraordinary declaration:

> We, the Japanese people, acting through our duly elected representatives in the National Diet . . . do proclaim the sovereignty of the people's will and do ordain and establish this Constitution, founded upon the universal principle that government is a sacred trust the authority of which is derived from the people, the powers of which are exercised by the representatives of the people, and the benefits of which are enjoyed by the people.

Regarding the principles of religious liberty and separation of religion and state, the new Constitution was explicitly clear:

> Article 19: Freedom of thought and conscience shall not be violated.

> Article 20: Freedom of religion is guaranteed to all. No religious organization shall receive any privilege from the State, nor exercise any political authority. No person shall be compelled to take part in any religious act, celebration, rite, or practice. The State and its organs shall refrain from religious education or any other religious activity.

> Article 89: No public money or other property shall be expended or appropriated for the use, benefit or maintenance of any religious institution or association, or for any charitable, educational, or benevolent enterprises not under the control of public authority.

On the basis of the new Constitution, the Occupation proceeded to reconstruct every important phase of Japanese life. Within the space of a few years, the entire structure of Japanese national life underwent an overhauling such as probably no other nation had experienced in so brief a time. The nation vowed to renounce war as a means of settling international disputes, and thus abandoned the military might which had so long been its pride. The secret police system which had held the Japanese people in the tyranny of "thought control" was abolished; protection of the law was now entrusted to a smaller police force under local, rather than national control. Political prisoners were liberated; civil and political liberty was proclaimed; freedom of speech, of press, and of assembly were guaranteed. Far-reaching agrarian reforms were instituted; the old absentee landlord system was dissolved, and farmers who had tilled for others for generations now were given the opportunity to secure precious land as their own. Restrictions on labor organization were removed, and within a few years the total strength of the unions would reach over six million members. The national educational system was reorganized, with militaristic and ultra-nationalistic teaching eliminated and a totally new system patterned after American education initiated. While all these changes had their separate identity and impact, freedom of religion was part of the warp and woof of the new Japan. As Edwin Reischauer has observed, "the United States, which has usually appeared to be the champion of the status quo elsewhere in the world, was clearly a revolutionary force in Japan."

With amazing good will and determination, the Japanese people joined the Occupation forces in the rebuilding of their nation. Despite a critical shortage of food, clothing and other necessities of life, the people gave themselves assiduously to checking economic disintegration and building their national life on a new foundation. Whatever hatred there may have been initially toward the conquering forces was soon dissipated in an atmosphere of warm friendship. Above all, the manner in which General MacArthur took over the administration of the nation, mingling firm justice with wise compassion, quickly convinced the people that the objective of the Occupation actually was not to wreak vengeance, but to impart to their nation a new and democratic way of life.

Yet it would be too much to expect that a mere change in outward structures would suddenly bring to birth a democratic nation. Underneath the democratic facade, the feudalistic social and thought patterns which had solidified through long centuries still controlled much of the everyday thinking and living of the vast majority of the Japanese people. Neither Rome nor a Japanese democracy could be built in a day.

THE OCCUPATION'S IMPACT ON JAPAN'S RELIGIONS, OLD AND NEW

How to assess the permanent impact of the Occupation upon the religious life of Japan? In some ways, it appeared that little had changed. Japan continued to be a nation with deep religious roots in Buddhism, Shintoism and the ethics of Confucianism. Post-Occupation Japan has witnessed a revival of the old religions in their multi-sect manifestations. Thousands of shrines and temples have been rebuilt through community subscriptions, much more elaborately than ever before. The annual attendance at each of the large national shrines numbers into the millions. Local shrine and temple festivals receive greater popular support with each passing year. In some aspects of the nation's religious life, there is evidence that "the pull backward is stronger than the push forward."

In particular, the separation of religion and government upon which the Occupation insisted was a principle which the general public found extremely difficult to grasp. Though Shinto was deprived of government support, the same Shinto shrines continued to be the centers of community life, to which all loyal citizens were expected to give their support. Following the Occupation, with a new upsurge of the spirit of nationalism, there appeared disturbing evidences of a reversion to the old identification of patriotism and national Shinto. No sooner had Japan's Prime Minister returned from the San Francisco Conference in 1951, by which Japan regained her independence, than a high government official made a pilgrimage to the Grand Shrine at Ise to report the signing of the Peace Treaty--the first time such a thing had happened since the end of the war. There soon followed similar government-sponsored religious observances throughout the nation, many of them honoring the spirits of those who had offered their lives for their country on the field of battle. Numerous cases have been appealed in which school children have been taken in classes to bow at Shinto shrines.

Certain nationalistic groups have made a concerted effort to revive the observance of *Kigensetsu*, or National Foundation Day, in commemoration of the mythological founding of the Japanese Empire by Jimmu Tenno, and to recognize the Emperor as the Head of the State rather than merely its symbol. There have been repeated attempts by the ruling Liberal Democratic party to nationalize the Yasukuni Shrine. However, at each crucial point of decision, democratic forces have been able to avert this turn backward.

Still another critical dilemma has been the teaching of ethics in the public schools. Witnessing the decrease of respect among post-war students for Japan's traditional system of ethics, some reactionary forces have sought to reintroduce the teaching of ethics based upon the concepts of respect for nation and Emperor which permeated pre-war education. *Dotoku kyoiku* (moral education) continues to be hotly debated, but thus far the trend has been toward the teaching of ethics which draws upon the highest ethical teachings of all the major religions, yet with an objective approach that does not compromise freedom of religion.

In addition to the old religions, the fallow soil of postwar Japan created an atmosphere conducive to the emergence of a plethora of new religions (*Shinko Shukyo*). The number had reached some 720 by 1951, but the enactment of the Religious

Juridical Persons Law in that year sifted out about one half the number and left a total of about 375. Some grew quickly into huge organizations, the more vital ones being the *Perfect Liberty* (PL) *Kyodan*, the *Rissho Koseikai*, and the *Soka Gakkai*. Some were revivals of prewar cults but most have been newly organized since the war. Taking advantage of the spiritual unrest which characterized postwar Japan, each religion had its own formula for peace of mind, security, healing, prosperity. The new religions range from those borrowing their main tenets from Christianity but leaving out the Christ, through those which seek to fuse hand-picked features from each of the major religions, to those which present a new messiah and play upon popular superstition. Generally they breathe the atmosphere of Buddhism--not solution but escape--and express the Shinto characteristic of limitation to the nation of Japan.

THE CHANGED STATUS OF CHRISTIANITY

And what of Christianity? With the end of the war, the Japanese Christian movement, which had so long suffered suspicion and suppression, found itself confronted with a new age of unprecedented opportunity. With the abrogation of the Religious Bodies Law and the removal of all other repressive measures, the Japanese Church now possessed a freedom for proclaiming its message such as it had never known before. Also, the general movement toward democracy offered Christianity an unparalleled opportunity to present to the nation a new and hopefully surer spiritual foundation.

This had its dangers as well as its advantages, for it easily led to equating Christianity with democracy or the American way of life, and brought some into the church either with the idea of winning American favor or simply because it was the fashion of the day. Be that as it may, the eyes of the nation were opened to the fact that there was a Church in its midst which offered a message of hope in the midst of despair.

Yet it was a church which, far from being exempt from the physical destruction which had come upon the nation, had suffered in even greater proportion because the majority of its work had been centered in the large cities where the bombing had been most severe. Of the approximately two thousand Christian churches in Japan proper, one-quarter had been completely destroyed. The heaviest loss was in the city of Tokyo, where 175 churches lay in ruin and only 9 were left intact. The destruction of Nagasaki, a stronghold of Roman Catholicism, caused serious hardship to the Catholic Church. Many Christian pastors shared the lot of the homeless, with a total of 331 parsonages destroyed. Among the Christian schools, almost half had been totally destroyed or very badly damaged.

The pastors themselves presented a pathetic picture of persons conscious of a tremendous responsibility in the reconstruction of their country, but tired, undernourished, struggling to exist, ill-equipped, since most Bibles, hymnbooks, Christian literature, even paper were gone. Seminary graduates had been so few during the war that the remaining ministerial personnel could not possibly serve all the previously organized Christian groups. Upon the prematurely-aged shoulders of this limited Christian leadership rested a Herculean task.

The Church which entered this new era was a Church with a deep sense of humility and contrition. The All Japan Christian Convention, meeting in Tokyo on the Day of Pentecost, 1946, began its declaration of rededication with the following statement:

> We, the people of Japan, feel deeply responsible for this great war just ended. Especially we, who profess the Gospel of Peace, do hereby express our profound reflection, confession and repentance. We believe, however, our Heavenly Father of infinite love and forgiveness will grant us sufficient grace to find a new way of life and the revival of faith.

> Confronting the immediate and unspeakable suffering and loss of our compatriots

by this war, we are fully conscious of the new meaning of the Cross pressing upon us. Whereby we have determined for the reconstruction of New Japan, founded upon the Cross of Jesus, to look forward to a day of a moral world order to be realized on this earth.

It was also a church which needed every assistance which Christians throughout the world could lend it. Into the chaotic situation which prevailed following the cessation of hostilities, there came a Christian Deputation from the United States in October 1945. Composed of four distinguished American churchmen, it was the first mission to arrive in postwar Japan in civilian dress, or, as one Japanese pastor put it, "in praying clothes." The deputation carried greetings from the Protestant Christians of America to the churches of Japan, reestablishing the bonds of fellowship with those Christians who for four long years had been cut off from all contact with the rest of Christendom. After conferring with both Japanese Christian leaders and Occupation authorities, they returned to the United States to report: "What the Japanese Church needs is our genuine interest, our prayers, our financial aid, a few experienced missionaries immediately and more later--when they are asked for."

A critical question which faced Japan's Protestant churches as they entered the post-war era was: What to do about the United Church of Christ, the *Kyodan*, which had come into existence under government pressure immediately before the war? The months immediately following the war were such desperate and confusing ones that ministers and congregations were able to consider nothing outside of maintaining their own physical existence from day to day. The wartime united church organization, therefore, continued for the time being. In December, 1945, however, its executive committee met to consider the future of the united church, now that all government pressure had been removed. The decision was made to draft a new constitution removing the government-enforced regulations, and to present the proposed constitution to a General Assembly of the church, which would convene as soon as physical conditions made it possible.

The General Assembly convened in June 1946, bringing together some 221 representatives from throughout Japan. It soon became evident that, while the large majority favored maintaining a united Protestant church, they also were convinced that every trace of the wartime government-coerced organization must be eradicated. The question of reversion to a federal-type organization was considered, but the final decision was that, even if it led to withdrawal of some groups, the *Kyodan* should continue as a truly united church.

There were particular Christian groups, however, which from the beginning had not been sympathetic with the idea of a united church and felt strongly opposed to the manner in which *Kyodan* leaders had yielded to the government during the war. After governmental pressure was removed, therefore, there came about a gradual withdrawal of such groups from the united church. By 1951, the number of Protestant denominations had increased to over fifty, most of them very limited groups which had been established by new missionary organizations entering Japan after the war.

Extremely difficult living conditions led the Occupation to restrict the entrance of any expatriate missionaries into the war-torn nation. The first group to receive clearance was a "Commission of Six," representing the Foreign Mission Conference of North America; they reached Japan in April 1946. As quickly as conditions allowed, other missionaries with years of experience in Japan were permitted to return. By 1947, over sixty Protestant missionaries had arrived. Then as conditions improved, the regulations were liberalized to allow new missionary recruits to enter. By 1949, over 500 reported. When all regulations were removed, there came the greatest influx of missionaries which the nation had ever experienced. By 1951, Japan had over 1,500 missionaries representing some 116 different churches.

While the immediate post-war years saw a remarkable increase in public interest in Christianity, the post-Occupation period saw the vision of a "spiritual revolution" fade into the light of common day. The total Christian constituency in Japan (Protestant and

Catholic) has continued to average approximately one percent of the population. Yet, strangely, Japanese society seems to show increasing evidence of the impact of the Christian message. The Bible continues to stay at the top of the best-seller list, as it has done consistently since the Second World War. A government survey of personal religious faith brought forth the surprising statistic that three percent of the Japanese people considered themselves "Christian"--three times as many as are included in church membership--an evidence of the impact of Christian schools and social work institutions. Christians continue to occupy positions of leadership in the nation, out of all proportion to their ratio in the total population. In every list of those honored by the post-war government for their contributions to education, medicine and social reform, Christians are conspicuously numerous. Certainly Christians "weigh far more than they count", and are at work as leaven in the lump of Japanese society.

As James Phillips observes, "The tremendous creativity in Christian literature, art, theology, lay witness, social service, and other areas that was to flourish in the succeeding years was due in no small measure to the dynamism that was generated during the comparatively short period of the Occupation."

THE NEW APPEAL OF COMMUNISM

In assessing the impact of the Occupation upon the religious life of postwar Japan, one cannot overlook the appeal of Communism. The extreme crisis of the postwar years pushed some to the materialistic philosophy of Marxism. Taking advantage of the free political atmosphere during the Occupation, the Communist Party strengthened its organization and stepped up its agitation. Appealing to the desire for an immediate solution to Japan's pressing economic problems, it gained fervent adherents among no small number of intellectuals, particularly university professors and students, and also among labor groups and peace organizations. Dismayed by such an unexpected turn of events, MacArthur resorted to banning the general strike of government employees early in 1947, banning the railway strike in the summer of 1948, and directing the purge of Communist leaders in the summer of 1950.

The true nature of Communism's international intrigue was manifested in the Korean invasion in 1950. With the outbreak of the Korean War, Japan was thrust into the middle of an international conflict. The American Occupation forces in Japan under General MacArthur's command were assigned to the Korean conflict and MacArthur assumed, in addition to his duties in Japan, the command of the United Nations' forces in Korea. The extent of hostilities in Korea was such that the attention of the United States became focused primarily on military developments in Korea rather than on civil reform in Japan. From 1950 Japan was used as a base for American military operations in Korea and elsewhere in Asia, and the United States-Japan Security Treaty that was signed at the same time as the Peace Treaty (1951) gave the United States the right to continued use of bases in Japan. In this situation, both for the protection of Japan from radical Communist influence and also to preserve Japan as an anti-Communist ally of the West, the Occupation authorities persuaded the Japanese government to establish a National Police Reserve of 75,000 men, which was later increased to 200,000 and was renamed the Self-Defense Force. Further, in the summer of 1951 the purge orders for most of the so-called "undesirable personnel" were lifted, as a result of which many conservative politicians became available again for public office, thus tilting the scales against the radical left.

More recent years have seen the Japan Communist Party resorting to a policy of quiet infiltration. Though less evident on the surface of national affairs, it would be a tragic mistake to assume that Communism in Japan is dead.

THE RESURGENCE OF JAPAN AS A SECULAR NATION

Beyond the supermarket of religions and ideologies which has emerged in postwar Japan, the most evident impact brought about by the new day ushered in by the

Occupation has been the rise of a predominantly secular nation. One cannot help but marvel at the thriving prosperity of this nation, emerging out of the ashes of such total defeat and devastation. Its amazing comeback accomplished in one generation has hardly any parallel in history.

Japan's present generation enjoys a prosperity never known to any previous generation. Its per capita income is far and away beyond that of any other nation of Asia and is comparable to that of most nations of the West. Its life expectancy is greater than that of any other nation. Its economy now dominates international economic affairs.

The picture of Japan as a modern, secular state is supported by many Japanese. As evidence of their country's secularity they cite widespread religious indifference. Government surveys indicate that about 65% of Japan's people claim no personal religious faith. Entrance applications to Christian schools, where students indicate every type of Buddhist and Shinto sect as their family religion, usually indicate in the blank for the student's personal religion, "I have none."

A professor of journalism at Japan's leading university, the University of Tokyo, in addressing the International Press Institute meeting in Tokyo several years ago, made the following statement:

> Our impotence--that is, the biggest problem facing the youth of Japan today -- is that we have lost all goals. We have lost our faith and we no longer seek moral standards in our lives. There is nothing that fires the hearts of the Japanese. Reliance on science no longer satisfies us. There is no doubt a need for a new faith.

Professor Joseph M. Kitagawa of Columbia University assesses the religious situation in postwar Japan as follows:

> When Japan surrendered to the Allied Powers in 1945, it was not simply the end of combat. What Japan lost was far more than the divine prerogatives of the throne or the gigantic institution of State Shinto. These were external symbols of something much deeper, that is, the source of the Japanese sense of destiny and security based on a cosmological world view which has been preserved from time immemorial....(T)he Japanese people as a whole have lost their traditional sense of values and of the meaning of history.

Certainly the Occupation ushered in a new day for the religious life of Japan--not the day which many had hoped or expected--but a day in which the Japanese people had opportunity as never before to choose their ultimate loyalties within the context of a democratic society. As William K. Bunce observes, "Today, the separation of religion and state in Japan is as complete as in any country in the world." For that we should all be thankful.

BIBLIOGRAPHY

Anesaki, Masaharu. *Religious Life of the Japanese People.* Tokyo: Kokusai Bunka Shinkokai, 1961.

Baker, Richard Terrill. *Darkness of the Sun.* New York and Nashville: Abingdon-Cokesbury Press, 1947.

Bunce, William K. *Religions in Japan.* (From the report prepared by Religions and Cultural Resources Division, SCAP). Rutland, VT and Tokyo: Charles E. Tuttle Co., 1955.

Cogswell, James A. *Until the Day Dawn*. Nashville, TN: Board of World Missions, Presbyterian Church U.S., 1957. Supplementary chapter, 1967.

Drummond, Richard H. *A History of Christianity in Japan*. Grand Rapids, MI: William B. Ererdmans Publishing Co., 1971.

Earhart, H. Byron. *Japanese Religion: Unity and Diversity*. Belmont, CA: Wadsworth Publishing Co., 1982.

Germany, Charles H. *The Response of the Church in Changing Japan*. New York: Friendship Press, 1967.

Holtom, D.C. *Modern Japan and Shinto Nationalism*. Chicago: University of Chicago Press, 1947.

Iglehart, Charles W. *A Century of Protestant Christianity in Japan*. Rutland, VT and Tokyo: Charles E. Tuttle Co., 1959.

Iglehart, Charles W. *Cross and Crisis in Japan*. New York: Friendship Press, 1957.

Kerr, William C. *Japan Begins Again*. New York: Friendship Press, 1949.

Kitagawa, Joseph M. *Religion in Japanese History*. New York and London: Columbia University Press, 1966.

Phillips, James M. *From the Rising of the Sun: Christians and Society in Contemporary Japan*. Maryknoll, NY: Orbis Books, 1981.

Reischauer, Edwin O. *Japan: Past and Present*. New York: Alfred A. Knopf, Inc., 1952.

Return to Japan, The. Report of the Christian Deputation to Japan, 1945. New York: Friendship Press, 1946.

Takenaka, Masao. *Reconciliation and Renewal in Japan*. New York: Friendship Press, 1967.

THE DEMOCRATIZATION OF THE JAPANESE, SEPTEMBER 1946 - SEPTEMBER 1948: A PREFECTURAL VIEW

Jacob Van Staaveren

JACOB VAN STAAVEREN, an independent historian, served during the Allied Occupation of Japan, initially, as Civil Information and Education Officer, Yamanashi Military Government Team, and, subsequently, as a historian in GHQ, SCAP. He later served as Historian, Fifth U.S. Air Force (in Japan) and with the Office of Air Force History in Washington. Mr. Van Staaveren received the B.A. degree from Linfield College, McMinnville, Oregon, in 1939, and a M.A. from the University of Chicago in 1943. He has published several articles on education in Japan in newspapers and journals.

In the still growing body of historical literature on the Allied Occupation of Japan from 1945 to 1952, very little has been published on the activities of military and civilian personnel who were assigned to Headquarters, Eighth Army's military government units and teams.

What follows is primarily an autobiographical account of my experiences as a civilian Civil Information and Education (CI&E) Officer while serving on the Yamanashi Military Government Team for 22 months, engaged in carrying out SCAP education policy designed to democratize the Japanese people. Except for Kofu, the prefectural capital, a city of about 100,000, and 100 miles southwest of Tokyo, Yamanashi was predominately rural. Thus I would be working at the "grass roots" level.

The military government team that I joined had evolved from a small detachment, established in December 1945 of only three officers and five enlisted men. In early November 1946, there were eight officers and five enlistees but by year's end more of the latter began arriving and soon there were 26--at one time as many as 30.[1] While being "processed" at Headquarters, Eighth Army in Yokohama, I had been informed that a majority of military government officers in Japan did not have college or university degrees. Thus, as the first professional civilian to join the Yamanashi Military Government Team, I sensed immediately that some of my uniformed colleagues believed I needed careful watching.

I had at the time B.A. and M.A. degrees plus a fair amount of administrative, research and writing experience. Some of my uneasiness dissipated, however, when I learned three officers possessed higher education: a 26-year old Captain and the Team's Adjutant with a B.A. degree and who had attended an Army civil affairs school; the Medical Officer who was a Doctor of Medicine, and the Labor Officer who had attended a junior college.

The Team commander, a Lieutenant Colonel, made it clear at the outset that he had strong reservations about civilians serving on military government teams, albeit he was duty bound to support Eighth Army's policy that so assigned them. Our relationship remained quite frosty until shortly after my arrival when he learned that my graduate studies had included the French Revolution and the rise and fall of Napoleon. As he had read numerous books about France's most famous general, there was now a Team member with whom he could discuss some of Napoleon's campaigns. Thus our relationship began to warm. The fact that he had fought the hated Nazis in Germany and not the Japanese also redounded to my benefit. He believed, in contrast with the Germans, that the Japanese people had been badly mislead by their military leaders. He thus became quite supportive of SCAP's democratization program and my CI&E activities. His attitude was not shared by several Team members who had survived *banzai* attacks on the Pacific islands and remembered more vividly the Bataan Death March and other Japanese atrocities.

THE TEAM'S JAPANESE AND AMERICAN STAFF

I was fortunate in having been briefed rather extensively at Headquarters, Eighth Army and by several members of SCAP's Civil Education Division on the many facets of the CI&E program. Informed that the overall Japanese compliance with SCAP's directives made the surveillance task minimal, my primary task would be to advise and assist prefectural officials and the populace in "democratizing" their educational and religious institutions in accordance with SCAP's directives, a forthcoming new Constitution, and other postwar Japanese laws.

After my arrival in Yamanashi Prefecture and a hasty orientation about my duties, I wondered how Team members managed to perform their multiple duties in education, public affairs, labor, agriculture, health and welfare and other areas. The answer lay in heavy reliance of the Team on a large Japanese staff. A translation section translated local newspapers and reports from all prefectural government offices into English--dictionary English--as none of its members had studied abroad. The Team also possessed several very fine interpreters who had studied in Canada or the United States. There were also numerous typists, mimeograph and phone operators, and other administrative personnel. In addition, some of the better educated enlistees were assigned to work with Team members--I soon had two and at one time three. I assigned shortly a talented Technical Sergeant to exercise most of the oversight for the storage and distribution of imported food used for the prefectural school lunch program which began in February 1947. Finally, there were soon three to four Nisei, all of whom were bilingual, although not as proficient in reading and speaking Japanese as our best interpreters who had studied abroad.

The Adjutant, who had been serving as the Team's CI&E and Political Affairs Officer as additional duties, had made a commendable start in establishing his Japanese staff. One member was a completely bilingual lady who was also an educator in her own right, a second was a retired former middle school teacher and principal, and a third was an energetic well-educated lady who was very adept in organizing educational exhibits. A few months after I arrived, I added to my staff an elderly gentleman who had spent his career with the Japanese YMCA. He became my consultant on youth associations and religion. It is worth noting that, with a few exceptions, the Team's most helpful Japanese staff members were Christians by virtue of their command of English and knowledge of the precepts of Canadian or American democracy.

ESTABLISHING CI&E PROGRAM PRIORITIES

As indicated, the military government CI&E portfolio was indeed a very large one which made mandatory a determination of which educational reform program deserved the highest priority. This was not difficult to do. Changing structurally and democratizing the Japanese educational system obviously had first priority as the first step in establishing a new 6-3-3-4 educational system was scheduled to begin on 1 April 1947 when new lower secondary schools would make their debut. In addition, Eighth Army required the inspection of a minimum of five schools per month and the completion of a 15-page form containing more than 300 questions about a school's status. This requirement dated from the early days of the Occupation to guard primarily against any display of "militarism" and "ultranationalism" in classrooms or on the school grounds. The inspection form also provided statistical and other data about a school. Although I soon concluded the inspection requirement was unnecessary, it was not rescinded during my 22 months service in Yamanashi. Filling it out became a perfunctory exercise.

I assigned second priority to adult education programs which by November 1946 had five components: encouraging the establishment of "democratic" youth associations, women's organizations, parent-teacher associations (PTAs), the building of numerous citizens public halls (CPHs), and educational exhibits. There were also documentary educational films for adults and students, but I had little to do with this program. SCAP's Civil Information Division made them available to prefectural Social Education Offices for showings in local theaters, and for mobile movie units that traveled to remote parts of prefectures.

The military government CI&E portfolio also mandated vigilance against any resurgence of State Shintoism, explaining to the populace when necessary the importance of religious freedom as directed by SCAP directives guaranteed in the new Constitution and other postwar laws, and dealing with any religion and state issues that might arise.

Finally, in January 1947, alarmed by the growing militancy and intransigence of many of Japan's unions led by Communists and radical Socialists, SCAP's Labor Division specialists--with what proved to be the reluctant concurrence of SCAP's Education Division--instructed military government CI&E officers through Eighth Army to supplement the Labor Division's efforts to teach labor and management how to settle disputes by "democratic" collective bargaining, i.e., by arbitration, mediation, and conciliation as in America.[2]

ON THE JOB

With the foregoing as background, how did a military government civilian CI&E Officer in a rural prefecture supplement SCAP's efforts to democratize the Japanese at the prefecture level? As has been stated, advising and assisting prefectural education officials and educators in Yamanashi on how to reform their entire educational system was my first priority. Thus, on 7 November 1946, barely three days after my arrival on the Team and exactly 45 years ago today, I visited--but officially "inspected"--my first school. The Adjutant, who would leave the Team in December 1946, promised to demonstrate for my benefit how a school should be inspected and teachers shown how to teach in a more democratic manner. It was a memorable day.

With a Japanese driver and Miss Aiko Enomoto, our interpreter, the four of us motored to a primary school on the outskirts of Kofu in the Team commander's 1939 black De Soto sedan which had been expropriated a year earlier from a Japanese citizen or prefectural office. Upon our arrival, we parked on the edge of the school ground. Our reception was unforgettable:

> Our unannounced appearance created pandemonium. Hundreds of students bounded out of their classrooms and surrounded us. Amidst their chatterings in Japanese were many shouts of "hello", "hello". Wading through the throng was the principal and head teacher who, upon greeting us with several bows, invited us to come to the teachers' room for tea. For lack of time we declined.

> We proceeded immediately to stroll through the school which contained, according to the principal, about 1,000 students and a faculty of 26. It was a rambling, one story, unpainted structure with several wings that had been added periodically. Nearly half of the windows were broken or missing which increased the draftiness of the school. There was no central heating. Classrooms were furnished sparsely containing only desks and chairs, most of them marred from extended use. An isolated light bulb hung from the ceiling in each classroom to provide additional light on dark, winter days.[3]

We found no manifestations of "militarism" or "ultranationalism" in the school, such as the display of the 1890 Imperial Rescript on Education, the use of a traditional textbook on "morals" (now totally banned by SCAP) or improperly censored textbooks on history and geography. Nor did the Adjutant expect to find any violations of SCAP directives. We then stopped at a classroom where a young woman teacher was nervously instructing her class by rote, i.e., in response to each question all of her students shouted the reply in unison. All American educationists who proffered advice on or were engaged in reforming the Japanese school system considered this pedegological method a mind-numbing exercise that stifled creative thinking. The Adjutant and I agreed. As this school inspection was primarily for my benefit, the Adjutant summoned other teachers from nearby rooms and proceeded to demonstrate how to teach in a more creative way. Tucking his gloves and riding crop (the Team commander had directed all officers to carry them) under his left arm.

> He assumed the role of teacher. Then, with the interpreter at his side, he asked the students to be quiet. He posed a question from a textbook and asked those who knew the answer to raise their hands without shouting. He called on one student to reply. He repeated this technique several times with the teachers observing intently. Did they now understand this better instruction method. All murmured their assent. Were there any questions? There were only two or three. It was a very stilted meeting.[4]

Thus ended my first and only "on the job" orientation for my CI&E duties on the Yamanashi Military Government Team. The always busy Adjutant, with many pressing administrative matters on his desk, was impatient to return to his office. As we ended our 40-minute visit, I informed the principal and head teacher I would return after the lunch hour to meet with the entire faculty. We then took our leave with hundreds of boys and girls again crowding around the De Soto sedan shouting friendly "goodbys".

Lunch over, I returned to the school and met in a large classroom with all the teachers, excusing the principal lest his presence inhibit responses to questions I might ask. I began the meeting with a short talk on the purposes of the New Education as described in the *Report of the United States Education Mission to Japan*, dated 30 March 1946, which served as a "bible" on the objectives of educational reform in Japan for CI&E officers and Japanese educators alike. I also discussed various Articles of the new Constitution which had been promulgated by the Emperor on 3 November. When I solicited questions:

> Several teachers said they felt very uncertain how to apply the precepts of the New Education. In the past, they knew exactly what to teach and how to control their students. Most difficult was how to present a lesson to allow students to "think for themselves." They had also tried to use a recommended group discussion method but this made it very difficult to maintain class discipline. All agreed they needed more specific guidance on how to teach their courses in a more democratic way. As for the new Constitution, they had been studying and discussing it amongst themselves and their students, but the meaning of some of the Articles was not clear despite frequent explanations in newspapers and radio broadcasts.[5]

I tried to persuade the teachers that, with practice, it would become easier to teach in a creative way than by rote. I also explained that more "democracy" in a classroom did not mean an absence of discipline in the classroom, and students should remain under control. With the issuance of new and better textbooks and teaching guidance materials, all teachers would be able to adjust to the New Education. When I raised the subject of extending coeducation in all classrooms throughout the school, a recommendation by the United States Education Mission of 30 March 1946, it drew a most restrained reaction.

I also asked the teachers if they had all joined a teachers' union. Most said they had or were considering doing so. Did they participate in union meetings? None had as they assumed union leaders "knew best what to do." My listeners did not appear enthusiastic about either unions or my counsel not to let a handful of union leaders make all decisions for them. One male teacher, apparently reflecting the sentiments of his colleagues, said most believed unions were for workers. Although all primary school teachers were urged constantly to join the local Yamanashi Teachers' Union, a branch of the Japan Teachers' Union headquartered in Tokyo, he said most teachers in the school believed union membership lowered the dignity of the teaching profession. Knowing that SCAP encouraged the growth of unions, I did not pursue the subject further.

I finally adjourned the meeting amidst many bows and "thank you's" from my listeners and departed the school grounds, again with shouts of "goodby" from hundreds of students who had been leaderless for nearly two hours. It had been a highly informative and exhilarating experience.

In my office I quickly composed a summary of the meeting and other observations. Boys and girls in the first three grades were taught in the same classroom, all by young women; those in the fourth grade and beyond were taught in separate classrooms, mostly but not all by men. The attire of teachers and students bespoke of their nation's severe economic straits. Several older girl students carried babies on their backs while their mothers labored in the fields. One girl carried the baby of a teacher. The extreme youthfulness of some women teachers was striking, a legacy of World War II when many young women who had not completed their normal school studies or mere middle school graduates had been given provisional teaching certificates.[6]

Meanwhile, I had already met the chiefs of the prefectural Education Section and the Social Education Office; then shortly the Chairman of the Yamanashi Teachers' Qualification Committee. After SCAP's major purge of former "militarists" and "ultranationalists" by a directive of 4 January 1946, the Committee continued to review the prewar and wartime records of prefectural educators if new information so warranted.

ADDITIONAL PRIMARY SCHOOL INSPECTIONS AND VISITS

My experience at a typical primary school in Yamanashi Prefecture on 7 November 1946 was generally replicated in subsequent weeks and months at scores of other prefectural primary schools. Accustomed to a highly structured and authoritarian educational system in which the Ministry of Education in Tokyo gave teachers virtually no discretion as to what, when and how to teach their subjects, the vast majority now were very much at sea in coping with the radical changes dictated by SCAP's school reform measures. In meeting after meeting, most faculty members agonized over their new responsibility to "develop a student's personality" or "inner self"; or how to encourage "imaginative" and "creative thinking." Like the Team's Adjutant during my first school inspection, I too assumed the role of teacher to demonstrate how students in America learned their lessons "the democratic way." Being a product of that system, this was easily done.

Primary school faculties also agonized over the possible dire consequences of more coeducation, along with the other aforementioned "democratic" concepts, in not only the United States Education Mission's Report of 30 March 1946, but in two basic postwar Japanese pieces of legislation: *The School Education Law* and *The Fundamental Law of Education* which came into force on March 29 and 31, 1947, respectively. Except for a small group of radical Socialist and Communist teachers in Yamanashi, none of whom chose to argue with me, all others appeared convinced that the New Education mandated a new morals course to help restore discipline in the schools. To be sure, most women teachers saw merit in coeducation in assuring more social, educational, and political equality for themselves, but instituting coeducation so quickly was another matter. Men teachers preferred to remain silent on the subject. As we now know, coeducation in classrooms was instituted faster and more successfully than most Americans and Japanese anticipated, first through the first six grades, then incrementally beginning with the seventh grade in the new lower secondary schools established on 1 April 1947, the beginning of a new school year.

From the onset of my meetings with faculties of primary schools--and also those in secondary schools and with leaders of youth associations--I was asked frequently to explain the "pioneering spirit" of America and/or the "secret" of American democracy. After several not too successful attempts to do so, I devised an answer that appeared to satisfy many of my listeners. I would cite the invention of the cotton gin by Eli Whitney in 1792, the electric telegraph by Samuel Morse in 1832, the grain reaper by Cyrus McCormack in 1834, the telephone by Alexander Graham Bell in 1877, the first phonograph and electric light bulb by Thomas A. Edison in 1878 and 1879, the first flight of an airplane by the Wright brothers in 1903, and the auto assembly line by Henry Ford. Although most of these inventors, I would explain, had poor formal educations, they all possessed "imagination" and "creativeness" which flourished in American democracy. I also wrote several short articles on this subject for use by three prefectural newspapers and the local radio station.

Another method for demonstrating how to teach "democratically" was through teaching clinics. In Yamanashi Prefecture, the first clinic was established by the Fuzuoka Primary School attached to the Men's Normal School. The primary school was headed by a fairly young and imaginative head teacher with a small faculty, better educated than most, who grasped surprisingly well the objectives of the New Education. In early February 1947, I witnessed some of its teachers employing advanced teaching techniques. I strongly urged the school's principal and head teacher to hold teaching demonstrations.

With some assistance from the faculties of the prefectural men's and women's normal schools, the first one day "teaching clinic" was held on 4 March 1947 with about 500 teachers in attendance. The morning was devoted to demonstrating how to teach other than by rote; the afternoon to lectures and discussions. Additional one day clinics followed. Meanwhile, the Ministry of Education, at the behest of SCAP's educators, directed prefectural education offices to designate in each prefecture a number of their best schools to serve as centers where the precepts of the New Education could be explained and demonstrated. Few designated schools in Yamanashi, however, possessed sufficient numbers of faculty members who could assume this responsibility very well, but the effort was made nonetheless. Special education conferences, in which I participated occasionally, were also held for the purpose of discussing the importance of more democratic teaching techniques.

In addition to newspapers, the New Education was also explained to students and teachers in radio broadcasts from Tokyo. In my view, these were not as effective as SCAP officials believed. First, many schools had nonfunctioning radios. A survey in January 1947 revealed that 161 prefectural schools, mostly primary but also some secondary ones, possessed radios that lacked vacuum tubes and other parts. Although the Ministry of Education had established in all prefectures a special radio repair project, many schools were unaware of it. I issued a press release on the availability of this service.[7]

Second, local electric voltage was often too weak for audible broadcasts. Third, special teacher broadcasts on Mondays, Wednesdays, and Fridays from 3:30 to 4:00 p.m. found many teachers too busy to listen with the result that one or two would be designated to listen and convey to others later what had been said. Fourth, the well educated men and women lecturers in Radio Tokyo used many words and phrases beyond the comprehension of many poorly trained teachers in Yamanashi. There were always some teachers, however, who said the broadcasts were helpful.

Meanwhile, I had made little headway in convincing primary school faculties to be more assertive in dealing with officers of the Yamanashi Teachers' Union. The Union, on orders from its Tokyo headquarters, frequently demanded that teachers halt their classes to "endorse" immediately and without debate, some proposal deemed essential, thus disrupting the teaching schedule.

YAMANASHI'S MIDDLE SCHOOLS

There were 11 middle schools in Yamanashi Prefecture, five for boys, six for girls. Each contained well over 1,000 students. The buildings were of sturdier construction than primary schools and had more facilities. Roughly 15 percent of all prefectural students who passed their "examination hell" to enter them knew they were among the prefecture's student elite and on the road to a college or a university, a respectable profession, and for girls especially, a reasonably suitable marriage. Students and faculties in these schools were extremely proud of their traditions. The students wore uniforms. All behaved with more restraint and did not display the boisterousness I experienced in arriving or departing most primary schools.

Democratizing these schools and making them a part of the evolving 6-3-3-4 educational structure would not be easy. There was considerable educational inequality between the boy's and girl's middle schools. The former were bastions of masculinity and provided for five years of study beyond the sixth grade. In addition to longer study of the Japanese language, their curricula emphasized mathematics, chemistry, physics and other sciences. They had no women instructors. Girls had a four year course of study and a predominately male faculty except for a sisterhood of teachers who taught language and the more classical subjects of art, sewing, flower arrangement, child care, and cooking. English teachers were present in all schools, and some students displayed a remarkable facility in speaking and reading their second language.

The faculties of the middle schools appeared to understand better than their primary school counterparts the purpose of the New Education. They and their students did not conceal their dismay, however, over the impending new school structure that would witness the breakup of their classes into new lower and upper secondary schools. The latter would be established on 1 April 1948 and stretch educational opportunity for both sexes from the 10th through the 12th grade.

To be sure, all women teachers and girl students in girl's middle schools favored the concept of educational, legal, and political equality provided by the new Constitution and postwar Japanese laws, but displayed great reluctance to forego most of their "domestic science" studies as the price for more substantive courses. My efforts to convince them they could learn nearly all they needed to know about cooking, flower arrangement, child care and similar subjects in women's magazines was, I fear, not very persuasive. They were as adamant as teachers and students in boy's middle schools in desiring to maintain their school's identity. They also manifested deep concern about coeducation in classrooms, fearing an increase in moral problems.

More than one girl asked: "Why can't girls obtain equal education in girl's high schools or colleges?" As some were aware of the existence of numerous single sex institutions in the United States, it was difficult to convince them, as the United States Mission Report on Education of 30 March 1946 stated, that coeducation in postwar Japan was necessary to assure equality of education and for financial reasons.[8] To stress coeducation's importance, I would cite the achievements of several outstanding American women, such as Clara Barton who founded the American Red Cross in 1881, and Susan B. Anthony and Frances Willard, leaders of the women's suffrage and prohibition movements in the late 19th and early 20th century. If their names were not familiar, I would cite Marie Curie of France, who with her husband Pierre received the Nobel Prize in physics and in her own right won a Nobel prize in 1911 in chemistry. As all appeared to have heard of Madame Curie, she became my best example of what Japanese women could achieve if given the educational opportunity to do so.

The emphasis of the new Constitution and new education and other laws on equality for all citizens once inspired this remarkable question: "If both sexes are equal, how can there be a head of a household?"

Despite the apprehension of all middle school faculties and students, 24 new upper secondary schools, 21 public and three private were established on 1 April 1948 with most offering college or university preparatory subjects and a few a "vocational tract."[9] Plans for coeducation were postponed until 1 April 1950, the beginning of the 1950-51 school year. I thought it should be postponed to even a later date. In June 1948, I wrote in a Team report: "Opposition to coeducation remains strong by all parties concerned: boy students, girl students, teachers, and parents."[10] Virtually no middle school girls and their women instructors in Yamanashi Prefecture believed it was absolutely essential to obtaining a "democratic" education.

VOCATIONAL SCHOOLS

About 47 prefectural youth schools taught vocational courses to part-time students and there were several full-time agricultural and technical schools. As vocational studies would be integrated into the new educational structure and the youth schools were to be phased out, I spent little time with them. The few youth schools I visited were very small, were housed in rudimentary structures, possessed few teachers and students, and lacked adequate workshops, laboratories or technical equipment. If nothing else, they underscored the strong desire of young men--and some young women--to obtain additional education, no matter how meager in order to better their lives. The agricultural and technical schools were housed in better buildings and had more teaching amenities.

In meeting with small groups of youth school students or their teachers in my office, I tried to assure them that under the New Education they would receive better vocational training than at present. It was very difficult to sustain their morale, especially after the Ministry of Education, prodded by SCAP, announced in October 1947 that all youth schools would be abolished on 1 April 1948. This triggered the formation of a "Laboring Students League" with 200 youth school students attending a meeting in Kofu on 25 November 1947. Several members of the Socialist and Communist parties in Tokyo assisted the students in voicing their discontent.[11]

My concern, based on conversations with the prefectural education chief, that the New Education would be unable quickly to replace existing vocational schools was soon confirmed. For lack of funds, classrooms, and teaching materials in Yamanashi, all of the 2,800 students who sought part-time vocational study in the new lower and upper secondary schools on 1 April 1948 could not be accepted immediately. Enrollment in correspondence courses in the two secondary schools was limited to 100 and 200 students respectively. Then course work was not available until 20 July 1948, more than three and half months after the new school year began. Because of these problems, numerous youth schools in Yamanashi were permitted to continue to operate for many more months. "Too much reform in too little time," I noted.

HIGHER EDUCATION

Yamanashi Prefecture possessed two regular normal schools, one for men and one for women plus a youth school normal school. All three offered a two-year preparatory course for graduates of "higher" primary schools (i.e., those who had completed the eighth grade) followed by a three year regular curriculum. The youth school normal school's curriculum was designed to provide teachers for the prefecture's 47 vocational youth schools. Not surprisingly, the curriculum for the women's normal school was less demanding than the one for men and included courses on "domestic arts." In another disparity, men had 12 weeks of practice teaching versus 10 for women.

SCAP's near-term objective as late as the summer of 1948 was to convert all of Japan's normal schools into four-year teachers' colleges and to assure at least one university in each of the nation's 46 prefectures. Their curricula would also be upgraded to produce higher quality teachers. As the last basic reforms in education would be primarily in the area of higher education, I conferred only occasionally with faculty members of all three normal schools. Their apprehensions about the New Education equaled those of teachers in primary and secondary schools. The lengthening of the preparatory school from two to three years beginning 1 April 1947 was particularly unsettling. Although it would affect only the newly enrolled 80 boys and 40 girls who would be required to study a year longer, present normal students would be expected to take additional course work to meet new and higher teaching qualifications.[12]

In late March 1947, I delivered the Commencement Address to 155 graduates of these institutions of whom 42 were from the youth school normal school. My discourse was on "Education in a Free Society," wherein I tried to persuade my listeners of the merits of the 6-3-3-4 educational structure, and to assure them that the transition to a more "democratic" educational philosophy and curriculum and also more effective teaching methods would probably be more rapid than they believed possible. I further emphasized that all teachers were at the forefront of creating a more "democratic" Japan.[13] This address, and some others that I delivered later, were primarily for the purpose of sustaining morale until the shortages in better teaching manuals, guidance and other reference materials were overcome, as well as the distress of daily living because of the war-torn and inflation-wracked economy.

ASSISTANCE IN THE SCHOOL REFORM TASK

Although some military government civilian CI&E officers rather quickly received an assistant, I worked alone with my Japanese staff until July 1947. That month Miss Eleanor Lee, a Women's Education Officer of the Kanto Military Government Region, visited Yamanashi for the first time. She spent several days meeting with prefectural women leaders and organizations including women teachers to talk about their new educational, legal, and political rights. She also addressed groups of women and teachers on the importance of PTAs once a decentralized educational structure became effective.

A former officer in the Women's Army Corps (WAC) and teacher, Miss Lee possessed B.A. and M.A. degrees. In July, Dr. Rollin C. Fox, the CI&E Officer of the Kanto Military Government Team, also came to Yamanashi for the first time to lend a hand for several days. An experienced former teacher, high school principal and superintendent of schools in three districts in New York state, he was exceptionally well qualified to discuss with prefectural education officials, principals and head teachers how to administer more efficiently schools, both at the prefectural level and in individual schools.

I was highly gratified to receive henceforth periodic assistance from Miss Lee and Dr. Fox. With occasional exceptions, each traveled and worked independently with an interpreter and made significant contributions in helping to "democratize" prefectual women's organizations and schools. My assistance to both was usually limited to arranging their schedules, thus leaving me free to perform my other CI&E duties.

ADULT EDUCATION PROGRAMS

Although the major effort of SCAP's Civil Education Section was devoted to reforming Japan's primary and secondary schools and its colleges and universities, its Adult Education Branch also devised a series of special programs to "reeducate" and "democratize" Japan's adults. With no American assistant during my first eight months in Yamanashi Prefecture, I relied primarily on the prefectural Social Education Office (upgraded to a "Section" in April 1947) to conduct programs for adults. However, I managed to speak a few times to adult groups, or meet with their leaders in my office. Perhaps more importantly, I participated with members of the prefectural Social Education Office and representatives of adult groups in three major adult education conferences in July and September 1947 and July 1948.

Youth Associations

At the urging of Russell L. Durgin, SCAP's chief of Youth Organizations and Student Activities Branch, I initially selected youth associations as my first priority. Observing that many of these youths were former members of Japan's Army and Navy, Durgin warned they had returned to a homeland defeated in war and in the throes of great economic hardship. It was thus essential, he believed, to prevent the rise of extreme left-wing or right-wing movements among these disillusioned young people.

My first contact with Yamanashi's youth occurred in mid-November 1946. A newly formed all-male Funatsu Youth Association had invited me to speak at their first meeting. It was held at the Funatsu Primary School. By the end of the meeting, it was a close call who had been "reeducated" the most: me or the 200 assembled youths, some of whom were well past 30 years of age.

The title of my address was "Discipline for Democracy," with the title and subject matter borrowed from a volume authored by a philosophy professor. The thrust of my remarks was on the necessity of all of Japan's citizens to understand their new Constitution, promulgated on 3 November 1946, and to develop sufficient "discipline" for preserving it. This called for individual as well as collective discipline. Although the political majority should rule, they needed to be mindful of the views of the minority; the minority, in turn, should abide by and respect laws enacted by the majority.[14]

This was not what my audience wanted to hear. Rather, they peppered me with many down-to-earth questions: "How should we get rid of old neighborhood association bosses?" "What should young workers do against mean employers?" "How can inexperienced youth make good decisions?" There were numerous questions about America: "How do young people get jobs?" and "How do young people play together?" "Are any marriages arranged?" I sensed many of my answers were not wholly satisfactory. As they seemed quite inquisitive about the relationship between young American men and women, I took the occasion to underscore the importance of equal educational, legal, and political opportunity for girls and women if Japan was to become a democracy. I also suggested that their association become coeducational. The response of my audience was silence. There were additional questions, however, about American and western democracies and what seemed to make them strong and prosperous. Also why they were so advanced scientifically. I attempted to keep alive the flame of hope, asserting that under a democratic system of government, Japan too could enjoy the many fruits of scientific advance including a higher standard of living.[15]

Needless to say, in a few subsequent talks before youth associations--all of whom quickly established "women's departments" as a gesture towards coeducation--I continued to address the fears and concerns of Yamanashi's youths. I recommended that all associations narrow their wide age range which extended from as young as 15 to as old as 40. This they did, although the conviction that those in their teens and twenty's needed strong "guidance" by older members remained strong.

Meanwhile, scores of associations continued to spring up on the assumption SCAP wanted all youths not in school to join one. By April 1947 there were about 200 of them in Yamanashi although many existed largely on paper. With my time very limited, I usually met periodically with youth leaders to discuss program activities by their associations. The most common were "athletic clubs," mostly to play baseball, the nation's favorite sport. A few established ping pong and tennis clubs, and discussion groups on "health and hygiene," "juvenile delinquency," and "agriculture." Most creative of all were "literary clubs" where members read their essays and poetry. My Japanese staff considered some of this literary output of fairly high quality. The young ladies' "departments" usually met to discuss the "domestic arts." There was no easy commingling of the sexes in the associations, however, because of their social and Confucian heritage.

Beginning in late March 1947, Mr. Hajime Akaike, a long-time worker in the Japanese YMCA, who had just joined my staff, gradually assumed most of the responsibility for talking with and advising Yamanashi's youth leaders. He also assisted them in developing a popular "coming of age ceremony" for those who reached the age of 20.

I twice received assistance from Mr. Donald M. Typer, who had succeeded Russell L. Durgin as chief of SCAP's Youth Association and Student Activities Branch. My most memorable meeting with Typer occurred in March 1948 during a two-day conference attended by 500 of Yamanashi's youths. To lighten the conference's overly somber atmosphere, we sang an unharmonious rendition of "Old McDonald Had a Farm." It brought the always serious-minded young men and women to their feet roaring with laughter and applause. In this manner did two Occupation officials try to demonstrate how a little singing, in the midst of an agenda weighted with lectures and discussion periods, could help move Japan's youth along the road to "democracy."[16]

Women's Organizations

Except for a few meetings with small groups of Yamanashi's women's leaders, it was also February 1947 before I found an opportunity to address a recently established women's organization called the "Kofu Educational and Cultural Society." Upon my arrival in a small but beautifully decorated meeting room were about 30 kimonoed ladies with carefully coiffured hairdos. The President proved to be the wife of the prefectural governor and the others were the wives of Yamanashi's political, educational and business elite. The subject of my address was "The Role of Women in a Democracy." When I asked for questions, there were very few. The ladies had something else on their mind, namely, a tea ceremony which they promptly demonstrated in my honor. Upon the ceremony's conclusion, I was then asked to repeat the ceremony with a beautifully attired lady assisting me. Again, it was the guest speaker who probably received the most education that afternoon.[17]

Like youth associations, many of Yamanashi's distaff members believed SCAP wanted all women to belong to an organization and there were soon scores of them in every town and village. For the wives of farmers and common laborers, the fact that the New Constitution and postwar laws gave them new educational, legal, and political rights was indeed a radical change.

For lack of time, I had to leave most of the task of supplementing SCAP's educational activity on behalf of new women's rights in Yamanashi to the prefectural Social Education Section and Miss Eleanor Lee of the Kanto Military Government Region, but I managed during the ensuing months to address several large organizations. The topics were: "The Development of Women's Organizations in America," "Women's Activities in America," and "The Place of Women in a Democratic Society." With few exceptions, the vast majority of my listeners sat mute, leaving the post-lecture questioning to a small coterie of acknowledged leaders in the town or village where the meetings were held. It was not difficult to discern that for most rural women, their new status in Japan's postwar democracy was quite unsettling, all with husbands generally non-supportive of the changes. This was, after all, basically a Confucian society in which male superiority had long been accepted.[18]

Fortunately, the city of Kofu, the prefectural Capital, possessed a fair number of well educated women who were capable of explaining to and encouraging other women to exercise their new rights. Also assisting in this effort was a small number of well-educated prefectural YMCA members who, working with YMCA headquarters in Tokyo, sponsored a number of conferences in Yamanashi devoted to the cause of women. Numerous Japanese suffragettes from Tokyo and two from abroad found their way to Kofu to discourse on the subject of women's new educational, legal, and political rights and their importance to developing a democratic Japan.

My participation in these conferences was minimal, consisting primarily of meeting briefly with the visiting dignitaries in my office and joining with Kofu's mayor or governor in delivering a few words of welcome to the conferees. In addition, Miss Eleanor Lee, the Women's Education Officer of the Kanto Military Government Region, cited earlier, came to Yamanashi periodically to meet with a variety of women's groups, teachers, and officials of the prefectural Social Education Office, and the Women's and Minor's Bureau. The last, of course, was charged with the enforcement of new laws governing the working conditions of young girls and women. The Team's Labor Officer also monitored the activities of the Bureau.

The women's movement produced two historical breakthroughs for Yamanashi's distaff citizens. During the April 1947 national elections, five were elected for the first time to village assemblies. In March 1948, Yamanashi's education chief, admittedly with considerable urging on my part, appointed five women as primary school principals beginning 1 April.[19]

Parent-Teacher Associations (PTAs)

Organizations of parents with students in a school were not new in Japan. In the past, in Yamanashi Prefecture, they had been called "School Supporters" or "School Maintenance Societies." Unlike American PTAs however, they were accustomed to meeting only two or three times a year to listen to reports delivered by a principal and head teacher on the status of a school. They left all substantive matters on school operations and the curriculum to the Ministry of Education and prefectural officials. As SCAP planned to transfer most of the authority over educational matters from the powerful Ministry of Education to prefectures, cities, towns, and villages, it was essential to prepare citizens to assume responsibility for the education of their children through elected Boards of Education. Most board members were expected to be drawn from new, "democratic" PTAs.

I had been adequately apprised by my well-educated Japanese staff that Yamanashi's parents did not look forward to assuming responsibility for local education as in America. In addition, prefectural education officials and PTA leaders who visited my office likewise conveyed their deep concern about establishing local school boards. Nor did public school teachers look forward to dealing with new Boards of Education. It simply was not part of Japan's tradition. Early in 1947, I had occasion to address two newly organized village PTAs. Both PTA presidents were village headmen who introduced their respective association officers, all men, appointed by the village headmen. At both meetings, men sat on one side of the room, women on the other. I was then introduced to give my talk.[20]

Suffice to say, my discourses at both meetings on the importance of decentralizing educational authority to further the objectives of the new 6-3-3-4 educational structure and democracy was received politely but without any enthusiasm. That SCAP would soon expect them to make decisions on a school budget, a curriculum, hiring principals and teachers and other matters, was most disquieting to my listeners. Several men asked in effect: "Don't education officials, principals, and teachers know best how children should be taught?" Knowing very well how a local board of education functioned in America--my father served on one in Oregon for many years--I was not at all sanguine about the ability of citizens in a rural Japanese prefecture to assume full responsibility for their schools. The concept appeared more plausible in large cities and towns, but there was sufficient evidence indicating that the education level in many villages was relatively low. In addition, the financial resources of most villagers was limited.

Nonetheless, I was obligated to be supportive of SCAP's planned decentralization of education (the Board of Education Law would not come into force until 5 July 1948). Pending its enactment, I continued to emphasize in meetings with citizens in my office, public meetings, adult education conferences and in press releases, the merits of strong PTAs from whence most Board of Education members would be drawn. The prefectural education chief warned, however, that the Yamanashi Teachers' Union would try to control local Boards of Education in the manner in which they already had succeeded in controlling negotiations on teachers' salaries, benefits, and other educational matters.

As we all know, the first Boards of Education were established on 5 October 1948 but only at the prefectural level and in five major cities. About 48 cities finally established them. After the Occupation ended on 28 April 1952, the process towards further educational decentralization halted for financial reasons and the lack of broad public support. The Ministry of Education gradually reassumed most of its prewar power over Japan's educational system.

Citizens Public Halls (CPHs)

Citizens Public Halls or CPHs, according to a 12-page document dated 1 July 1946 prepared in SCAP's Adult Education Branch,

> should be opened in all cities, towns, and villages throughout the country where people may assemble to talk, discuss, and read books...to obtain information about their work and life...and cultivate friendship...The CPH should be a fountainhead of local progress and development...a link between various associations and organizations...and born of the people's wishes and cooperation and supported ideally by their own purse and brain.[21]

Each CPH, the document continued, should initially have four departments: general culture, library, industry, and social gathering: then add departments of physical training, social work, and social welfare. A children's playground and other facilities, such as movie projectors, and corn-powdering and threshing machines were recommended. In short, the CPHs would be a "grass roots" beehive of community activity. In light of the postwar economic distress in a rural prefecture like Yamanashi where there was little time for leisure, it appeared that the document's author apparently had not visited Japan's outlying areas.

Construction of a few CPHs in Yamanashi was under way in late 1946 and the first one was completed on 3 November; the second in January 1947. With prefectural citizens possessing little purse, the Ministry of Education directly or indirectly financed their construction. I had very little to do with the program except to discuss with the prefectural Social Education and other offices how many and where they should be built. Eventually, 40 were planned. After the first two were completed, there were no funds to staff them or for any of the facilities they were supposed to possess. I visited only two CPHs, participating in the dedication of one of them with the Team commander. Although others built in subsequent months were also largely bereft of any facilities, they were quickly used by youth and women's groups and other organizations which heretofore had no suitable meeting place except at the local school. Thus they fulfilled one of the purposes of this particular adult education program.

Educational Exhibits

The sponsoring of educational exhibits for adults and students was another function of the CI&E Office of the Yamanashi Military Government Team. Miss Aramaki Fusuoka, a well-educated Japanese lady, served as the curator of these exhibits. Assisted by two or three enlisted men on my staff and prefectural officials, teachers, and others as needed, the exhibits, in my judgment, helped maintain citizen moral. They also demonstrated what local citizens could do on their own initiative instead of relying constantly on directives and guidance from officials in the national and prefectural governments.

My predecessor, the Team's Adjutant, had held three exhibits in the Team's library reading room prior to my arrival. The first two consisted of two separate sets of photographs loaned by SCAP's Information Division. One set showed the nature of atrocities committed by Nazi Germany, Japan's erstwhile ally, the second represented scenes of American life, and the third exhibit featured paintings by a Mr. Yamamoto, a local artist. Many adults and students attended these showings.

In December 1946, Miss Aramaki arranged a showing of 400 pieces of student art of all ages. Committees of judges were appointed. Many thousands of adults and students visited the exhibit during a five-day showing. Near the exhibit's close, a trove of prizes was awarded for the best art work according to the age and grade of students with the Team commander officiating in presenting the prizes. Through my personal contacts, many of the entries were sent to the United States where they were shown in schools and museums. American students, in return, sent art works to Yamanashi Prefecture which were also shown in the exhibit room and then donated to various schools.[22]

Other exhibits in the Team's library reading room followed, many of which were likewise shown in other parts of the prefecture. With few exceptions, local talent was used. The following is a partial list of these educational exhibits: papermaking; local archeology; student handicraft; local photography; American books on history, literature and other subjects; the cause and prevention of schistosomiasis, an endemic worm disease in Yamanashi; the preparation of imported American food, and the care of preschool children.[23]

Dr. Maurice Jakofsky, the Team's Medical Officer, assisted with the exhibits pertaining to health. The most popular exhibit was on schistosomiasis caused by "flukes" that incubated in a small snail which inhabited rice paddies, ponds, and streams. In addition to Dr. Jakofsky, Dr. Donald M. McMullen, and Dr. Saburo Sugiura, foremost parasitologists of America and Japan, were on hand to deliver lectures and answer questions during this major exhibit. Both had been experimenting for many months in Yamanashi on how to break the life cycle of the deadly flukes which entered the body through the skin or by drinking contaminated water.

The vast majority of Yamanashi's populace managed to see this exhibit which was also shown in many other prefectural towns. During his frequent visits to Yamanashi, Dr. McMullen lived in the BOQ with other members of the Yamanashi Military Government Team. Happily, he and Dr. Sugiura succeeded in breaking the life cycle of the flukes which redounded to the benefit of millions of Japanese farm people who were inclined to work barearmed and barefooted in their fields. Very few Occupationnaires were aware that a major scientific breakthrough to improve the health of millions of Japan's citizens was achieved in Yamanashi Prefecture. In recognition of his many parasitological accomplishments, especially in the Philippines and Japan, Dr. McMullen won the Medal of Freedom, America's highest civilian award, and was granted an audience with Emperor Hirohito.

AN ADDITIONAL DUTY: LABOR EDUCATION

In January 1947, Captain John Kopke, the Team's Labor Officer and I were summoned to Headquarters, IXth Corps in Sendai to attend a two-day Labor Management Relations and Civil Information Conference for all military government Labor and CI&E Officers in the IXth Corps area. Several officials of SCAP's Civil Education and Labor Divisions were present. They were alarmed by the marching, sloganeering, and flag waving of millions of unionists and especially the fiery speech-making of Socialist and Communist union leaders who were threatening a nation-wide strike about 1 February to improve their economic lot. To help curb the growing labor turbulence, the officials desired to step up an information program to teach union leaders how to negotiate with management, private or government, to settle their disputes through collective bargaining as in America.

The upshot of the conference was a request for military government CI&E officers to assist their Team labor officers in accelerating the information campaign on the virtues of "democratic" collective bargaining, i.e., through arbitration, mediation and conciliation. SCAP's Labor Division officials quickly sent military government teams additional materials on unionism in America and postwar Japan to facilitate the educational task of CI&E and Labor officers. I was not happy to get the additional assignment. In fact, I found little time during the ensuing five months for this additional duty other than issuing a few press releases, making available Japanese language booklets on democratic unionism in the Team's library, meeting occasionally with members of the prefectural Labor Relations Committee, mandated to resolve local labor disputes, and visiting four small "factories" in or near Kofu. I spoke to only one group of unionists.[24]

Belated assistance arrived in late June 1947 when I was finally assigned my first American civilian CI&E assistant, a 23-year old university graduate who had also attended a Navy language school where he had developed a very good facility for speaking Japanese. Although he totally lacked any educational, administrative, or any other experience, I assigned to him, with the Team commander's assent, the labor education duty. As he quickly announced his admiration for Henry A. Wallace, dismissed by President Harry S. Truman as Secretary of Commerce in September 1945 because of Truman's "anti-Communism," the Team commander asked me to keep "a close eye" on our new civilian employee's performance. As he would be speaking with prefectural union leaders and officials in Japanese, it was not clear to me how this should be done.

My new assistant and I received a fast baptism in Japan's volatile postwar union movement during the period 15-25 July 1947 when SCAP and Eighth Army officials directed military government labor educational personnel to participate in a series of Labor-Management Institute Conferences in all of Japan's prefectures. In Yamanashi, one-day conferences were held in Kofu and six other prefectural towns. It was a grueling travel and lecture schedule. The agenda called for lectures and discussions on the following topics: The Purpose of Labor Laws, Labor Unions, The New Standard Labor Law, The Present Situation of Enterprises and Unions, The Theory of Labor Unions and Management, and Labor Surveillance under Current Conditions. Japanese participants consisted of representatives of the Yamanashi Labor Relations Committee, management, local trade union officers and members, primary and secondary school union members, and other professions. My new assistant and I participated as neutrals.[25]

Using materials produced by SCAP's Labor Division, my new assistant, as expected, made his presentations in Japanese while I made mine, of course, in English. Many conferees appeared more transfixed listening to an American speaking their language than to the substance of his remarks. Discussion periods were enlivened when some union leaders repeatedly asked for our views on the Taft-Hartley Labor Bill, enacted over President Truman's veto on 23 June 1947 or less than a month before the conferences began. Branded a "slave-labor" bill by unionists in the United States and also privately by SCAP's Labor Division specialists, we Americans were all enjoined nonetheless by Eighth Army to support it and it was the "law of the land." I explained to the conferees that the law, passed by a democratically elected U.S. Congress, attempted to rectify certain excesses in American union activity and that the bill undoubtedly would be modified if not repealed eventually once the excesses had been corrected.[26]

At the end of the seven one-day labor education conclaves and on the basis of Captain Kopke's labor experiences thus far, I summarized briefly, 22 months after the Occupation began, my impressions of labor management relations in Yamanashi Prefecture:

> Except for union leaders, worker's education has not progressed very far. Knowledge of new Japanese labor legislation and especially matters pertaining to collective bargaining procedures and how "democratic" trade unions should function still appears quite negligible.

> In addition, a recent survey on educational facilities in different unions in this prefecture revealed that only 11 of 111 separate unions had a small reading room to enable them to read about their union rights. Consequently, during the seven conferences, I emphasized constantly to union leaders the importance of making union literature available to workers.[27]

The traditional paternalism between many prefectural employees and employers was another impediment to democratizing local unions as was generally known and as I had also observed early in July 1947 during visits to two small silk spinning mills and two crystal factories which employed only young girls.

Although the Team commander left me in overall charge of the labor education program after this conference, I had no option but to delegate most of my work in this area to my politically uninhibited new assistant. Most of the task of resolving labor disputes in Yamanashi was left, of course, to the prefectural Labor Relations Committee. Then, after several indiscretions and repeatedly offending the Team commander and some of his uniformed colleagues with his seeming "leftist" political views, my assistant was summarily transferred in February 1948 to another military government team to a less sensitive position. He was replaced by an older civilian, Richard Zachry, who had served in the Team's administrative section for quite some months. Zachry had studied briefly at a junior college. He managed to handle the labor education task without creating political waves.

Almost concurrently, the Team received a new civilian to serve as the Team's full time information officer. This was Paul Patrick Judge, a seasoned veteran of the U.S. Army. In his early 30s, he possessed B.A. and M.A. degrees and immediately proved himself a dedicated and highly capable employee. His mission, to speed up the information programs in education, labor, land reform, health and other areas, signaled that the Occupation might end sooner rather than later. I retained only a few information duties in the area of education and labor education.

I would miss the most volatile period of efforts to "democratize" unions. In late July 1948, General MacArthur launched his famous "Red Purge." This required the Japanese Government to amend the National Public Service Law prohibiting all government workers, including members of the large Japan Teachers' Union, from striking.[28] The Government complied quickly.

When I departed for the United States a month later, it appeared doubtful, despite many meetings and conferences, whether Yamanashi's trade unionists could effectively emulate in the near term American unionists in engaging in collective bargaining with management. The ideological radical Socialists and Communists, who led the major unions in Japan, certainly had no intention of operating in "the American way." Nor had the traditional bonds of paternalism in union-management relations been completely broken.

RELIGION AND STATE ISSUES

Teaching the Japanese the merits of "religious freedom" as in America was not a problem per se, but consisted of monitoring and dealing with breaches of SCAP's directives, the new Constitution, and other postwar laws guaranteeing such freedom.

The practice of State Shintoism was quickly abolished by a SCAP directive of 15 December 1945 and other directives. Sect Shintoism remained legal but its practice created frequent problems in not only Yamanashi Prefecture but throughout Japan. The most common state-religion problems arose from activities by neighborhood associations which existed in every village, town, and city. Traditionally, they collected money from every household, based on tax records, to support local Shinto shrines and Buddhist temples and for periodic shrine festivals. Such "forcible" contributions were now deemed unlawful by SCAP's Religions Division. Upon my arrival in Yamanashi in November 1946, no less than 30 public complaints had been received by the Yamanashi Military Government Team about these contributions exacted by present or former heads of neighborhood associations. The Team's Adjutant and my CI&E predecessor, had already brought some of these violations to the attention of the prefectural Penal Affairs Office which arrested or admonished some of the association violators.[29]

I continued to do the same, issuing periodic press releases explaining why "forcible" contributions, especially to support Shinto Shrines and their festivals were now illegal. Nonetheless, the practice continued. In April 1947, I asked Mr. Hajime Akaike, my new consultant on youth activities and religion, for a report to determine if it was realistic to end the time-honored practice. His report stated in part:

> All villagers or parishioners in a rural prefecture like Yamanashi feel protected by the local Shinto shrine. Because they live in a particular settlement, they cannot be members of another. Unlike Christians who select a church of their choice, regardless of location, Japanese parishioners are bound by the settlements. Their duties are to hold festivals in the spring and autumn and repair and maintain the local shrine. According to a very old custom, money is collected according to ability to pay.

> SCAP's warnings about forcible contributions create an enormous problem for parishioners of local Shinto shrines and Buddhist temples, especially in areas where villagers look forward to the spring and autumn festivals. With few other amusements, shrine activities especially are important to rural people. For SCAP to insist all contributions for shrines and temples to be voluntary will cause deficits so large they may eventually cease to exist.

> The relationship between parishioners and the local Buddhist temple is similar. Priests hold mass for their ancestors and thus their relationship to the local Buddhist temple cannot be broken.[30]

It was a problem, Mr. Akaike added, "that can hardly be understood by foreigners." He went on to say that those who complained about "forced contributions" were in four categories: those who disliked strongly many present heads and officials of their neighborhood associations, those presently too poor to contribute, those who reported illegal fund raising to avoid getting into trouble, and local political leftists and Communists who wished to change drastically Japan's social, religious, and political institutions.[31]

Mr. Akaike's report reinforced my growing feeling that a SCAP directive of 6 November 1946 specifically prohibiting neighborhood associations from collecting funds for any purposes was unrealistic. Although duty-bound to enforce SCAP directives on this issue, I turned over to local authorities for investigation hereafter only the most egregious complaints, letting Mr. Akaike monitor and deal with the others. Although SCAP abolished neighborhood associations on 1 April 1947 to end forcible contributions for religion and other reasons, such as the practice of denying scarce food rations to repatriated Japanese who were adjudged not "legal" residents of a community, Yamanashi's neighborhood associations, now "democratically reorganized," continued to function. Certainly in Yamanashi, most citizens could not perceive how anything could be done efficiently without them.

Meanwhile, other religion-state issues arose. Mr. Akaike dealt with many of them. If sufficiently serious, I handled them in conjunction with the prefectural Penal Affairs Office which investigated the violations. The following is a partial list of religion-state issues that arose: The failure of a village headman to remove completely a shrine, formerly containing a picture of the Emperor, from the entrance of a primary school; dismissal of a primary school principal who persisted in taking students to a local shrine during the school day; denying a village headman permission to collect money for a Shinto ceremony for eight deceased soldiers from his village; denying permission of a Buddhist priest to lecture in public schools on Buddhism, student discipline, and to sell talismans to ward off "poor behavior," and assisting villagers in replacing a local Buddhist priest who was incapable of meeting their needs.[32]

There was one incident in the religion-state area that proved quite traumatic for me. It followed an inspection in May 1947 of Yamanashi's *Gokoku Jinja* (shrine) for the local war dead while the shrine was celebrating its first postwar "festival." The purpose of the inspection was to determine if the "festival" would trigger a local revival of "militarism" and "ultranationalism." The shrine's chief priest, believing I had come to pay my respects to Yamanashi's deceased warriors, dating from the beginning of the Meiji Restoration in 1860 through World War II, excitedly informed Yamanashi's largest newspaper of my "official visit" which carried the story the next morning with a large headline and a lengthy account.[33]

Several breathless hours elapsed before a member of SCAP's Religions Division assured me by phone that the erroneous report did not appear in one of Tokyo's national newspapers, and the local newspaper editor explained to me how the story managed to be printed. At my instruction, his paper published a "correction" the following day.[34] As World War II had ended only 20 months earlier, it was an untimely incident as many Americans still harbored very harsh feelings about the Japanese. Thus the knowledge and quick resolution of the "flap" was confined to Yamanashi Prefecture. At the time, I feared my immediate dismissal, if not by high SCAP officials, then perhaps by General MacArthur himself and my dispatch on the next boat to the United States. Also happily, the Team commander was not in his office that day. I explained the incident to him later, assuring him I had "cleared everything with SCAP."

CI&E AND LABOR EDUCATION CONFERENCES

Military Government CI&E officers and their assistants did not work in complete isolation. During my 22 months with the Yamanashi Military Government Team I participated in 11 conferences. There were two combined CI&E and Labor Education conferences for American attendees at Headquarters, IXth Corps in Sendai and Tokyo, respectively. There were five other CI&E conferences, all but one solely for American attendees. One was held at Headquarters, IXth Corps in Sendai. The other four were convened by Dr. Rollin C. Fox, the CI&E officer of the Kanto Military Government Region which exercised nominal supervision over eight prefectural CI&E offices. They were held at the following places: military government team headquarters in Niigata, Saitama and Gumma Prefectures, and at the Kanto Region's headquarters near Tokyo. Seven prefectural education chiefs participated at the conference in Gumma Prefecture.[35]

In Yamanashi Prefecture, I participated with the Team's Labor Education Officer in a series of four major conferences in which all other lecturers and attendees were Japanese. One was a series of one-day labor education conferences held in Kofu and six other towns in the last half of July 1947. In addition, a series of adult education conferences was conducted in Kofu and other towns from September 1947 to July 1948.

Ranking SCAP officials were present to lecture and participate in the discussions for some of these conclaves, especially the two military government CI&E and labor education conferences held in Sendai and Tokyo in January and August 1947, respectively. At some of the others, SCAP participants included Dr. Helen Heffernan, a specialist in primary education, Ethel Weed, chief of women's education, Dr. Virginia A. Carley, a specialist in higher education, and Donald M. Typer who headed SCAP's Youth Associations and Student Activities Branch.

At all of the conferences, whether exclusively for military government CI&E and labor education officers, or jointly with the Japanese, the formal agendas and informal discussions covered the gamut of progress and problems in SCAP-instituted reforms: new lower and upper secondary schools, higher education, education associations, teachers' unions, overcrowded classrooms, insufficient school supplies, inadequate teachers' manuals, school curriculums, student discipline, teaching clinics, coeducation, a proposed five-day school week, remedial teacher training, and vocational and religious education. Also the social education programs, particularly youth associations, women's organizations, PTAs, plus labor education. Sessions with Japanese participants from prefectural offices, educators, unionists and others included in one instance lectures and discussions on the democratizations of towns and villages, cultural improvement, and the prospects of Japan in international relations.[37]

At the time of the CI&E-Labor Education Conference at Headquarters, IXth Corps in Sendai in January 1947, which drew attendees from 15 prefectures in northern Honshu, including the special regional/district of Hokkaido, only a few civilians had replaced uniformed officers. At the Kanto Military Government Region's first CI&E conference in June 1947 in Niigata Prefecture, seven of the eight invited prefectural military government CI&E officers were civilians (one was absent). Most had previous teaching experience in public schools. I had previous administrative experience in the office of the Dean of Students at a university, with the U.S. National Labor Relations Board, and in the area of public administration.

In July 1947, Eighth Army authorized a maximum of 605 civilians to serve on military government teams, but I have no data indicating how many were actually recruited.[38]   I can only surmise perhaps half of this number were obtained. The majority, I gathered, were CI&E officers, their assistants, and Women's Education Officers. On the Yamanashi Military Government Team there were for a brief period four professional civilians in the following positions: CI&E, labor education, public welfare, and information. The full time Information Officer did not join the Team until February 1948.

In conversations with my military government CI&E colleagues at numerous CI&E conferences, I found that the similarities in problems experienced by my counterparts, especially those within the Kanto Military Government Region, in attempting to "democratize" the educational system and adults, were quite similar to those I experienced in Yamanashi Prefecture. Except for the largest urban areas, it appeared evident to most of us that the legacy of a highly centralized and authoritarian system of education and government and a strong Confucian culture could not be replaced easily by an American style democracy. This legacy made it relatively easy for the radical Japan Teachers' Union in Tokyo and its branches in all of the prefectures, to be the new "authoritarians" in educational matters.

In addition, we agreed generally that SCAP pursued too many educational programs simultaneously and too rapidly for Japan's teachers and other educators and the populace to absorb quickly, a populace that had the additional daily burden of obtaining the bare necessities of life in a war-torn and inflation-wracked economy. Several SCAP educationists I knew at the time agreed. By early 1946, we were all aware that the Occupation might end sooner than expected. Many of us also believed that, given the nation's economic disarray, a prolonged Occupation was also a threat to "democratization." Admittedly, by the time I departed for the United States in late

August 1948 to resume my graduate studies, there were still Occupationnaires, mostly uniformed including some on my Team, who believed Japan should be occupied indefinitely, a view with which I disagreed.

Most of us CI&E civilians and some uniformed personnel who were responsible for CI&E programs on military government teams far from Tokyo nonetheless did the best we could in the limited time available. Generally, what the Occupation achieved or failed to achieve in the educational area in Japan already is history. What remains to be written, however, is the full extent CI&E and other officers on 45 military government teams effectively supplemented the massive educational and other reform programs, directed by General MacArthur and his large professional staff in Tokyo, for the purpose of "democratizing" the Japanese people and its institutions.

On the basis of my personal experiences in Yamanashi Prefecture and knowledge of the activities of my CI&E counterparts within the Kanto Military Government Region, which encompassed eight prefectures, I believe we accomplished more than is generally realized.

NOTES

1.   Yamanashi Military Government Team (hereinafter cited as YMGT) Reports, December 1946-February 1947.

2.   Transcripts of addresses presented at Labor Management and CI&E Conference at Headquarters IXth Corps, 21-22 January 1947; personal letters, 23 and 25 January 1947.

3.   Personal letters, 13 and 15 November 1946.

4.   Ibid.

5.   Ibid.

6.   Personal letters, 11 and 15 November 1946.

7.   YMGT Reports, 16-31 November 1946.

8.   *Report of the United States Education Mission to Japan*, 30 March 1946, p. 26.

9.   YMGT Reports, April 1947.

10.   Ibid., June 1948.

11.   Ibid., November 1947.

12.   Ibid., March 1947; notes on Normal Schools, 14 March 1947.

13.   YMGT Reports, March 1947.

14.   Ibid., 1-15 November 1946; notes on Meeting with New Youth Association, November 1946.

15.   Ibid.

16.   YMGT Reports, April 1947 and March 1948.

17.   YMGT Reports, February 1947; personal letter, 30 February 1947.

18.   Ibid.

19.   YMGT Reports, April 1947, An. G., subject: Election Report.

20.   Personal letter, 20 February 1947.

21.   Memo, *The Citizens Public Hall: An Outline of its Creation and Management* (prepared by Adult Education Branch, Civil Education Division, Headquarters SCAP), 1 July 1946.

22.   YMGT Reports, September-December 1946.

23.   Special Report, *Record of Exhibits Held Under the Auspices of the YMGT*, prepared by CI&E staff member, December 1946-September 1947.

24.   YMGT Reports, February-June 1947.

25.   YMGT Reports, July 1947, and notes July 1947.

26.   Ibid.

27.   Personal letters, July 1947.

28.   Benjamin C. Duke, *Japan's Militant Teachers: A History of the Left-Wing Teachers' Movement*, (An East-West Center Book, The University Press of Hawaii, Honolulu, 1973), pp. 85-86.

29.   YMGT Reports, November 1947.

30.   Memo, Mr. Hajime Akaike, Consultant on Youth Associations and Religion to CI&E Officer, YMGT, no subject, 15 April 1947.

31.   Ibid.

32.   YMGT Reports, January 1947 through July 1948.

33.   Personal letter, 7 May 1947.

34.   Ibid.

35.   Ibid.

36.   YMGT Reports, January 1947-July 1948; personal letters, January 1948-July 1948.

37.   Agendas of Conferences, January 1947-July 1948; personal letters, January 1947-July 1948.

38.   Horner, Layton, *The American Occupation of Japan at the Prefecture Level* (M.A. Thesis, University of Denver), December 1949, p. 18.

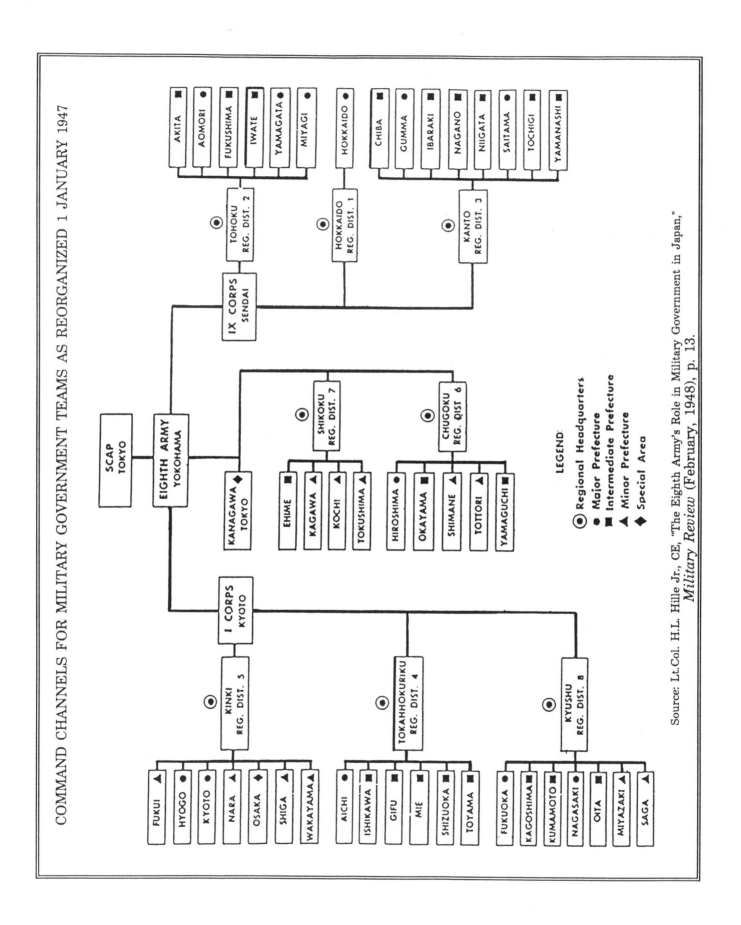

COMMAND CHANNELS FOR MILITARY GOVERNMENT TEAMS AS REORGANIZED 1 JANUARY 1947

LEGEND:

- ⊙ Regional Headquarters
- ● Major Prefecture
- ■ Intermediate Prefecture
- ▲ Minor Prefecture
- ◆ Special Area

Source: Lt.Col. H.L. Hille Jr., CE, "The Eighth Army's Role in Military Government in Japan," *Military Review* (February, 1948), p. 13.

LEADERSHIP OF MILITARY GOVERNMENT TEAMS AND CI&E IN THE EDUCATIONAL PURGES AND PUBLIC REACTION

Reiko Yamamoto

REIKO YAMAMOTO is a researcher and staff member at Meisei University Research Center for Postwar Educational History of Japan. She is a 1983 graduate of Sophia University in Tokyo and received a M.A. in History from the University of California at Santa Cruz in 1985. She is a Ph.D. candidate at Meisei University. Miss Yamamoto published *The Educational Purge Under the Occupation* in the *Nihon Kyoiku Shimbun* [Japan Education Newspaper] in 1992. (Note: The presenter expresses gratitude for suggestions on style and content made by Dr. Harry Wray, Professor of History, Yokohama National University.)

LEADERSHIP OF MILITARY GOVERNMENT TEAMS AND CIE
IN THE EDUCATIONAL PURGES

This paper is a two part study of educational purges carried out by the Civil Information and Education Section (CI&E). My first section deals with the leadership of Military Government Teams in particular with local educational purges, and focuses on their involvement in the establishment and reorganization of local screening committees. In the second part, this paper discusses public reaction to the screening process through an investigation of grass roots correspondence to GHQ.

A thorough study on the administrative system and activities of Local Military Government (MG) has been done by Akira Abe, Professor of Osaka University.[1] Focusing on interactions on the prefectural basis between Military Government Teams and Japanese administrators, he described Occupational personnel, the roles and activities of MG, and the impact of the educational reforms. The first half of this paper, however, focuses on the leadership of Military Government Teams in one of their special activities, the project of screening local teachers and educational officials, and discusses two points. One problem was a general disorganized implementation of policy caused in part by MG Teams' precipitous implementation of screening without coordination with SCAP policy. The other point discussed is the dilemma which existed between MG Teams' excessively active leadership and the CI&E's more deliberate goal of teaching democracy through the screening process. My examination of CI&E records discloses frequent disputes between CI&E and MG regarding these two points.

The Implementation of SCAP Directives
on Educational Purge

Two directives were issued to eliminate the influence of militarism and ultra-nationalism from education in Japan. One was the "Administration of the Educational System of Japan" (22 October 1945), and the other was the "Investigation, Screening, and Certification of Teachers and Educational Officials" (30 October 1945). The latter instructed the Japanese Government to establish machinery for screening teachers and educational officials and for evaluating their acceptability in the educational field.

For the Japanese implementation of the two directives, Imperial Ordinance 263 (7 May 1946) was promulgated. By this Ordinance, the Japanese Government established detailed criteria for purging educators and educational officials, and set up five kinds of committees for evaluating the acceptability or lack of acceptability of the above criteria.[2]

At the local level, Prefectural Inquiry Committees for Teachers' Acceptability investigated teachers of elementary and secondary grade schools and school inspectors. These local committees were placed under the jurisdiction of prefectural governors, and each committee was composed of thirteen members. Seven were teachers from the concerned local area. They were recommended by the Japan Educational Association, and six were representatives of organizations deemed suitable by the prefectural governor, an appointed official, still in 1946.

Involvement of Local Military Government (MG)

The involvement of MG was active in the early stage of the implementation of screening. The conservative nature of the seven teachers selected by Japan Educational Association, which had been an established organization subservient to the Ministry of Education in the prewar period, drew the immediate attention of the Education Officer of I Corps, Ronald S. Anderson. On 9 July 1946 he sent a telegram to each prefecture within I Corps territory and requested the postponement of the selection of screening committee members under his jurisdiction until such time as representatives of I Corps Headquarters could visit and instruct the local screening committees according to the I Corps Policy.

Informed by Iichi Sagara, chief Secretariat of the Screening Administration Office of the Ministry of Education [Mombusho], of MG orders to have all the meetings of the Inquiry Committee open to the public, and to have a representative of Labor Unions placed on the prefectural inquiry committee, Major Roy Arrowood, in charge of the screening of Education Division, had a conference with Anderson on 22 July. Anderson told Arrowood that some of the prefectural screening committees were made up of at least 50 percent former members of the Imperial Rule Assistance Association (IRAA), many of whom formerly held important positions in it. Anderson believed that even though I Corps had exceeded its authority in ordering the screening proceedings to stop, this action had facilitated the establishment of more efficient screening committees.[3] Consequently, he implemented his own views without prior consultation with CI&E, and regardless of the subsequent opposition of CI&E.

On 22 July 1946 Anderson submitted to CI&E a "Report on Investigations of the Teacher-Screening Arrangements in Twenty Prefectures under I Corps Jurisdiction." It was the product of MG's reports from each prefecture. The report consisted of "Reasons for the Investigations," "Purposes of the Trips," "Procedure of Meetings," "I Corps Recommendations," and "General Recommendation." Anderson stated in the report: "It was reasoned that unless drastic action were taken immediately the purposes and spirit of the screening directives would be defeated." He emphasized the importance of MGs frequently checking on the screening process. He even recommended more radical standards for screening. According to the "I Corps Recommendations" and "General Recommendation" categories, it was boldly suggested that former IRAA members be relieved of membership on the committee, that the committee should be as broadly representative as possible of the major elements in the prefecture, including the forces of the New Japan such as women, youth, and labor, and for example, bona fide representatives of real farmers instead of agricultural associations.[4]

Opposition of Education Division, CI&E to Anderson's Implementation

The Education Division of CI&E felt that it was better to let the local governors make selections for committee members in accordance with provisions of Imperial Ordinance 263 without any influence from the MG Units. If Military Government or Counter Intelligence Corp (CIC) concluded that certain selected screening members were not acceptable, it should request the prefectural governor to change the committee. The Education Division asserted their view as follows:

> Inasmuch as it is the policy of CI&E to allow the Mombusho to carry out the screening by itself and to hold it responsible for the success or failure of the program, it is suggested that some steps be taken to keep such interference at a minimum, and if possible, to correct the situations outlined above.[5]

In contrast with Anderson's view that the screening committees should be instructed by the Occupation, the Education Division, CI&E advocated that Japanese implementation of the educational reforms should be autonomous and self-determined, and regarded the involvement of the MG as nothing but interference, and criticized Anderson's drastic measure.

Confusion Caused by "Interference" by Military Government

Prefectural authorities experienced much trouble and confusion in operating the screening committees. Almost every day in August, Sagara reported to the Education Division complaints from prefectural screening committees. For example, in Shizuoka prefecture, the screening committee was ordered by MG in the midst of their proceedings to reorganize their committee after 300 teachers had been screened. This action forced them to rescreen the 300 teachers.[6] Requesting minimum interference from MG, the Ministry of Education submitted to the CI&E a report entitled

"Negotiations Between Prefectural Governments and Military Government Investigated by the Education Ministry." According to the report, some orders were given by MG education officers that committees be suspended or reconstituted to select women, more farmer members, and so on. (Gifu, Nagasaki, Kyoto, Yamanashi, Ishikawa, Fukushima, Toyama, etc.) Other orders required them to submit the English version of the screening questionnaires.[7]

Sympathetic with Japanese local authorities, CI&E called for improvement of the attitude of the Military Government, and requested minimum interference by the Military Government units. Major Arrowood wrote that MG should feel free to make suggestions but it was not felt advisable to state that committees must contain specific categories such as women, etc.[8] CI&E seems to have emphasized that implementation of their policy should comply with Imperial Ordinance 263 because that practice would be an implementation of the SCAP objective of educating Japanese in democracy. On the other hand, MG actions were too drastic and too hasty, and went beyond the role prescribed in the Provisional Manual of the Military Government.

According to that Manual, while GHQ, SCAP was to execute policy and planning, the military government mission was effective surveillance and supervision of the Japanese in executing directives issued to their government by SCAP. In fact, however, the latter often operated almost independently of SCAP. It was a constant frustration of SCAP officials, who were looking at a larger picture of teaching democratic process, that they could not order MG teams and discipline them for exceeding SCAP plans. This was because they were under the direct jurisdiction of the Eighth Army located in Yokohama. The Occupation's enthusiasm for the job of democratizing Japan at times outran its grasp of the situation when MG neglected systematic cooperation with CI&E.

Reorganization of the Prefectural Screening Committees

In October 1946, a few months after the purging process began, the screening of about two hundred thousand teachers (about one-third) was completed, and only slightly more than one hundred were found unacceptable.[9] This was an extremely small number of purgees. In order to improve the screening program, CI&E agreed with MG that certain screening committees should be reorganized. In contrast with the confusion in establishing the original screening committees, reorganization of the new screening committees was carried out in a smooth and democratic way under the CI&E initiative.

CI&E requested MG to submit recommendations and to report which committees were required reorganization and to give the reasons why it was felt necessary to request such reorganization. They were asked as well, in case reorganization took place, to justify the necessity of rescreening personnel previously screened.[10] At the same time CI&E ordered the Ministry of Education to conduct its own investigation with the assistance of prefectural officials. The Ministry of Education stated to CI&E that an expansion of the scope of the Public Officials Purge Directive would affect the committee members' acceptability, and reorganization might be necessary. The Ministry of Education telephoned prefectural officials and requested them to report on their investigation by 20 November. The CI&E and Ministry of Education compared recommendations from MG and local Japanese officials, and both agreed that 20 committees from among 46 prefectures plus 3 school block inquiry committees should be reorganized.[11]

CI&E, in clarifying "Standards for New Committees," strongly emphasized the role of MG as follows:

> The ruling that all new members must have the Approval of MG does not mean that MG should unduly hold up the reorganization of the committee. MG and Appointing Authority should confer together on Appointments. MG should make suggestions to the Appointing Authority and be sure that the Appointing Authority fully understand that they are suggestions. MG will not tell the Appointing Authority that they must appoint so-and-so.[12]

The former experience of undue MG interference led CI&E to give strict warnings to MG in order that Japanese initiative in the reform might not be violated. But it did not mean that CI&E gave the Japanese authorities a free hand. Surveillance and investigation were reasonably undertaken with the intention that the CI&E policy should encourage Japanese autonomy. When reorganization was to be undertaken, CI&E cautiously wrote, "MG should not let the Japanese know the committees recommended for change, because the Japanese are running the same survey and should not be influenced.[13]

Local Military Government Contributions to Reorganization

The Ministry of Education studied the recommendations made by MG for committee reorganizations, and approved all the recommendations. As stated above, 23 committees were ordered to be reorganized. The chiefs of the Prefectural Bureau of Education, for each of the prefectures where the changes recommended, were ordered to come up to Tokyo for a joint conference with the Ministry of Education and CI&E, and there they were told the names of the committee members to be changed.[14] In this case as well, to encourage Japanese autonomy nothing written was handed to those representatives, but the changes decided upon by CI&E and Ministry of Education were given to the prefectural representatives in the form of a verbal order in order that the prefectural authorities should have the opportunity to give their opinions to the Ministry of Education.[15] Afterwards, a written order was sent out officially.

At this conference a significant suggestion, which R.S. Anderson had asked CI&E to make, was made to each prefecture about the screening procedures, if a change took place. Anderson specified the persons who should be rescreened by the new committees. They were as follows:

a. All principals
b. All head-teachers
c. All inspectors
d. All educators who have served as inspectors, head-teachers or principals in the past.
e. Those who have published books or articles as described in Appendix I of 263.
f. All founders of schools
g. In addition, others considered necessary by the new committee to be rescreened. In these cases the new committee will consult with Military Government.[16]

His suggestion was called a "Seven Point Plan" and became the base of a later Formal Instruction of Eighth Army on 5 January 1947. It effectively worked to improve the screening process because it was specific in its instructions for rescreening by the newly reorganized committees. The "Seven Point Plan" also served as encouragement of a speedy settlement of problems raised in the process of screening as well as the instruction that postponement of a case would take place only under exceptional circumstances.

In the meantime, CI&E clarified the "standard for determining a good committee."[17] But the MG reports of investigation of prefectural committees proved the committees to be far from their expectation. Those reports submitted to CI&E concerning the operation of prefectural committee were critical and can be summarized as follows:

a. Removal of committee members was recommended because of absence and general lack of interest in the committee work. (Aomori, Tochigi, Kyoto, Shiga, Toyama, Tottori, Kagoshima)

b. The election of the committee members was typical Japanese election in which the relatively well-known people in authority were automatically elected. But they were too busy to devote adequate time to the activities of the screening committees. (Shiga, Niigata, Kagoshima, Tottori)

c. Since seven of thirteen committee members (representatives of educators) were mostly principals, they were recommended for removal and more classroom teachers had to be elected. (Hokkaido, Tokyo, Osaka, Saga, Miyazaki)

d. Time allotted to each person screened was limited to only about two minutes. (Yamaguchi, Osaka, Tottori, Tochigi, Gunma)

e. Since committee members did not receive even "one cent" for their work, MG, especially Anderson, commented that they should be paid adequately for an extremely important job. For the sake of dignity of the committee it was recommended that a salary be offered, in accord with the "Principle of democracy." (Kyoto, Tokyo, Hyogo)

f. The majority of the committee members had never experienced taking individual actions. At this most important time of requiring action they showed no tendency to indicate individual thought and assertion. (Shiga, Kagoshima)[18]

The sources of information for the above recommendations and comments were an important factor in determining the nature of the MG reports to the Education Division. In some cases sources came from MG observations of the committees, the prefectural education sections, chairmen of the committees, interviews with other external officials of the organizations, etc. (Miyagi, Mie, Tottori, Oita), but in other cases from CIC (Aomori, Akita, Shimane, Yamaguchi). The former contained positive information in general, such as "carefully and well chosen for their task and the present board is considered to be doing a thorough and conscientious job of screening teachers."[19] The CIC reports, however, were critical and negative.

Reorganization was orderly due to cooperation between both MG and CI&E, in contrast with the critical troubles and confusion on the Japanese side caused by the interference of MG in the establishment of the original screening committee. The nation-wide investigation of the committees initiated by CI&E and cooperated with by MG was, in general, successful in increasing the number of unacceptable teachers. It served to improve the quality of committee members, and to select more representative members, while the drastic action initiated by MG only caused confusion.

Result of Reorganization and its Legacy

As shown by the table below, reorganization resulted in a remarkable increase in the number of unacceptable educators. Most of the purged were from those who were rescreened by the "Seven Point Plan," those who were put aside for further investigations, and those who were returned from Central Inquiry Committee to local screening committees for re-examination.

	As of 30 November 1946	As of 30 April 1947
Total screen	395,801	568,228
Those unacceptable by first examination	422	2,268
Those unacceptable by second examination	1,506	2,943

An issue of regional discrepancy, however, occurred in strictness of judgment. A heated debate developed about whether a decentralized system and program of screening or a central supervision of the national screening program provided a more democratic juridical process. Aomori, Ishikawa, Shizuoka, Aichi, Gifu, Shiga, Nara, Kumamoto, and Kagoshima prefectures, all of which were under Anderson's jurisdiction except Aomori, provided a great increase in unacceptable educators. Among them Nara showed the most noteworthy increase in purgees.

Up to the time of the reorganization, the Nara Prefectural Teachers Screening Committee had examined 5,200 teachers and educational officials. Out of this number, 101 individual cases were deferred or put aside for further consideration, and ultimately none were purged. The MG Team report, after thorough investigation, gave detailed reasons for the original committee's failure to purge more persons.[21] After the reorganization, by the end of April 1947, 66 were judged unacceptable. The number of unacceptable per 1,000 persons became 13.2, the highest number of all prefectures.[22]

The previous process of examining questionnaires prepared by those who were to be screened was thought to be an ineffective and unsatisfactory method for determining guilt. Accordingly, after the reorganization, the MG and local officers asked the people of Nara Prefecture to report information regarding undesirable educators in all Nara newspapers. This information was used as a source for the screening committee's decision. MG reported to CI&E that the information seemed to be a more likely method for achieving justice, and for representing the will of the Japanese people. Some other causes were reported as well for failure of the earlier screening in Nara prefecture such as a reluctance to carry out "excessive" screening, and misunderstanding, on the part of officials and committee members, of the true function of the committee, etc. They concluded, "the new members are becoming gradually conscious of the fact that their most important responsibility is, more than the mere compliance with existing screening regulations, the interpretation and definition of those regulations."[23] On the 25th of February, through Headquarters Eighth Army to SCAP, the Nara Military Government Team reported that "the reorganized screening committee was taking hold of the job in a positive manner and it confidently expected definite results in the near future."[24]

Those educators who were judged unacceptable made a judicial appeal to the Central Inquiry Committee. That committee with the approval of the CI&E Review Board reversed and qualified some decisions of the prefectural committee. Others were referred back to the original committee for "lack of concrete evidence." The Nara Military Government Team and Nara Prefectural Screening Committee were critical of the reversed decisions made by the Central Inquiry Committee. The Nara Military Government Team commented bitterly.

...there is considerable evidence to indicate that the Central ISC is following a conservative policy, which, if it results in considerable reversal of our decisions, will be disastrous to the democratization of education in Nara Prefecture.[25]

Furthermore, the Nara Military Government Team stated that members of the Ministry of Education had put pressure on the prefectural screening committee to "desist from their active screening policy." MG suggested to CI&E that reversed decisions be carefully examined by the authorities concerned with the approval of SCAP (in fact they had already been examined by the CI&E Review Board), and that they be referred to the local CI&E officer for comment.[26] Immediately, CI&E responded as follows:

Officials of the Ministry of Education and of the Central Inquiry Committee have reported that the Nara Screening Committee, upon ascertaining that it had established categories additional to and in contravention of those contained in Imperial Ordinance 263...Inasmuch as Imperial Ordinance 263 and Japanese Government Ordinance 62 are in implementation of directives issued by the Supreme Commander for the Allied Powers, it is considered that strict compliance with the letter and spirit of these ordinances should be required of all screening committees.

Furthermore, CI&E stated that returned cases to the original committee indicated the necessity for more substantial documentary evidence or authenticated statements in support of the committee's decision. Moreover, they stated that decisions of the Central Inquiry Committee had been reviewed by officials of SCAP, and they would not be referred to the Military Government for comment.[27] The dispute between the Nara MG and the Central Inquiry Committee drew the attention of Lt. Col. Mark T. Orr, Chief of Education Division and Donald R. Nugent, Chief of CI&E. Orr told Leon A. Kief, Liaison and Investigation Branch officer, to "prepare draft reply per his recommendations."[28]

On 6 October 1947, Kief wrote a Memorandum to the Chief of Education Division. In it he asserted the screening policy of CI&E. He declared himself in favor of "continuation of the System in operation," namely since central supervision of the national screening program was provided for a democratic court system, final decision on appeals was to be made by Ministry of Education (and SCAP) as the highest tribunal. By this time, Kief had become confident of Sagara's (Chief secretariat of Ministry of Education) "tactful diligence and conscientiousness in his execution of a difficult assignment." He also opposed adoption of the decentralized system of screening recommended by Nara as follows:

Adoption of the decentralized system of screening might understandably result in a marked increase of impassioned decisions motivated by personal prejudice, local politics, bigotry, etc. It can easily be envisaged how, under this system, personal animosities might gain the ascendancy over dispassionate judgment.[29]

This case was not the only example of the frustration experienced by local teachers' screening committees. In Kumamoto prefecture, a report to CI&E through channels stated that the percentage of reversed cases appealed to the Central Inquiry Committee against prefectural judgments and of returned cases for further evidence and documentation was 38 percent and 55 percent respectively. The report of the Kumamoto Military Government Team read, "The Central Screening Committee of the Education Ministry in Tokyo is exerting undue pressure on the decision making function of the Kumamoto Teacher Screening Committee." They requested that some clarification of the local committee's power be made as distinguished from the power of the Central Screening Committee, and that the Central Screening Committee be restrained from requiring further documentation.[30]

All reversed cases by the Central Inquiry Committee were submitted to the Education Division, CI&E for approval of CI&E Review Board. Significantly, therefore, the judgment of final acceptability of an educator was not only that of the Central Inquiry Committee, but also that of CI&E. Furthermore, the CI&E Review Board's emphasis was based on a strict compliance with the letter and spirit of the law. For example, it made a strict distinction between ultra-nationalism and patriotism. As a result of the foregoing levels in the screening process, discrepancies in screening results among the different prefectures, between prefectures and the central screening committee, and, finally, even among the members of CI&E Review Board invited significant discussions.[31]

In contrast with the demands for autonomy by local screening committees, and an assertion of justification of their judgments, the CI&E supported the central committee from the viewpoint that screening should be fair and limit discrepancies among prefectures. In a sense, then, the screening process reveals a dilemma in the fundamental Occupational policy of decentralization. Namely, complete autonomy of local committees without central review would promote the SCAP policy of decentralization, but it could, as we have seen above, weaken the goal of teaching democracy. The system of appeal provided greater justice in the screening process and was indispensable for the purpose of pursuing democratization. This thinking is described in the following CI&E policy document of the Education Division written by Leon A. Kief, chairman of the CI&E screening Review Board, with the consent of Nugent:

In its consideration of appealed cases, the Screening Review Board has, from its institution, adhered strictly to and been motivated by the following:

a. Conscientious interpretation of the letter and spirit of Imperial Ordinance 263 and Government ordinance 62, as well as of the Ministry of Education notifications clarifying, elaborating, or modifying the Ordinances.

b. Directions and specific policies set forth in memoranda from Chief, CI&E.

c. Unprejudiced reasoning.

d. Abiding realization that screening of educators is necessarily more severe than that of other public service officials.

e. Fundamental concepts of American legal justice.[32]

The activities of MG were no doubt a significant factor in considering the matter of Japanese interactions with the Occupational Authorities at the prefectural levels. MG Teams had a great impact on Japanese attitudes toward the Occupation. Professor Abe has repeatedly reported how MG and local Japanese officials contacted each other. This paper discloses how the attitude and leadership of MG affected the local level in one area of their activity, the teachers' screening program. When MG Teams moved too precipitously to achieve their goals, they deviated from SCAP objectives and created bad public relation with Japanese. By contrast, well-organized and collaborative work between CI&E and MG operations, such as that seen in the reorganization of the local screening committees, proved to be effective in the practical achievement of Occupational policy.

One of the most important things that has ever been described about CI&E policy and attitude toward democratization of Japan is revealed in CI&E Records. From an educational point of view, the Education Division, CI&E made a strenuous effort to demonstrate the "American Creed," "American Legal Justice," and "American Justice" in its judicial operation of the screening committees. It can safely be said that in these screening activities the CI&E found an important stage for demonstrating democratic principles. Furthermore, as far as the educational purge is concerned, a general sense of justice and fairness seems to have been the fundamental principle at which the CI&E adhered. This can be seen at the beginning of the Occupation even in the investigation of purges by Memorandum Cases. That attitude and practice was maintained all through CI&E Screening Review Board Judgments. The existence of a democratic court system of screening plus the final reviewing decisions on appeals made by the Ministry of Education with the approval of CI&E functioned as an organ for fair decisions. Those procedures avoided discrepancies in interpretations of screening regulations by prefectures, even though such a process limited the decentralization of the screening system.

PUBLIC REACTION TOWARD THE SCREENING OPERATION

One of the most exciting features of public participation in the educational reforms was the correspondence to GHQ or General MacArthur from the grass roots level. Emancipation from wartime nationalistic and militaristic indoctrination and restrictions on free speech inspired Japanese people to express themselves, and they became vociferous. Moreover, this was backed by MacArthur himself, a powerful sympathizer of democratic movements. Professor Sodei, our keynote speaker, wrote in his book that about 500,000 letters were sent to GHQ, and that most of them never failed to begin their letters with sincere admiration of MacArthur.[33] This is also true of all the letters related to the educational purges.

Because of the smaller number of purgees than had been expected, some prefectural screening committees, acting on instruction from prefectural Military Government Teams, asked the newspapers to encourage the people to send relevant information to help with teacher screening. A considerable number of letters were written by the people to local screening committees or MGs, and directly to MacArthur or GHQ, CI&E.

CI&E reactions toward the letters, in general, seem to have been cool and indifferent, and very few direct actions seem to have been taken as a result of them. At the local level, however, the impact of letters from the general public was significant. Among the correspondence were grudge letters by persons who simply attacked one another. This type of correspondence added to the confusion and burdens which screening committees faced. Proof that these acrimonious grudge letters constituted a problem in achieving real justice can be seen in the Ministry of Education's warning to each local screening committee that they should not be unduly affected by irresponsible censure.

It is true that one element of the contemporary Japanese general public was expressed in the correspondence to GHQ, but it is not all inclusive. Obviously, most of the Japanese did not write letters, and in most cases the accused kept silent. This fact must not be forgotten in evaluating the public reaction under the Occupation.

Nonetheless, those letters written relevant to the screening process eloquently express grass roots reflections and evaluations of what happened in the teachers screening from the public point of view. Accordingly, this paper discusses the problems incurred from the American initiative in calling for grass roots contributions to the screening process and analyzes the public view toward SCAP's aim of eliminating militarism and ultra-nationalism.

American Idea of Calling
for Information
from General Public

The idea of encouraging people to write letters to the Occupation originated not only at the MG level, but also as a proposal of Lt. Scott George, a member of the Education Division, CI&E. In the beginning of August 1946, George made the suggestion to the Chief of the Education Division, Mark T. Orr, that "democracy" should be taught to Japanese people through their direct participation in the reform process. In my view George's suggestion originated from two ideals: a) the American principle of individualism which had been strengthened through the frontier experience, and b) the belief that democracy should be learned through a democratic process.

George suspected unproductive results from the screening process, even at an early stage. For he had seen a conservative mood and tendency exerting a great deal of influence on the contemplated educational reforms. According to George, to ask screenees themselves if they were militarists or ultra-nationalists would result in nothing but immediate negative answers based on self-preservation. He predicted that, without any third-party testimony, screening programs would be completely ineffective. He believed as well that parents of Japanese children knew much more about bad teachers than CI&E or the screening committees. Accordingly, he thought parental correspondence should be sent to the local MG, and be turned over to screening committees for their action. According to him, public participation was an essential practice of "democracy."[34]

In a memorandum to Orr of 31 July 1946, dealing with teacher screening, George appended a "Statement to the Japanese people," which read as follows:

As Japanese citizens, you must know that a large part of the responsibility for the war lies with wicked school teachers, those teachers who cooperated gladly with the militarists in power, taught their students that it was right to wage aggressive war, and gave them, not an education for useful living, but an education for death. Japan can never resume her place among the nations as a peaceful, respected country until such teachers are no longer in the schools. The removal of such people is one of the aims of the Occupation forces, it is also the aim of all forward-looking Japanese.

As the parents of the boys and girls of new Japan, it is your duty to help remove your children from the evil influence of militarism. You, the people of Japan, know who the bad teachers are, and you know who should be removed. If these bad teachers still remain, in spite of the best efforts of the screening committee, if mistakes have been made, write to the Military Government Company in your own prefecture. Tell them the name of the teachers you think should be removed; give them reason why you think so. All such complaints will be turned over to the screening committee, who will give them a fair, honest judgment.

People of Japan, you have asked the meaning of this mysterious word "democracy," and been puzzled and bewildered. But it is no more than this, that the ordinary people have the privilege and the duty of determining who shall administer their government, make their laws, teach in their schools. We must come down from meaningless generalities to concrete facts, and in this case the concrete fact is that you people have it in your power to put into your schools the kind of teachers you think should be there. Take that responsibility seriously, break with the dead past, help us. We are willing to help you, but remember that it is your Japan you are building, and yours is the responsibility for what that Japan will become. Hold up your heads, speak out boldly against the bad teachers still remaining. As long as you are afraid to do so, as long as you hide behind each other, as long as you wait for someone else to speak for you--just so long will the evil remain in power and the new democratic Japan remain only a dream.[36]

George's proposal induced a serious discussion among the education Division staff. Captain Donovan, Captain Osborne, Wigglesworth, Durgin, and Harkness made comments on it. Two of them, except Harkness, wrote that it was excellent. Osborne wrote, "Practically any project which would give the people of Japan a voice in their school was worthwhile." Others wrote that in general the idea was good. Most of them expressed the fear that the MG Teams would be unable to handle their part of the plan. Harkness concurred with others in the view that it was advisable to re-check the work of screening commitees.[36]

Major Arrowood, who was in charge of the screening project at that point, however, turned down the proposal. He considered it improper for CI&E to make such a direct appeal to the Japanese people. According to him, "a large majority" of letters would simply be grudge letters and create more confusion than clarity to the entire screening process. He believed that the screening project was a job to be accomplished by the Japanese people themselves. It was their project to serve as an experimental lesson in democratization, and a "drama" to be performed by their own effort even if the performance was awkward. His emphasis was placed strongly on the educational effect of the screening process for the future Japan. Arrowood reflected an American educator's view that screening should serve a long range educational purpose. Arrowood wrote:

We have approved Imperial Ordinance 263. It is a Japanese show, let them carry the ball. All Committees in all prefectures have been selected and are operating. Such a statement to the Japanese people as the enclosed would cause the committees to lose face. In my opinion too much fault is being focused with the screening program. Of course, there are faults to it, but it is the most democratic thing that Japan has ever done and one must crawl before one walks. (Not original.) I say, "Let's give them a chance to run their own show."[37]

Local Military Government's Encouragement of Grass Roots Correspondence

On the other hand, at the local prefectural level, under the MG's instructions, some prefectures encouraged people through the newspapers to write letters so that the screening committee might be helped with actual information. Many anonymous letters poured into the screening committee office and MG, most of which were grudge reports. The accused were embarrassed greatly by them.

For example, in Nara prefecture, "after the alleged failure of the screening committee," the committee was reorganized in November, and all teachers who had already been screened had to be rescreened. The new committee intended to supplement the former records of individual screenings with information received from various other sources. As a result an appeal to the people for information regarding undesirable educators was publicized in all Nara newspapers. Many anonymous letters poured into the screening committee and Military Government Office. The Nara Military Government Team wrote approvingly in its report to Eighth Army:

> The use of information gathered from the people themselves as a basis upon which to base decision, rather than the word of the teachers themselves, not only seems to be a more likely method of achieving justice, but also one which delineates the T.S.C. in its true light; namely as a body not only composed of but representing the will of the Japanese people.[38]

This view seems similar to that opinion of Scott George of CI&E. Strict implementation of Arrowood's thought would have prevented the whole operation of screening from confusion. The encouragement of MG Teams, however, brought about a reckless attempt to gain information from the general public without taking any foreseeable confusion into consideration. As a result, at the local administrative level, some screening committees suffered from grudge letters and much confusion.

Confusion in the Prefectural Administration

In Ishikawa prefecture the unsatisfactory number of purged teachers caused MG Officials to exert a tacit and implicit pressure on the screening committee by attending screening meetings. One of the screening committee members, reflecting later on the contemporary climate, wrote, "Moreover they (MG) provided proof for a list of teachers whom they considered to be unacceptable for their teaching position. Most of the proof was in the form of anonymous letters addressed to the MG or screening committee." Consequently the number of the unacceptable was increased.[39]

In Oita prefecture the letters only provided trivial information on such matters as the concealment of worn out wooden rifles, that the Hoanden (a sacred place where the Imperial Rescript of Education used to be kept) still remained only half-destroyed, and that American dolls had been burnt during the war.[40]

According to The Hyogo Prefectural Educational History, there seems to have been 34 letters regarding screening. The committee members investigated each information offered except very unworthy ones, only to find most letters to be absurd slanders.[41]

In Nagano prefecture, the "Shinano Mainichi Shimbun" dated 22 November 1946 called for information regarding the screening of teachers and educational staffs. Most of the letters sent to the offices requested the purge of certain individuals; only a very few writers extended sympathetic feeling toward the purgees.[42]

In Kanagawa prefecture, a radical Military Government Officer was so absurd in picking up trivial matters and claiming them as violations of SCAP directives that people were threatened by a potential purge. Shigenobu Suzuki, chief of the School Educational Section, refuted these criticisms on each occasion, and, he finally became offended by the officer's actions. The officer, then, requested the Governor of the prefecture, and subsequently GHQ to purge Suzuki on the basis of anonymous letters. Later, Suzuki wrote it was a pity to know that people became so malicious against their friends and colleagues.[43]

Information gathered from the "grass roots" was, in most of the cases, abused and absurd. The prevalence of this condition throughout the country is proved by the fact that Chief of Acceptability Inquiry Board, Minister's Secretariats, Ministry of Education issued an official notice to chairman of each screening committee stating as follows:

> You are expected to be deliberate and impartial in carrying on teachers' screening. It is reported, however, that recently many letters are sent to the committee which are written with a malicious intention of making some false charge against others. You are hereby notified that you will be cautious enough in handling such letters, especially anonymous ones, to be used for your information in screening.[44]

In theory the American idea of direct public participation in the Occupational operation was good, however, the Japanese people had no such experience. In practice, they only made personal attacks against their opponents. The idea of providing direct public participation was, in general, neither a "democratic" nor a helpful lesson to the Japanese people under the enormous social and economic confusion of postwar Japan.

Letters to GHQ as Historical Sources

The above letters to GHQ to fulfill a practical democratic function did not work out. These letters, however, serve as significant historical records. They are eloquent in telling how the Japanese general public reacted to the screening implementation on both the local and government level, and how they interpreted militarism. The general public's reactions made constructive contribution to some extent in creating a structure for the screening program. They sometimes made an impact on CI&E public and MG Teams actions. This has only come to light through this investigation.

Among the letters sent to the Occupation Forces, approximately six or seven hundred letters on the educational purge are filed in the CI&E documents of Washington National Records Center. The writer's investigation of about 500 of these letters[45] revealed three major points.

First, profound hatred of militarism was expressed in the immediate postwar attitudes toward career military people. Furthermore, that feeling was even extended to young students and graduates of wartime military schools who had been encouraged by the Japanese Government immediately after the termination of the war to seek admission to higher educational institutions. In fact, however, through CI&E policy they came to be discriminated against in admission to higher educational institutions. Second, principals of elementary schools, secondary schools, and colleges were severely charged by the Japanese general public, students, and teachers with responsibility for militarism and ultra-nationalism in the prewar and wartime Japan. A major reason for the teachers' purge was the public's widespread resentment of their manipulation by these educators during the war. Third, the general public's comments on the screening system and its procedures were to the point, and they could tell the defects of the screening process. Let me substantiate these assertions.

Discrimination Against Ex-Military School Students

On 5 September 1945, right after the war, the Japanese government issued a notice by which all the military school students became entitled to be transferred to middle schools, higher schools, colleges and universities.[46] The policy illustrated the Ministry of Education's sympathetic attitude toward these students. Occupational policy, however, turned out to be directly contrary to Japanese policy. On the basis of CI&E instruction, on 22 February 1946 the Ministry of Education issued a notice by which the number of students and graduates of military schools who were to be admitted into a university or a college was not to exceed one-tenth of the total number of students of the university or college.[47]

These two regulations invited many complaints, both pro and con to each policy. Between late 1945 and the February 22 regulation, all letters concerning the admission of ex-military students opposed granting any advantage to them concerning entrance to higher educational institutions. What the letters were afraid of was, first, that the military students could defeat, in the entrance examination competitions, the students who were exhausted owing to forced labor services during the war. Second, the correspondence feared that a mass entrance of military students would revive militarism. They definitely stereotyped ex-military students as anti-democratic and worried that a prevalence of militaristic thinking among them could suppress democracy and freedom. One of the letters went as follows:

...there is a remarkable fact that the former students of military or naval schools, were permitted to study as the first year students of universities after April of this year. Those students were educated as professional soldiers for at least three years and they took ultra-advanced actions [sic] during the Japanese aggressive militarism, but permitted to be the first year students of universities without a fundamental education of democracy. (T. Yuki: Niigata)[48]

While most letters were critical of militaristic indoctrination of youth at military schools, there were some letters which showed sympathy toward ex-military school students. One stated:

Not only military schools but also every school in Japan, regardless [of] the kind of school, elementary, middle school or colleges and universities have conducted the education of militarism, anti-Anglo-Saxon, and ultra-nationalism since 1931 or 1933 under compulsion of the militarists. Therefore, every Japanese must be re-educated, to the ways of democracy. Every school in Japan should be reformed thoroughly. Why do you talk only [of] the graduates of military schools, limiting their admittance to 10% of the graduates. (F. Hashiguchi: Tokyo)[49]

After the 10 percent restriction of admission against ex-military school students, students and graduates of the Army and Navy Military Academy suddenly faced an unexpected disadvantage because of their past choice of entering military schools. That choice had resulted from a feeling of patriotic duty at the age of sixteen, or less, and sometimes the choice was forced by the prevailing climate and government. So resolved were the ex-military students to overcome this discrimination in order to achieve a promising future that they made eloquent appeals. Their pleas were made more trustworthy by signing their letters clearly with their names and addresses.

To accomplish the objectives of demilitarization set forth in the guiding policy of the Occupation such as in the "Potsdam Declaration," and the "United States Initial Post-Surrender Policy for Japan," it is evident, and hardly surprising that elimination of militarism was strictly emphasized. The crucial point discussed here, however, is the forced sacrifice of the teen-aged ex-military students. Since they were banned from employment, they made up their minds to achieve a self-enlightenment through democratic education. Their restriction had an enormous impact on the starting point of their new life, furthermore, rejection of their reeducation may have resulted in a great loss of social energy for new Japan's reconstruction.

Ambivalence toward demilitarization among military Occupational forces, however, has been discovered. Robert K. Hall, CI&E officer who was involved in drafting the educational purge directive and the Imperial Ordinance 263 (Japanese Government implementation of the educational purge), stated that "one of the equivocal and at times ludicrous aspects of the Occupation" was for "military officers of the Allied Powers to preach a doctrine denouncing militarism." He added that at the same time as "the President and a considerable proportion of the military and political leaders of the United States were vigorously advocating the establishment of compulsory military service, increased budgets for the armed forces, and unification of Land, Sea, and Air Forces in order to increase military efficiency, the officers of those three services were directed to convince the Japanese public that a military machine was intrinsically wrong."[50] The following letter shared this opinion and pointed out the forced sacrifice of the student.

> We, who grew up during the war, were not allowed any criticism and the Government Policy covered our eyes, ears and mouth. The simple and honest boys in the high school were driven to the entrance gate of the naval academy by the instigation of the government and militaristic education. We believed our motive in giving up our lives in the war was entirely the same as your feeling for the same purpose for their beloved land by naval cadets at Annapolis and Dartmouth [sic]. (As a result, we were labelled wrong, and they were right only for the reason our war had been aggression, while theirs had been a sacred war.)

> Since the termination of the Pacific war, the national feelings in all quarters for us has completely changed. We are now accused and cruelly treated as the direct partisans in the aggressive war. However, are we really responsible for our past devotions? No, we believe, national leaders and educators who instigated the nation to blindly enter the so-called "Holy-war" should bear the responsibility...

> We made a firm determination to start a new life for the establishment of peaceful Japan. But suddenly those who had been in the military service were banned to enter the higher educational institutions. In order to develop a true democracy in Japan, it is much more necessary to re-educate those demobilized young people than other civilians. (K. Tsuruoka: Tokyo)[51]

Policy Making Process
Against Ex-Military Students

Letters from the Japanese general public affected CI&E's policy. There were several factors which led CI&E to instruct the Ministry of Education to adopt the discriminatory policy against ex-military school students. What is considered to be the most influential was the letters against their privilege for admission to higher educational institution. These factors will be discussed subsequently.

The target of the purge policy was on the military and ultra-nationalists, who were "culpable for having deceived and misled the Japanese people." The number of the purgees, therefore, falling into the category of military elite was the largest, 79.6 percent of the number of purgees of the public officials, according to Hans H. Baerwald, Professor of University of California, Los Angeles.[52] In the educational purge, as well, the administrative process designated career military officers as unacceptable for teaching, without any judicial process. Professor Baerwald explained:

> This implementation was not based on the view that all career officers had deceived and misled the people of Japan. To equate the power of General Tojo with second-lieutenant Suzuki, graduate of the Japanese military academy in the summer of 1944, would be patently absurd. The all-inclusive category was based instead on the elimination of the influence of the army and navy.[53]

With regard to categories applied to soldiers, Professor Hiroshi Masuda of Tokyo Eiwa Women's College wrote in his paper entitled, "The Formulation of the Purge Directives, (SCAPIN-550, 548)", that General Willoughby, chief of Civil Intelligence

Section had recommended the purge be limited to the rank of captain and above, because he believed that the "drastic reforms intended by Government Section would result in Japan's deterioration." Thus American career officers were critical of the provisional purge designation suggested by Government Section. The Government Section, however, overcame all the opposition made to them by emphasizing an interpretation that young officers had been more aggressive and used to be more powerful in fighting; hence, they offered a broader interpretation to the purge category to be applied down to all career officers. According to Professor Masuda, this was the only phenomenal exception to general "backwardness" seen in setting purge categories.[54] There is no denying that the CI&E's purge policy was influenced by this dispute and "inner politics" that took place between Government Section and General Staff Section.

Concerning the implementation of ten percent quota on ex-military students, the following facts were disclosed by my research. A CI&E weekly report in January reads: "a study is being made of the many charges of the militaristic attitudes of university students who formerly enrolled in the military academies.[55] Subsequently on 2 February, Major Arrowood submitted to Nugent, chief of CI&E, fourteen letters from the Japanese general public to GHQ and two letters obtained by censorship. On his routing slip Arrowood noted "The attached material constitutes all available complaints concerning ex-Army Navy students in the civilian schools."[56] This is clear proof that among the CI&E officials an issue was raised on the students who had been transferred or entered from ex-military schools into universities, colleges and other higher educational institutions, and that Arrowood had been required to submit materials on the problem. Those letters were from civilian students who made a severe criticism of ex-military students. They strongly opposed the privilege of ex-military students being admitted to higher educational institutions for fear of prevalence of their militaristic thinking. My research has not been able to disclose how Nugent reacted to the letters, but we do know the CI&E instructed the Ministry of Education that it should reverse its existing policy.

On 7 February CI&E staff and Kyosuke Yamazaki, Secretariat of the Minister of Education had a conference. The CI&E report of this conference declared that the Ministry of Education was aware of "the danger of any concentration of such students" in higher educational institutions, and that they would submit a plan to prevent the "danger."[57]

On the same the Ministry of Education reported to CI&E the number of ex-military students who were supposed to apply to higher educational institutions in April. It was expected to amount to one third of the number of all applicants. The CI&E pointed out the "danger" involved and suggested that the Ministry of Education should submit a plan to solve the problem.[58]

With the information obtained from letters, even some anonymous ones and through censorship, CI&E regarded the consolidation of ex-military students in higher educational institutions as a "danger," and rejected the Ministry of Education's action of giving a privilege to ex-military students. Hence the Ministry of Education found it necessary to restrict the number of their admission to ten percent.

Accusation of Militarism

The Japanese people directed their bitterness after the war against the militarists, who had led the nation into aggression. Their direct wartime experiences and terrible suffering produced a revulsion against militarism. The Japanese soldiers were the first target of the accusation. They had left home as heroes but were spat upon by resentful city crowds on their return. A citizen of Tottori City, after listing undesirable categories of military men, requested that any military man or military school student should be prohibited from holding teaching positions and entering any school as the purge of military men was the most crucial issue for Japan's democratization.[59]

The second target of the accusation of militarism was principals, judged by the people as the most strenuous advocates of militarism because principals were linked with educational school-inspectors and governmental cliques and were believed to be of a bureaucratic type. In fact, they were active in imparting militaristic education during the war.

Large numbers of principals of elementary, secondary and other schools were accused of militaristic thought and behavior. Parents, their subordinate teachers, and students requested them to be designated as purgees because of wartime activities or because of positions they held, which were deemed sufficiently undesirable and ultra-nationalistic.

Since they had direct contacts with the general public on an every day living basis, principals were subject to the greater public denunciation. Out of 71 letters denouncing principals, 36 were written to designate specific individuals as undesirable. An educator in Gifu prefecture wrote, "All the principals of our schools, who had made the utmost devotional service to our militarists' government during the war should be expelled from our educational world."[60] Another educator in Osaka requested elimination of every principal who had had an educational post during the war.[61] Another letter from Tokyo recommended that principals over fifty years of age should be removed to make way for a new educational leadership.[62] The following letter described the typical public image of principals.

> I would like to ask you to purge the headmaster[s] of all the public and private middle schools. During the war, they became the tools of the army, and made pupils, students of preparatory course or military cadets compulsorily [sic], [and had been proud of the official prize for accomplishment of the national policy. And then, after we were defeated, they made believe that they were representing themselves as democrats.] (N. Yamashita, a teacher: Osaka)[63] (Words within the bracket are the authors translation because of the mistranslation.)

Subordinate teachers and students castigated principals about their trend after the war to do an about-face and become alleged disciples of democracy in order to escape the purge and remain as educators. Furthermore, the general public was severely critical of the fact that the purge struck down many figureheads and minor officials who had not been responsible for Japan's militarism, but had not been carried far enough to remove the most dangerous elements. Those 71 letters were written in a fierce tone exemplified by the following quote: "I wonder why SCAP do [sic] not enforce more strict purge against teachers. I tell you the persons who had played an important role in the War were principals of elementary school[s]...There again I repeat it is the principals of the elementary schools that organized the masses of people to accelerate hostile intention. (Anonymous: Gifu)[64]

Denunciation of particular individuals was mostly anonymous without sufficient proof. The reasons they gave for purging were mostly trivial such as principals' authoritarian behavior, undemocratic school management, concealment of food and other materials, and an unpleasant disposition. The CI&E's interpretation of the purge provision as clarified in the documents of the CI&E Review Board, however, did not refer to principals' wicked school management as having anything to do with ultra-nationalism or militarism.[65]

Some denunciation of particular teachers came from students for the reason of violence perpetrated in the school against the students. They interpreted militarism simply as "teachers' violence backed by militaristic training." One of the letters said "what we hate is our teacher's cruel behaviors manipulated by militarism." (A student: Tokyo)[66] Another wrote as follows:

> Today Mr. Naka, our mathematics teacher, ordered his two students to stand and made them beat each other, because they made mistakes in their calculation in class. The students hesitated. Then, he repeated his order, told them to feel hurt, and they would be able to do a good job in calculation...Is this a democratic education? It is nothing but militarism. Please dismiss the teacher from our school. (M. Honda: Tokyo)[67] (Author's translation)

With the student's handwriting demonstrating his sincere appeal, this letter showed that he made a clear distinction between the new democratic education and the old authoritarian one they had been forced to endure. They realized that violence was far from a democratic education, and deserved to be purged. Students, parents, and teachers disclosed their bitter enmity against the past militaristic education, hence, they displayed considerable antagonism against "militaristic teachers that made them suffer." The "Purge" that the Occupation implemented was the best possible measure allowing them to resist past educational instruction in the new age.

Critical Opinions from the General Public about Screening Operations

There were 49 critical letters on screening operations, and the letters were mostly sent from late 1946, when the result of screening became known, through early 1947. First, they blamed the lenience of screening for its unfavorable result. Second, they criticized the arbitrary process of screening by the so-called "Automatic Purge."

The first point regarding leniency seems partly to have resulted from the discrepancy in interpretations of the purge provision noted above. The letters accused prefectural committeemen and the Ministry of Education for "the negative and lukewarm attitudes," a point strongly made by a teacher. They were said to have been unwilling to designate their colleagues as unacceptable, to look for loopholes in the provisions, and to give no specific instructions regarding problems that occurred in the process of screening.[68] A similar mood was frequently pointed out by Professor Abe. His thorough study includes many statements and quotations of persons about the purge. They support my discussion of the contemporary mood, but since they were made years later when it was easy to make such statements, the contemporary letters are a much greater corroboration of contemporary feeling regarding screening.

Among the letters dealing with the screening committee, fourteen claimed an unfair designation by "Automatic Purge." This provision, Appendix II of the Imperial Ordinance 263 of 1946, read: "The categories of those who are to be designated as non-acceptable persons for educational service without being referred to the inquiry committee are defined as 'career military and naval personnel,' and 'persons who, though they were not career military and naval personnel, have served in the Army or the Navy as their principal Occupation for more than ten years'" etc. That is to say, according to this provision, those who had served as career military and naval personnel for only a few months, or those who had been in military service 20 or 30 years before that time were purged without any chance to defend themselves through due process of law. The following letter was from an old teacher who felt sacrificed by this arbitrary definition.

> I am a sixty-year-old teacher. I was purged from my teaching post in the name of democratization of Japan, because I served in the Navy over 30 years ago. Due to my old age, I am unable to work in any other field, and suffer from living. Even a convict receives living expense after serving the penitentiary for 30 years, and is no longer considered a criminal. I have been teaching for 30 years and was deprived of my job. I agree to the purge directive, I know I must obey the law. But, disappointed at the refusal of Ministry of Education against my request for pension, I sincerely asked MacArthur for my pension right. (M. Horiuchi: Nagano) (Author's translation)[69]

On a routing slip attached on this letter, Orr recommended a special action on the request. The letter was written before "Application for Special Exemption of Appendix II" became available. Subsequently Arrowood suggested to the Ministry of Education that undemocratic procedures such as the "Automatic Purge" should be modified. Consequently, in this case letters from the general public as well as Arrowood's, due consideration made the screening procedure fairer, which, of course, the CI&E intended.[70]

A few comments on the screening operation doubted the competence of the quasi-judicial review process to correct errors and injustices. As a result of many overrulings of prefecturally designated purgees by the Central Inquiry Committee, MG and prefectural committees became furious. One man wrote:

> ...Wartime activities of local teachers were carried out in local districts so the investigation committee members and any people of the local districts have thorough knowledge of these teachers' true thoughts and activities. To date, teachers found to be ineligible by the local committees were recognized without exception by the people as being most qualified.

> I believe the system whereby the central committee, which conducts investigation by written material only, can overrule the decisions made by the local committees when disqualified teachers' appeal to the central committee is unreasonable. Furthermore those written appeals without exception hide true facts.

> Therefore, I believe that a single decision system should be created. (A member of a teachers' union: Shimane[71]

The same opinion was discussed in the previous part of this paper, namely when the Nara Military Government Team made a strenuous opposition to CI&E about overrulings by the Central Inquiry Committee. The CI&E, however, countered this criticism by arguing the validity of "central supervision of national screening program providing for a democratic court system, final decisions on appeals to be made by Ministry of Education (and SCAP) as the highest tribunal." That is to say the CI&E supported the centralized system of the teachers' screening operation as efficient and in the best tradition of democratic juridical process.

Anonymous letters, in general, tended to be irresponsible grudge letters. The CI&E and MG's idea of public participation in the screening process, as a democratic measure, therefore, fell short of the original expectation based on American idealism. Because of the bitter wartime experiences that had been forced upon the Japanese people, the general public thrust the responsibility for militaristic and ultra-nationalistic education on those leaders close to them, to be more specific, on principals and headteachers, and military men. Direct accusation, through correspondence to GHQ, of their wartime attitudes was a much greater public concern than the significance of screening as a means of constructing a new Japan.

Two kinds of letters, however, seem to have exerted influence on the policy making process of Education Division. One type seems to have motivated Arrowood to modify the "automatic purge." Undue application of the provisions of Appendix II of Imperial Ordinance 263 to particular ex-military personnel was considered to be undemocratic. Arrowood's action was consistent with his zealous advocacy of a democratic screening process. Arrowood's strenuous efforts allowed the Ministry of Education to set up machinery for appealing special exemptions by those ex-military personnel who believed their purge to be unreasonable. The other kind caused teenage ex-military students to be restricted from entering higher educational institutions. This correspondence resulted in a simplistic solution by discrimination against ex-military students mainly because the ultimate aim of the Occupation was exclusion of militarism from the education field, and partly because public accusation of militarism was strong enough to welcome the discrimination of ex-military students. Fourteen letters written by ex-military students throw light on their contemporary feelings of being victims of immediate postwar prejudices. As a whole, however, CI&E did not consider the contemporary correspondence to be an adequate and trustworthy example of public opinions,[72] even though all letters had been translated.

Correspondence from the Japanese general public did not serve as effective information for the screening operation, but it did reveal the trends of thought of a portion of the population about the Occupation, particularly concerning the purge. The general public fervently welcomed the education purge. Their antagonistic feeling against wartime leaders burst into a demand for purging of the undesirable. Once the accused, whom the general public believed to have been unacceptable, were judged to be acceptable, they demanded more severe actions to be taken. This emotional attitude stands in striking contrast with principals' and teachers' reluctance to accept purging for patriotic wartime actions. The latter justified themselves by saying, "I was obliged to obey the order from the above." According to screenees' contentions, principals had been passive victims, rather than a source of theoretical manipulation of militarism. Their reluctance to accept responsibility for wartime cooperation is also seen in the tendency for screening committees to avoid purging their colleagues. Thus, although the removal of ultra-nationalists and militarists from the educational field seemed to be a logical first step, the general public regarded the purge policy as a punitive measure or an act of revenge rather than a step to secure the future of a peaceful democratic state.

There was a discrepancy between the public interpretation of militarism and ultra-nationalism and that of the Central Inquiry Committee and CI&E Review Board. The reversal of local screening committees' judgment by the Central Inquiry Committee and the CI&E Review Board brought severe criticism from Military Government officers and the general public. They voiced demands for further elimination of remaining unfavorable elements. The general public castigated a wartime leaders' attitude which had suppressed freedom. Their interpretations, therefore, of militarism and ultra-nationalism were arbitrary and unfair. Not only classroom violence, authoritative school management, bureaucratic attitudes, and unpopularity of principals, but also the abuse of privilege in food provision and concealment were claimed by them to be adequate reason for educators' purge. In contrast, the Central Inquiry Committee and CI&E Review Board emphasized strict compliance with the letter and spirit of the purge law. The above reasons, according to their interpretation, were not evidence of militarism or ultra-nationalism. Furthermore, the CI&E Review Board made a clear distinction between ultra-nationalism and patriotism. Those who were members or had taken nominal positions within the IRAA were not accused. The CI&E interpreted the general public's contribution to the state's defense and cooperative spirit for wartime activities as nothing but a citizen's duty and a manifestation of patriotism. This interpretation of CI&E Review Board is clearly expressed in the CI&E Review Board records, mainly from late 1947 when CI&E review began.

NOTES

1.   Abe Akira, *Sengo Chiho Kyoikuseido Seiritsukatei no Kenkyu* (A Study on the Process of Establishment of Postwar Local Education System). (Kazama Shobo, Tokyo 1983).

2.   Five kinds of Inquiry Committees and their functions.

   (1)   Metropolitan, Hokkaido or Prefectural Inquiry Committee for Teachers' Acceptability to investigate teacher of elementary and secondary grade schools and school inspectors.
   (2)   School Bloc Inquiry Committee for Teachers' Acceptability to investigate teachers of higher schools and colleges.
   (3)   University Inquiry Committee for Teachers' Acceptability to investigate teachers of faculty concerned.
   (4)   Inquiry Committee for Educational Officials' Acceptability to investigate head of universities, higher schools and colleges, and to investigate teachers and various educational officials as enumerated in Item 2 through 6 of Appendix

III of Screening Ordinance Enforcement Regulations.

(5) Central Inquiry Committee for Educational Service Members' Acceptability to handle all requests for re-investigation from teachers and educational officials investigated by other committees.

3. Washington National Records Center (WNRC), GHQ/SCAP Records, CI&E(C)04083, "Report of Conference" 22 July, '46.

4. WNRC, GHQ/SCAP Records, CI&E(C)04083, "Report on Investigations of the Teacher-Screening Arrangements in Twenty Prefectures Under I Corps Jurisdiction."

5. WNRC, GHQ/SCAP Records, CI&E(C)00493, "Interference with Teacher-Screening."

6. WNRC, GHQ/SCAP Records, CI&E(A)00668, 00663, 00669, "Report of Conference."

7. WNRC, GHQ/SCAP Records, CI&E(B)05760, "Negotiation between Prefectural Government and Military Government: Investigation by Ministry of Education."

8. WNRC, GHQ/SCAP Records, CI&E(A)00668, "Report of Conference."

9. WNRC, GHQ/SCAP Records, CI&E(B)05810, "Report of Conference."

10. WNRC, GHQ/SCAP Records, CI&E(B)05761, "Report of Conference."

11. WNRC, GHQ/SCAP Records, CI&E(B)05810 or (A)00682, "Report of Conference."

12. WNRC, GHQ/SCAP Records, CI&E(B)05836, "Standards for New Committees."

13. Ibid.

14. WNRC, GHQ/SCAP Records, CI&E(B)05810 or (A)03016, "Report of Conference."

15. WNRC, GHQ/SCAP Records, CI&E(A)03016, "Report of Conference."

16. WNRC, GHQ/SCAP Records, CI&E(B)05810, "Report of Conference."

17. WNRC, GHQ/SCAP Records, CI&E(B)05836, "Standard for Determining a Good Committee."

18. WNRC, GHQ/SCAP Records, CI&E(B)05716-05719, Report of MG.

19. WNRC, GHQ/SCAP Records, CI&E(B)05717, Report from Miyagi MG "Screening Board."

20. GHQ/SCAP, CI&E "CI&E Bulletin" II, 16 July 1947 and WNRC, GHQ/SCAP Records, CI&E(B)06009.

21. WNRC, GHQ/SCAP Records, CI&E(B)06012, "Special Educational Sectional Report."

22. Abe, *Sengo Chiho*, p. 451.

23. WNRC, GHQ/SCAP Records, CI&E(B)06012, "Special Educational Sectional Report."

24. WNRC, GHQ/SCAP Records, CI&E(B)06012, Letter to SCAP attached "Special Educational Sectional Report."

25. WNRC, GHQ/SCAP Records, CI&E(B)05925, "Special Report on Teacher Screening."

26. Ibid.

27. WNRC, GHQ/SCAP Records, CI&E(B)05687, Letter to Eighth Army from CI&E.

28. WNRC, GHQ/SCAP Records, CI&E(B)05925, Orr's pencil memo to Kief.

29. WNRC, GHQ/SCAP Records, CI&E(C)04177, "Screening Policy (Nara TSC Report)."

30. WNRC, GHQ/SCAP Records, CI&E(C)04182, "Special Report Re: Education Screening Committee."

31. WNRC, GHQ/SCAP Records, CI&E(C)00458, "Screening Review Board Judgement."

32. Chief of CI&E, D.R. Nugent wrote several pencil-memos on the Records of Brief of CI&E Review Board and emphasized CI&E screening policy. L.A. Kief wrote his instruction in a memorandum "Screening Review Board Judgements, WNRC, GHQ/SCAP Records, CI&E(A)00458.

33. Rinjiro Sodei, *Haikei, MacArthur Gensuisama* (Dear General MacArthur) (Otsuki Shoten, Tokyo, 1985).

34. WNRC, GHQ/SCAP Records, CI&E(B)05754, "Screening of Teachers."

   Robert K. Hall, CI&E officer who was involved in drafting the educational purge directive expressed the same opinion, saying, "it (the purge) proposed to provide a demonstration of the democratic processes as applied to an educational field; to increase the individual parent's interest and participation in education; and to increase the degree of local control through the establishment of a decentralized screening machinery." Robert K. Hall, *Education for a New Japan* (Yale University Press, 1949), p. 432.

35. WNRC, GHQ/SCAP Records, CI&E(B)05754, "Statement to the Japanese People."

36. WNRC, GHQ/SCAP Records, CI&E(B)05755, "Comments, Officers, Education Division: Re-Screening of Teachers."

37. WNRC, GHQ/SCAP Records, CI&E(B)05755, "Education Division Routing Slip."

38. WNRC, GHQ/SCAP Records, CI&E(B)06012, "Special Educational Sectional Report." A different but complementary view was held by Nugent. He reflected the view that "American justice" should be demonstrated through a sound judicial process to pass the future "scrutiny of history." WNRC, GHQ/SCAP Records, CI&E(C)03528. Nugent Intra-Section Memorandum. Nugent's view of the screening was described in my paper "Educational Purge (PArt II) Reversed Case by Central Inquiry Committee," *Research Bulletin of Educational History of the Postwar Japan*, No. 5 edited by Meisei University Research Center for Postwar Educational History of Japan, 1988), 84-103. Harry Wray wrote about Nugent's view as well in his paper, "Dyke and Nugent as Chiefs of the CI&E: A Contrast in Style and Personality," *Research Bulletin of Educational History of the Postwar Japan*, No. 6, 1989), pp. 1-31.

39. Edited by The Association of High School Principals, *Ishikawa Ken Kotogakko Kyouiku Jyunennshi* (Ishikawa Prefecture High School Ten Years' Educational History) 1959, p. 33.

40. Edited by the Occupational Study Association, "Senryoka no Oitaken Kyoiku Gyosei," (The Administration of Oita Prefecture under the Occupation) (Tokyo Keizai Daigaku Kaishi, 1977), p. 85.

41. Edited by Committee of Hyogo Prefecture Educational History, *Hyogoken Kyoikushi* (Hyogo Prefecture Educational History) 1963, p. 721.

42. Yasohachi Morimoto, *Sengo Kyoiku no Shuppatsu: Naganoken Kyoin Tekikaku Shinsa Iinkai no Kiroku* (The Departure of Postwar Education: The Record of Nagano Teachers' Screening Committee) (Ginga Shobo, Tokyo, 1977), p. 83.

43. Edited by the Committee of the 20 years' Anniversary Publication of Yokohama Elementary and Junior High School Principal Association. *Ishizue: Shin Gakusei 20 nen*, (20 years from the New Educational System) 1967, p. 97.

44. WNRC, GHQ/SCAP Records, CI&E(C)00495.

45. The 500 letters dealt with in this paper were sent to GHQ in 1946 and 1947.

The period includes some time before the Imperial Ordinance 263 was promulgated on 7 May 1946 and 8 months after the screening at the local level almost completed. Well identified letters with writers' names and addresses on them are considered to be trustworthy and dependable as historical documents, but even anonymous letters, if several of them shared the same opinion, provide factual proof.

The number of the letters dealing with each item:

(1)	Opposition to ex-military students entering higher educational institution, and in favor of the restriction	25
	Opposition to the restriction	13
(2)	Accusation for militarism and ultra-nationalism	131
	Accusation of principals and school inspectors	73
	Accusation of particular individuals	83
(3)	Comments on the screening operation	49
	Opposition to judgement	23
(4)	Others	168

The total number of letters here exceeds the actual number investigated because there is some overlap. Some letters dealt with more than one of the above area.

46. The Ministry of Education Notice, "Hatsusen No. 120," 1945. *Kindai Nihon Kyoikuseido Shiryo*, Vol. 26 (Collection of Materials on Contemporary Japanese Educational System) (Kodansha, Tokyo), pp. 178-185.

47. Ibid., 196-198.

48. WNRC, GHQ/SCAP Records, CI&E(A)06544. Letters referred in this paper were translated by ATIS unless the author's translation is specified.

49. WNRC, GHQ/SCAP Records, CI&E(A)06542.

50. Robert K. Hall, *Education for a New Japan* (Yale University Press, 1949), p. 98.

51.   WNRC, GHQ/SCAP Records, CI&E(B)05906.

52.   Hans H. Baerwald, *The Purge of Japanese Leaders Under the Occupation* (Connecticut: Greenwood Press, Publishers, 1959), p. 80.

53.   Ibid., pp. 16-17.

54.   Hiroshi Masuda, "The Formulation of the Purge Directors" *International Relations, The Occupation of Japan: Studies from Various Viewpoints*, The Japan Association of International Relations, 1987), pp. 87-94.

55.   WNRC, GHQ/SCAP Records, CI&E(C)00265.

56.   WNRC, GHQ/SCAP Records, CI&E(A)06535.

57.   WNRC, GHQ/SCAP Records, CI&E(C)00270.

58.   Ibid.

59.   WNRC, GHQ/SCAP Records, CI&E(A)06539.

60.   WNRC, GHQ/SCAP Records, CI&E(A)06557.

61.   WNRC, GHQ/SCAP Records, CI&E(A)06549.

62.   WNRC, GHQ/SCAP Records, CI&E(A)05647.

63.   WNRC, GHQ/SCAP Records, CI&E(A)06556.

64.   WNRC, GHQ/SCAP Records, CI&E(B)05908.

65.   The CI&E was severely critical of the small number of the unacceptable as of late 1946 and many reversed cases by the Central Inquiry Committee. As a result on 14 January 1947, the Education Division, CI&E notified the Central Inquiry Committee that "after a decision had been reached by the Central Inquiry Committee it would then be approved or disapproved by the CI&E." Then the CI&E Review Board was set up as a checking machinery of judgements of the Central Inquiry Committee. That is to say, decisions of the Central Inquiry Committee were controlled by the CI&E Review Board. Subsequently, however, the CI&E interpretation of the purge provision enabled two thirds of the reversed cases by the Central Inquiry Committee approved by the CI&E Review Board according to the 170 reversed cases that I investigated through the CI&E documents.

66.   WNRC, GHQ/SCAP Records, CI&E(A)06540.

67.   Ibid.

68.   WNRC, GHQ/SCAP Records, CI&E(A)06553.

69.   WNRC, GHQ/SCAP Records, CI&E(B)05910.

70.   It was Major Arrowood who raised the issue of "Automatic Purge." His point was "...not to allow a purged individual to present his side of the case is a poor way to teach democracy." (WNRC, GHQ/SCAP Records, CI&E(A)00667, "Report of Conference.") Through several negotiations with the Ministry of Education, Arrowood showed untiring zeal in the pursuit of educational effect. Finally on 30 January 1947 those who had

been designated as unacceptable were allowed to ask for "Special Exemption" of their designation.

71.   WNRC, GHQ/SCAP Records, CI&E(B)05915.

72.   Edited by Mitsuo Kodama, *CI&E Bulletin (2 June 1947 - 21 December 1949)* Tokyo: Meisei University Press, 1985), p. 31.

One of the SCAP Civil Information and Education libraries, strategically located throughout Japan, and in great demand.

SCAP higher education official discusses varied phases of Japanese overall educational reform with key Japanese Government officials.

Teaching English and preparing Japanese for language simplification.

PANEL DISCUSSION

(First Day)

Moderator: **Craig Cameron**
                                Yale University

Panelists: **Rinjiro Sodei**
                                Hosei University, Tokyo

                                Carmen Johnson
                                Washington, D.C.

                                Helen Hosp Seamans
                                Coral Gables, Florida

                                Cornelius K. Iida
                                with Mrs. Isako R. Iida
                                University of Yamaguchi, Japan

                                James A. Cogswell
                                Independent Historian

                                Jacob Van Staaveren
                                Independent Historian

                                Reiko Yamamoto
                                Meisei University Research Center
                                for Postwar Educational History of Japan

Craig Cameron. We are at the half-way point for the symposium and we have heard three panels today. While I will certainly be glad to leave the overall summary to Tom Burkman for tomorrow, it is interesting that we have three panels that deal with some of the most sensitive of the cultural aspects, cultural interchange between the Americans and Japanese, namely the issues of gender, religion and education of the succeeding generations.

While we've heard relatively little from our panelists so far about the GHQ reference from this morning from Professor Sodei--the "Go Home Quickly" aspect--that is certainly in the background. I think it has already been made clear a couple of times what the general procedure should be, and again, I will be happy to recognize anybody in the audience who has a question.

Frank Sackton. I was Staff Secretary to General MacArthur during the first few years of the Occupation and I can't tell you how fascinating it has been to hear about the grassroots because I was at the far other end of the whole operation. But I thought I would do this--I don't have any implied questions, but I have a couple of comments that I would like to make--if I might do that. Let me say at the outset, and I would like to comment on Professor Sodei's comments because I thought he did a wonderful job in laying out the problem for all of us and one of the things with which I was impressed was his allusion to some of the mistakes that were made at the grassroots.

I want to tell the Professor that we made a lot of them at our end, too, and I'll tell you why. You know we had never done one of these things before. The General, General MacArthur, brought to Japan senior officers who had been trained to fight and this was a new operation. Our whole orientation was a little bit different than the occupation of a country about which we did not know too much. We had problems of language, terrain and culture. Also, there was a substantial problem of confusion in those early days because there was a lot of communication going on and much of it was miscommunication. And I know that mistakes were made. However, like Professor Sodei, I think the general outcome was not too bad in the end and perhaps that's the thing about which we take a lot of comfort.

Moving to the women's issue panel--that I thought was very heartwarming and inspiring--because General MacArthur, was so very strong on the emancipation of women and worked very hard, very early to get a new constitution from which would stem the civil code to give the mechanism to which you alluded. During the panel discussion of that panel, there was a question from the floor about the interpretation, the translation problem. That struck a responsive cord that I wanted to address because I entered Japan in early September of 1945 and initially the Japanese State Department gave us Japanese interpreters. They were very courteous and very well trained. However, it wasn't very long for me to realize that they were always saying things that would please me. They wouldn't change the truth necessarily but they would smooth it out and I thought in some cases that was not appropriate for what I was trying to reach, so finally I did switch to American interpreters of the Japanese language and that worked a little bit better for me because then I got the unvarnished translation. But, the point here is the women made a point, and I think a very good one, that there is something about the ability of women to communicate with women and language is never a barrier. I think that is absolutely right. I agree with you. I think that probably is a very important point that I picked up from the panel.

On the religious panel, I thought that was very heartwarming and it was so reflective of the General's personal point of view in the fact that he was a religious person and wanted to insure there would be religious freedom in the country. I don't know if you are aware, I should tell you, that he set aside one whole evening for Bible study and Bible reading with his family--that was on Sundays. By the way, he worked until 9:30 or 10:00 every day, seven days a week. That's if we were lucky--sometimes he worked later. But on Sunday, when he did go home after a light supper, why he would gather the family and read the Bible to them. A very religious person and was interested in the religious freedom for the people there--the Japanese. So, I know he had total support of what you all were doing at the grassroots.

A brief word on the education panel. Very early I remember the General alluding several times to the fact that the new generation of Japan held the promise for the future of Japan and that was very important that they receive the best possible education. The General invited many distinguished scholars and panels to Japan in order to help him in policy making and I think that did a lot of good. He kept in close touch with the education of the children. I think almost as much as any other facet of the operation. He was that interested in it and he had the vision of the future and what it is that the children would bring to the operation in later years. One of the very important aspects of the operation, I thought, in education was one day the General invited Dr. Seuss to Japan. You remember Dr. Seuss, the distinguished writer of children's stories, and he was a delight to have in Japan. One of the things he did was to develop a survey among the young children seeking the answer to what it is they wished to do later in life. They did the usual things--some wanted to be firemen, others wanted to be policemen, some wanted to be scholars and professors, and the interesting thing is--this was only about a year and a half after the start of the Occupation--there was no feeling of any of the children wanted to be military people and this was an enormous, I think, recommendation for the progress that was being made in so short a time in the education system. There was one exception. One young boy, later I found out he was seven years old, said he did want to be a soldier but only on condition that he would be General MacArthur. (Laughter) Thank you. I have no questions, but I couldn't resist the opportunity to make some comments.

Robert Textor. I'm from Stanford University and formerly of I Corps Military Government CI&E, later Wakayama Military Government Team. I want first to say that virtually everything that Jacob Van Staaveren gave us this afternoon has its parallel in my own experience, even though the communication between I Corps CI&E officers and IX Corps was very limited. Second, I would like to say to Sodei-san that I tremendously appreciated the way in which he keynoted and framed our terms of dialogue. The variability, however, within the Occupation from prefecture to prefecture is a subject that I think can hardly be overemphasized. As the General has just said, nobody had ever run an Occupation before. We all made mistakes. We were all subject to quick decisions that we later regretted. For the record, however, I know of no CI&E officer anywhere in the I Corps Area (that's 20 prefectures) who ever threatened to send anybody to a forced labor camp in Okinawa. Maybe it happened, but if so I don't know about it and it's not because I didn't want to know.

Finally, Yamamoto-san's paper I find extremely fascinating. I do want to say, and I will work with you to the extent that you may want to pick what's left of my brains--I was Ronald Anderson's right hand man at I Corps 10 hours a day and I want to correct what might be something of a misimpression. He was the gentlest and mildest of people. He was not by temperament a hell-raiser or a loose cannon. He did, however, know something about Japan. And he actually had a certain amount of experience and training in military intelligence. Ergo, when Ronald discovers that in social reality at the local level you have prefectural *chosa iinkai* (screening committees) which include former active members, if not officials, of the Imperial Rule Assistance Association, it's not particularly perverse or unnatural to suggest that maybe this isn't a very good idea. Nor was it unusual for these gaps in communication to exist as between people like Dr. Orr at CI&E/SCAP and people like ourselves out in the field in the actual synapse where the policy implementation has to occur. These misunderstandings, these miscommunications happen all the time. You have stumbled across one of them. Well, there are probably ten more that one could recall and I think that as things finally worked out, I believe this is also your conclusion, the trade-off between participation/education on the one hand and fairness of final decision on the other hand worked out fairly well. That is the end of my comment.

Tom Burkman. First of all, I would like to correct a misstatement I made this morning. I checked Professor Sodei's paper again. He did not say that there were only military government teams in a few prefectures but they were in all prefectures. I'm sorry.

I'm concerned about the question of communication between the grassroots level and the GHQ level. I think this has very serious implications for whether there is in fact unified Occupation or whether there is really a two-level Occupation going on. So let me address my question to Jacob Van Staaveren and to Mark Orr in the audience because you were at the grassroots level in educational policy and you were at the GHQ level. I remember the first symposium I came to here. One Occupationnaire from GHQ very candidly said, "Boy, we got reports from the prefectures. Did we read them? Heck no, we didn't read them, we weighed them!" (Laughter) And so, and I know you wrote reports, over and over again you wrote reports. Did you feel your reports were being read? Did you ever get feedback from your reports? Did you feel that your reports had any influence on revising policies in Tokyo; and, likewise, you received reports--did the grassroots input play a role in policy-making in Tokyo?

Jacob Van Staaveren. The main feedback that we got, the direct feedback, was from Headquarters IX Corps and sometimes from the Kanto Military Government Region. I discovered going to the Kanto Military Government Region conferences--this is under the aegis of Dr. Fox--that some of the commanders on the teams (I don't recall how many) were very strict about communicating to higher authority. They had to go through 8th Army channels if they wanted to get anything done and I think this was probably the militarily correct thing to do. But, I had the advantage before I came to Yamanashi prefecture of being, as I indicated, pretty well briefed not only at Headquarters 8th Army but by several members of SCAP's education division. I met these people--one of them, Abe Halperin who was a language anthropologist, came over with me to Japan on the boat and he introduced me to Dr. Orr and other members and from the very beginning, if I wanted to ask a question and communicate with these people, I just picked up the phone and talked to them. Some of the people I know at the Kanto Military Government Region, the CI&E officers said, "We aren't allowed to do this." So, my commanding officer didn't seem to mind. He had enough other problems, and my section seemed to be running okay. He was quite always impressed when anyone from SCAP came out--we had quite a few visitors from various commands. But anyone from SCAP carried a lot of weight and if they put in a good word for me, that was okay. So, he never interfered with my direct communication with the civil education section.

I cannot, to answer your question specifically, I don't recall that I ever made a recommendation and got a direct feedback. I did convey my impressions to SCAP people. There were at least two large labor/education CI&E conferences where I spoke informally with members of SCAP and told them rather candidly, as I recall, that we were having too many reforms--they were going too fast. It was more than the Japanese could absorb. Some of them seemed to be aware of it. But the rationale for all of these reforms was certainly by early 1948 was that the Occupation may not last very long and we had to make these reforms as quickly as possible. I think Dr. Orr may confirm this. There was a general consensus--yes we were going a little too fast, but we had to get this thing done before we leave. So, I hope this rather lengthy answer partially answers your question. I can't point to anything that resulted in a change of policy, but again the feedback was mostly from IX Corps and from Kanto Military Government Region. Dr. Orr?

Mark Orr. Thank you, my memory doesn't serve me too well on this subject, but I do recall that we frequently had complaints from the field that communication down through Japanese channels was working much more effectively and quickly than through our own channels and that this was causing a great deal of unease at the local level where the Japanese side seemed to know much more than the American side did. I remember that. Now, as to these reports flowing upward toward Tokyo. As I recall, these written reports were primarily directed to 8th Army Headquarters and there was a very careful selection of what came on to SCAP. So that we saw only a very small proportion of these things that were flowing up from the military government teams. I do want to change the topic now.

I have a neat little anecdote that is useful at this time of day. I think that

Helen Seamans is needed back in Japan, quickly, because of the following anecdote. Two years ago, my wife and I were visiting a university in Tokyo and had the usual reception and nice dinner. She was the only lady present for the party. And during the party one of the young professors came to me and whispered in my ear, "Do you always bring your wife when you come to Tokyo?" (Laughter)

Jacob Van Staaveren. May I make one quick comment. Yes, the Japanese channels were faster than the American channels, but remember the laborious channels set up by 8th Army. Our communications went from 8th Army to IX Corps to the Kanto Military Government Region and then finally to the Yamanashi Military Government Team and some communications would take 12-14 days to reach us. I think we got all the communications, but there was considerable annoyance that it took so long to go through these channels.

Constantine Vaporis. First a short comment, and then a question. Ms. Seamans made a remark about separate washtubs for men and women and separate bamboo poles. I wonder whether--I'm not sure if you were implying that this was evidence of subordination of women or not--but if, in fact, you were then I would like to suggest the opposite--that perhaps it was evidence of women wanting to keep their own sphere of life separate from men. And I would suggest that that continues today where a manufacturing company is pushing its washing machine which has separate compartments for men's wash and women's wash and the advertisement which has appeared on TV has a young woman saying, "You can put your husband's or your father's dirty laundry in this one, but don't tell them." So perhaps Occupation reforms went too far. My question is quite different--to Reiko Yamamoto.

About, perhaps your work doesn't touch upon this, but I'm interested in the question of people who purged themselves--in effect--those who resigned upon hearing about purges to come in the field of education. I believe that they were at least equal in number to the number that were purged. Is there information known about these people who resigned and what happened to them? Was there a lot of pressure at the local level for people to resign first?

Reiko Yamamoto. I think I should mention first the number of people who were purged. Well, I have a lot of statistical material. Today I dealt with the reorganization of the committees and how it affected the number of the screened. So, I will try to give you the number. When the comparison of the number--when before and after the reorganization took place. The Imperial Ordinance was issued in May 1946, and in July the screening started. By 30 November, the total screened was almost 400,000 people. Only 422 persons were screened out by the screening committee. The automatic purge was 1,500. But after reorganization took place, about 5,000 people were purged. Of course, before the ordinance was issued, 115,000 people resigned. So, it naturally caused a shortage of teachers and a lot of trouble occurred in the educational field. Almost at the same time, 1947, the new school 6-3-3 system started and a lot of teachers were needed. Surely there was a lot of shortage of teachers and the confusion was great. My particular emphasis was the CI&E policy--so I have no actual data on the problem that occurred with the school system actually.

W. Soren Egekvist. Maybe I could add two bits worth. During the Occupation I had three hats: I was chief of price control and rationing; I was administrator of the food relief program; and I was also chairman of the economic stabilization policy board. I worked for General Marquette and Ray Kramer. That's why some of these people I recognize their faces. Regarding the relationship, initially the idea was to have direct military government. I was on the planning staff for that and I brought a whole briefcase full of directives from California to Manila and to Tokyo. We issued a directive and I believe the first one was 3 September 1945, for example, freezing prices on a certain date. Then General Whitney and I had a little falling out on that because his idea was that we should not become involved directly with the Japanese government. So, we found out that it was a military government team--I can't remember what prefecture it was--but they had complete price control. They hadn't raised any prices a cent. We found out about it and I had to write a letter--I don't know if it was to

General Krueger or to one of the generals--telling them--Do not issue any more directives to the Japanese government. In other words--the policy was, economics was the responsibility of the Japanese government. We'll do all we can to help them with relief and that sort of thing, but we will not get involved in telling them how to do it. And that's where there was a little breakdown. Now, we found out that later, a couple of years later, it helped very much to have the military government team supervise or just--for example, on crop collections, rice collections--it just helped to just nose around a little bit to help the Japanese government. But our job was to help the Japanese government.

Betty Lanham. You know, there is one aspect of this that I don't hear any reference to in the Occupation and it seems to me to be one that would be fascinating. This is the personality of the Japanese that enables them to react and respond to an Occupation in the way that they did such that they came out favorably. And so if you are talking about the personality of the Japanese, you are talking about to accept a position of subservience and not to get angry with people, but accept it the way it is and just go about your way when things don't come out the way you want them to. If you are talking about it, you're talking about pragmatism of the Japanese. For instance, when someone says to me--one of the speakers was saying in an excellent presentation--was speaking of the time when at one of the university women's organization that they had as the treasurer a person who was wealthy who could supplement funds when they need to. This is the pragmatism of the Japanese and I could name multitudes of cases where this indeed comes out and this is one of the things that enabled the Occupation to go through. It wasn't just what the Americans did, but it was the admirable traits of the Japanese. It was their own value system. A study should be made and it should be made by somebody who is cognizant of the personality of Japanese--a Japanese who is American who can talk about the traits that are not common in general to Americans--that contrast with this because the Japanese would see these traits as ordinary and not unusual. I think this would make a very interesting presentation and certainly something that should be done to give a full perspective to this whole problem or question.

Mike Ditto. I'm pursuing a masters in secondary education at Old Dominion University. One of my favorite subjects has been Cultural Anthropology and I've always been impressed by the colonialization process whereby the Europeans came into South Africa and the South Pacific. The societies that were conquered, suffered. I'm wondering--and I think my question is directed to Miss Yamamoto--as far as the curriculum goes, during the Occupation of Japan, you mentioned the purges of the educators--who had ultimate control of the curricula that these teachers presented to this new generation of Japanese children?

Reiko Yamamoto. As far as curricula are concerned, probably I should have brought Professor Wray here. I haven't studied about curricula yet, but according to the suggestions of US education mission to Japan, they had committees in both sides, CI&E and Education Mission, and to cooperate with the Education Mission, the Japanese side established committee members consisting of leading educational specialists. They made a lot of suggestions on the curricula. After the Mission, that committee was extended to a special steering committee and among the audience there is one student who is now studying about the steering committee. I'm not sure about the details.

Rinjiro Sodei. I'm not a specialist on this, but let me add just one fact that the Occupation wasn't concerned about mathematics or science but they were very much concerned about the education of history and geography and Japanese language, for that matter. They prohibited teaching of history and geography immediately. They started rewriting the history books first. They took a long, long time because they assigned it to the Japanese scholars, you see; but scholars just could not comprehend--they just kept submitting the old stuff--starting from all the way down. They just couldn't--didn't know how to write the new type of history--I think eventually the draft was rewritten three times. So I think there was a big CI&E involvement with writing of the history textbook.

98

Also, if I can speak from my childhood memory, when the war ended I was in the eighth grade and the teacher of Japanese language, or national language, just didn't know what to teach because the old textbook was full of this gung-ho, you know, military stuff... so, I remember he read for us the Jean Jacques Rousseau's *Emile* every day. (Laughter)

Reiko Yamamoto. Well I would like to add something more to Professor Sodei's comment. Well, as he said, first, as you know, the directives to suspend the morals, national history, and geography was issued on the last day of 1945. A new textbook was going to be written, but there was a lot of heated debate between the CI&E and Japanese special historians. The courses were opened probably 1946--September 1946--and as far as curriculum is concerned, it is another problem. He talks about just three subjects which were suspended at the very punitive phase of the Occupational policy. And that was, I can say, was a major punitive policy for the Japanese education. Japanese tried to correct the textbook materials. First of all, there was a lot of militaristic and nationalistic writing in textbooks, and the teachers had the students bring brush ink and line out the objectionable material, but then there was almost nothing in the textbooks left. After that, as from my experience, they issued sort of a newspaper-type of textbook we cut it out and made a very simple fan textbook. That's from my experience. And curricula--with goals--had to be debated with the establishment of the new 6-3-3 system. So, in the first punitive phases, militaristic and nationalistic material was erased from the textbooks. And after that, the constructive phase, they wrote suitable textbooks according to the Mission's suggestion, I think.

Mark Orr. I was chief of the education division from 1947 to 1949 in CI&E. I also have a nice suggestion for a future conference. I was quite discomfited today that this is the last of the conferences on the Occupation. But when someone mentioned the nicknames that were applied to certain Occupation officials, it occurred to me that that would be an excellent subject for our next conference. (Laughter) All of the participants would be Japanese. We would be singing--or they would be singing--about "Behind Closed Doors." I would like to know what they were talking about when they talked about us after their meetings with Occupation officials, what nicknames we had, what peculiarities were noticed and so on. I'll be happy to be present for that conference. (Laughter)

This is more of a comment on the history question that shouldn't be overlooked; that this controversy is still going on. It is a very real one. For the past ten years, the governments of Korea and China have complained about the Japanese history books; that they gloss over the invasion of Manchuria and of China, the treatment of prisoners of war, the horrors of the war, the question of Japanese war guilt. All these things are still highly controversial and the Ministry of Education, being the very conservative body that it is, still glosses over the real history of Japan. This is something yet to be really faced.

Cornelius Iida. If I may, I would just like to add two comments. I welcome both suggestions--first the last one being that the symposia of this type should continue on. The first one is a very poignant point--because even last week or within the last several weeks, the Japanese textbook having to do the history of Okinawa has been in discussion. Apparently the Japanese military issued grenades to Okinawan civilians and children to kill themselves because they felt that the Americans, once they got there, would mistreat them. So, these grenades were issued and the scholar who was writing the textbook wanted to put that in very clearly--that the children were forced by the Japanese military to commit suicide--and the Education Ministry said "No." Censorship continues on very strongly. You mentioned China and Korea--yes, those points were very well taken. Okinawa--even though a part of Japan--is still very much mistreated in this manner. And this type of distortion of history, I think, is unconscionable. I think that the conference ought to go on--continue on--emphasizing some of the true merits that really transpired 45 years ago.

Crawford Millen. I'd like to direct my question to Professor Sodei. But I would like to comment that unfortunately the rewriting of history is not a unique problem to the Japanese as so many of us in our country at the present time are seeing happening. It is a real tragedy of our times. My question to Professor Sodei is: how is the constitution--the 1947 constitution--being viewed at the grassroots level in Japan now and also, how is it being viewed among the academic legal profession and also among the practicing legal profession in Japan?

Rinjiro Sodei. I think another 30 minutes--I need another 30 minutes for answering to this. But because of this Gulf War, there is a new controversy over the merit of Article 9, whether we should keep this so that Japan can dispatch defense forces abroad. But there is still strong opinion that Japan should stick to the letter and spirit of Article 9 of the Constitution. They are mostly rather the older people or the middle aged and who still remember--at who least know--how this constitution was brought over. But, I'm afraid that the younger generation who have no historical memory to hold on to tend to have a rather contemporary idea that why don't we amend the constitution so that we may be able to dispatch troops. But, still, you know, it is a big controversy and it will continue for some time. For the academic world, most of, the absolute majority of the jurists think that the present defense forces is against the letter of Article 9--they are unconstitutional. And that much the academic world agrees on.

REPATRIATION AT THE GRASS ROOTS LEVEL

Allen H. Meyer

ALLEN H. MEYER, an attorney in Chicago, Illinois, was a U.S. Army officer assigned to the Allied Occupation of Japan in 1946 and 1947. He was a Japanese language specialist in the Allied Translator and Interpreter Service where he served in a variety of functions, e.g., editorial translator, election monitor in Hokkaido, and repatriation coordinator at Uraga, Sasebo, Hakodate, and Maizuru. He is a 1948 graduate of Harvard University and holds a Doctor of Jurisprudence degree from Northwestern University (1951). He has published several articles in law journals, has provided legal assistance to Nisei Veterans groups, and has lectured on Japanese-Jewish relations.

On V-J Day, Repatriation was a scientific operation with which the United States was ill-prepared to cope. In no prior (or subsequent) wars or military engagements was the scope of magnitude of the operation comparable to what confronted us with Japan. Even Germany, less than a year earlier, presented no precedent. At V-E Day, we merely put the POWs on trains or busses, and the job was done. Here, we were confronted with six million Japanese, requiring transport by ship from vast distances around the Pacific theatre.

By way of personal background, I had studied the Japanese language in college in 1943, and had been trained by the Army as a translator and interpreter in the Military Intelligence Service Language Schools at Ann Arbor and Fort Snelling.

During the period from late 1941 through early 1946, the U.S. Army had a series of programs which involved intensive training of the Japanese language of a limited number of its personnel. Rough estimates have been about 6,000 Americans of Japanese (AJA) ancestry and about 700 others. The 700 were ultimately given army commissions and, as the war progressed, hundreds of the AJAs were most appropriately commissioned. This non-AJA group consisted of a small percentage of Chinese, Koreans and Filipinos, but was largely comprised of Caucasians. A small percentage of the Caucasians was made up of people who had lived and worked in Japan, as businessmen or missionaries, but the vast majority was made up of people with aptitudes in foreign languages. As one of the latter who learned the language here, my remarks will be concerned with working with the AJAs during the early 24 months of the Occupation.

The initial trainees began in November 1941, at Presidio of Monterey, California, and all had strong connections with the Japanese language. The two Caucasians were given commissions, while the other 43, Nisei (2nd generation Americans) or Kibei (Americans who had received some schooling in Japan and returned to the States) were sent to the Pacific Theatre or, in a few instances, remained in the States in the War Department, Signal Corps, or were sent to the Army camps where advanced training was given to others, or to various colleges, to act as teachers in the less intensive Japanese language training courses. Due to general relocation of Japanese-Americans from the West Coast in spring 1942, the school was moved to facilities at Camp Savage, Minnesota, and, as the space needs expanded, was ultimately transferred in 1943 to Fort Snelling, Minnesota, where it remained until early 1946.

As the purpose of this paper relates only to the Occupation, I will not dwell on the pre-Surrender period, but the role of the AJAs cannot be understated. Many volunteered from Relocation Centers, leaving families behind in the camps. During the period through 1944, very few received Army Commissions because of unfounded apprehensions about loyalty. Those who dealt with the problems of Intelligence gathering recognized their contributions to the ultimate victory in war, and any remarks are likewise directed to their achievements during the Occupation.

During the war, the Japanese man on the street, as well as his or her military and naval personnel, considered their language to be of such difficulty that they were genuinely surprised to be confronted with exposure to Caucasians, or even persons of Japanese ancestry who were a generation removed from their homeland, who could deal with them in their own language. Although, today, this would not shock the average Japanese, it had a substantial impact during the period I was there--from shortly after the end of the war until August 1947 when I was discharged and returned to the States.

The impact of such confrontation was initially one of being put on the defensive, and then, when they realized that we were not the ogres depicted by their war-time characterization of the Americans, they tended to open up to us. This general observation related to virtually all of the areas of contact I will discuss. Although we received no written or verbal guidelines on how to cope with this series of reactions, common sense instructed us that we had two, sometimes conflicting, goals: (1) to do the job assigned to us as military occupiers of a defeated enemy, and (2) to avoid temporary or permanent alienation of the people among whom we were to live, and hopefully, to "democratize."

Initially, when we disembarked near Tokyo, we spent a few days at Camp Zama for shots and general orientation. As the linguists had been given training in area studies, history and culture, the orientation was rather simplistic, and at times, conflicting, even for the 20-year old, like myself, who had been immersed in language study for over two years. Many of us were assigned to billet at the NYK Building in Tokyo, as members of the Allied Translator and Interpreter Service (ATIS). The Building, the formidable former headquarters of the leading shipping company, was located at the corner of an intersection of considerable activity. On one side, we overlooked the Emperor's Palace grounds, and the other street was the two small blocks leading to the partially bombed-out main Tokyo railroad station.

We lived and worked in the NYK, which most translators and interpreters considered their interim home between assignments. Also living there were some linguists in Japanese of the armed forces of England, Australia, China, the Netherlands and Russia. The latter, trained in a language school in Vladivostok, could converse with us only in Japanese, but we were all on good terms before the Cold War set in, and they were then moved out.

My initial assignment in Japan was that of a translator of daily newspapers and periodicals and editor of translations of others.

During the period of my time in Japan, Colonel Sidney Mashbir, and later, Colonel Austin, would call upon those living at the NYK to perform emergency tasks unrelated to our work. Our proximity to Tokyo's main railroad station resulted in a few emergencies, when the Military Police were confronted with fights among what we would now call the "homeless," and they were in need of interpreters to calm the disturbances. I also worked on election patrols in Rumoi prefecture, as interpreter for staff officers on special projects, as well as a variety of other tasks requiring language skills.

During late spring, 1946, I had my initial encounter with the issue of Repatriation. I was requested to join Robert Fair (then a 1st Lieutenant, who retired as a General) for a dinner meeting at the Home Ministry Office. The Ministry of Welfare had handled well the general problem of Repatriation, but the trickle of personnel being returned from Soviet or Red Chinese regions made this a concern of the Home Ministry. Those attending the meeting included former high-ranking military personnel who, with the Home Ministry, were concerned about communist indoctrination the Japanese were receiving, coupled with the impact it would have when they ultimately returned. I was told to study background material, and, some weeks later, I was sent to Uraga to work on Repatriation of non-Red returnees, in order to learn the general routine of Repatriation as practiced by the Ministry of Welfare and to report periodically to those in charge of ATIS, to permit them to determine the composition of teams of linguists to be sent to various Ports when these people began to return in great numbers. There was only limited mention of this issue in the media, because little was known by the Japanese; however, there was an abundance of letters to the editor, beseeching help to get these people back. We would read about discussions at Allied Council for Japan meetings, covered by the media, but only frustration confronted the Japanese and GHQ.

My research revealed generally where they were, how they were being used as labor and attempts at indoctrination; these came from Nationalist Chinese, foreign nationals in Manchuria who left by way of Japan, and the few Japanese who escaped or were returned for reasons of health. I shall not attempt to cover the overall story, because that has been more recently analyzed in William Nimmo's book, *Behind a Curtain of Silence.*

There were two distinct phases to Repatriation port work, the initial being concerned with Japanese in areas other than Soviet-controlled, and the latter involving persons caught in Manchuria, North China, North Korea and Sakhalin (Karafuto).

During the early phase, without written guidelines, the role of the language officer was to act as liaison to the Port officials, and thereafter, with his team, perform interrogation of the repatriates and occupational translation of what they brought with them. By early 1946, with the increase of AJA language personnel in the Pacific, and the impetus to commission more of the Nisei/Kibei servicemen, teams were set up with one officer and three enlisted men. Unlike the war-time ratio of 1 to 10, this meant more time for interrogation by the officer and, fortunately, less editing of notes and reports of other members of the team. The verbal skills varied from team to team. Mine was on a par with, but by no means superior to, that of some of the other members of my team. My personal experience was that the best team was one that consisted of at least one Kibei or a person from Hawaii because, although their skills in English reports occasionally required extra time in editing by me, they understood some verbal nuances better than I or the Stateside AJAs. The reading skills were another matter. If the material was printed or in a standard cursive written form, I could handle that as well as the others, but, if in *sosho* (grass-writing), generally only the Kibei or Hawaiian was able to cope with it. If none of us could handle the translation, the document was confiscated, the repatriate being given a receipt, and sent to Yokohama or ATIS for clarification and ultimate return to the owner.

The normal procedure was one where we, living at the Port city, would be alerted (by telephone) by the Port Officer (as an agent for the Japanese Ministry of Welfare, who was frequently a discharged Naval Officer) that a particular ship was coming in from a particular area and the approximate time of arrival (usually 12-24 hours prior to arrival). We would alert Yokohama and request instructions as to any particular information they were seeking or as to any particular individuals they considered as more likely to interrogate or search. Only after the beginning of the Cold War did instructions become more detailed.

The physical atmosphere of interrogation would vary, depending upon the Port and the size of the returning ship.

According to the official *Reports of General MacArthur: The Occupation: Military Phase* (pp. 148-193), the breakdown of Japanese to be repatriated, as of late August 1945 was:

China	1,501,200
Manchuria	1,105,800
Siberia	700,000
Karafuto/Kurile	372,000
North Korea	322,550
Dairen/Port Arthur	223,100
Islands near Japan	62,400
Formosa	479,050
Ryukyu Islands	69,000
Philippines	132,900
North Indo-China	32,000
Southeast Asia	710,000
Netherlands E. Indies	15,550
Australia/New Guinea	138,700
New Zealand	800
Hawaii	3,600
Other Pacific Islands	130,900
Totaling:	5,999,550

These did not including Japanese, mainly diplomats, in Europe (as part of the Axis or neutrals), nor the few thousand in the U.S. and England captured and detained for Intelligence purposes.

Although there was, early on, a Repatriation Section in SCAP, we had no direct contact with them, and, if they had published guidelines and procedures, they were given to the Japanese government, not to us. The point here is that, when we arrived at a Port, procedures were already in operation, and our duty was to work within that framework.

As of SCAP's report in April 1947, the general "Plan" was spelled out in G-3 GHQ SCAP, *Report on Mass Repatriation in the Western Pacific* (April 1947), which stated, in part:

> The Imperial Japanese Government was charged with the execution of the provisions of the repatriation directives published by SCAP. This included establishment, organization and operation of repatriation reception centers, transporting of repatriates to and from these centers and providing of crews and supplies for repatriation ships. At the reception centers, the IJG was required to subject each repatriate to physical examinations and quarantine procedure, as were necessary; inoculations against cholera and typhus, vaccination against smallpox, and disinfestation by DDT of person and baggage; screening for war criminals; inspection of baggage and persons to prevent unauthorized traffic in goods, financial instruments and precious metals. In addition, the following functions were performed at reception centers: rail and ship movements were coordinated; food and clothing, to be placed aboard repatriation ships or to be used at the centers, were assembled and distributed; returning Japanese soldiers and sailors were demobilized and furnished free rail transportation to their homes.

Given the limited space and facilities, we could have encountered serious problems. For example, the MacArthur *Reports* mentioned the problem of the need for quarantine due to epidemics of cholera among the repatriates. I quote from the Reports (p. 155):

> This situation interfered considerably with the repatriation program since infected ships were quarantined and the passengers held aboard, examined, and treated until medical authorities were satisfied that they no longer constituted a hazard to the public health of Japan. Some of these ships were held in quarantine as long as thirty days. To indicate the magnitude of the problem, there were at one time twenty-two ships with a total of 76,000 repatriates in quarantine at Uraga, Japan. A total of 438 persons died of cholera before the epidemic was brought under control; only the determined efforts of the Public Health and Welfare Section of SCAP and port quarantine agencies prevented introduction of widespread epidemics into Japan.

Uraga was the first port to which I was assigned, and my team was involved in that problem.

Uraga was a relatively large, unmined port, about 25 miles south of Yokosuka, but far enough removed that it would not interfere with U.S. Naval operations. It had no railroad facilities large enough to process the 664,000 repatriates who ultimately passed through there. It was separated by a hill (and tunnel) from Kurihama (whose claim to fame had been the monument commemorating Perry's landing at that village in 1853). The Japanese government provided us with a billet and mess in Kurihama, in a former Naval office building, which, as of my last visit there in 1973, was a Japanese Self-Defense Force training school--off-limits to sightseeing Americans. Kurihama had the railroad station, the southerlymost stop on the line north to Tokyo, a 40-minute ride through Yokosuka and Yokohama.

At Uraga, we had two (and, for a brief time, three) teams. A telephone call from the Port Officers would bring us there within 5-10 minutes by jeeps, but, once there, we had no interrogation area, and whatever we did was conducted virtually in the open.

When we were working, the Port facility always had large numbers of military support (8th Army and, in particular, First Cavalry), as well as substantial groups from the Welfare Ministry. Occasionally, special interpreters were sent from ATIS to work with the Army doctors, but, in their absence, we would help. Also, Japanese doctors or non-medical personnel who spoke some English were of great assistance.

Although a doctor and interpreter were generally the first to board a ship, our role, as interpreters, was usually not in the medical field, but was more concerned with general liaison. SCAP's original policies, set forth in MacArthur's *Reports*, were fairly specific, but did not always contemplate periodic problems. These policies were:

a. Maximum utilization will be made of Japanese naval and merchant shipping allocated for repatriation of Japanese nationals.

b. Japanese naval vessels and those Japanese merchant vessels designed primarily for the transport of personnel and not required for inter-island or coastal passenger service, will be utilized for the repatriation of Japanese nationals.

c. Personnel to be repatriated will be transported on cargo vessels only to the extent that the cargo-carrying capacity of the vessel is not curtailed thereby.

d. The Imperial Japanese Government will operate, man, victual and supply Japanese shipping used for repatriation to the maximum practicable extent.

e. First priority will be granted to the movement of Japanese military and naval personnel, and second priority to the movement of Japanese civilians.

f. All Japanese personnel will be disarmed prior to return to Japan proper.

g. In the evacuation of Japanese nationals from areas under the control of CINCAFPAC and CINCPAC, the former will prescribe the percentage of shipping allocated for repatriation purposes, to be employed in servicing the respective areas. Priorities for the evacuation of specific areas will be established as necessary...

h. In the evacuation of Japanese nationals from areas under the control of the Generalissimo, Chinese Armies, SACSEA, GOCAMF and the Commander in Chief, Soviet Forces in the Far East, SCAP will make the necessary arrangements.

At Uraga, we did not often encounter the need for Intelligence gathering, unless we were forewarned by the Port Officers of some trouble en route. Fights would occur between people who blamed the Emperor for their plight, and those still loyal to the system who refused to deny his divinity, or among people (usually Officers or NCO's) who were blamed for their oppressive treatment or exploitation of their troops and those who felt oppressed. As a group, the team would first interview the ship's commanding Officer for insights into the problems and the identities of the combative participants. The latter would then be interrogated by each of us, one-on-one, but before we made our final report, we would wander through the other repatriates eliciting casual discussion. We usually confiscated any written material from those involved in confrontations and, if we could translate them rapidly and found them to be insignificant, returned them to the owners; otherwise, we would ship them on with our reports.

While en route, standardized cards were distributed and filled out by the returnees, giving name, address and prior occupation and military unit data. Unfortunately, this was prior to access to photostating equipment, and, for an interrogation, we had to pull these cards out of order and write out duplicates in both Japanese and English (for our reports).

Our basic concern always had to be with the impression we left on these people before they returned home. Inasmuch as accusers were always willing to come forth, The interviews with them tended to be fairly brief, so as to avoid any impression that the accusers were being doubted. Considering the lack of privacy, and the fact that we

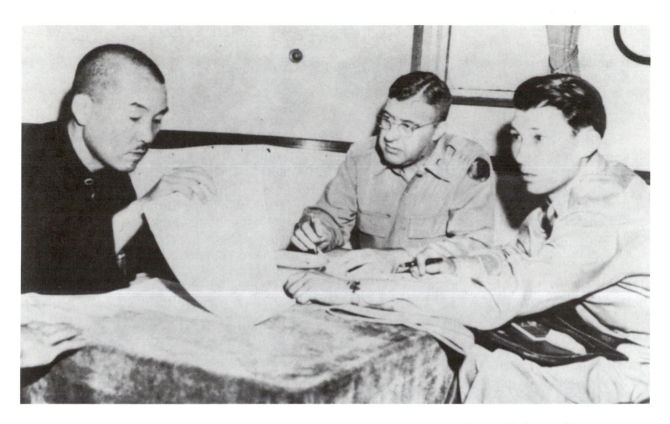

Interrogation officers check passenger list with captain of the *Tokuga Maru.*

were being observed by hundreds of others at a distance, an appearance of not being overbearing was essential.

At Uraga, upon disembarking, the repatriates passed through a large warehouse building, where the Japanese customs and identification searches were processed. During this phase, we kept a low profile, usually interviewing the ship's officers and higher ranking officers of the military units on board. As they left the warehouse, in multiple rows, DDT and inoculations were applied in ample doses. As an aside, the fear of contracting diseases caused my team to have our hair cut almost to the scalp, to avoid lice and, more importantly, so that the DDT would cover us completely. We took daily "bathes" of DDT, and, if we worked more than normal hours, had the Welfare Ministry people spray us a few more times. Later medical studies in the 1960s revealed the dangers of DDT, but the Army doctors pointed out the greater dangers of the diseases it was intended to avert.

When the repatriates, still in rows, reached the open end of the warehouse, we called out names and took these particular individuals to the perimeter areas to interrogate them. In the absence of desks and chairs, we frequently squatted or sat on the ground for these interviews, making notes as we spoke.

All around the perimeters, Army personnel, usually armed with carbines or M-1 rifles, stood or sat observing this massive array of humanity. Fortunately, their armed assistance was never required during my experience in Uraga. Our interrogations took place within, but at the edges of, the perimeters, so that all could see that nothing unusual was happening to their fellow personnel. Our team always wore fatigues, and we intentionally did not carry weapons. The fact that Americans were speaking to them in their own tongue was sufficiently disarming to them that the initial surprise caused them to open up. When our guards, out of curiosity, came too close, we ordered them to move back, and then translated to the repatriate what we had just said, in order to put him more at ease. The contrast of our conciliatory approach with the appearance of the armed Army personnel, we would like to think, had an impact of dispelling latent fears of the Occupiers, while still recognizing that the soldiers with weapons represented a recognition of the defeat of Japan. Finally, when we interrogated an accused, we took him outside the perimeter, and, if there appeared a valid basis for the accusation, he was turned over to the Army officers for further processing in Yokohama. When he did not return to the line-up, the others knew that we were on the side of the underdog, and left the same with a feeling of support for the people they had been trained to hate or fear.

What I have described up to this point was the unspectacular. Now, I would like to impart more unusual events at Uraga, not contemplated by the SCAP policies. Two particular ships proved the exceptions to the rule: one contained over 8,000 armed service personnel, and the other transported diplomats from Europe.

The day before its arrival on 3 November 1946, we were informed that a large naval vessel, the Katsuragi, was returning from the Netherlands East Indies. What we were told was that the Dutch and British had accepted their surrender and that some of the personnel were still armed. We were also informed that, coming from the tropics, cholera was a problem. When we asked why the return of this group was so long delayed after the end of the war, the Port Officer responded that the Dutch, with the help of the British, had used the prisoners in forced labor to rebuild areas to the needs of the victors. When I asked the reason they were coming to Uraga, rather than the port of Kure, where British and Dutch had their own personnel, he suggested that the ship might be too large for other ports. His comments were a gross understatement, not through his fault, but because he was misinformed.

When our two teams drove to the Port early the following day, we were astonished to see a mammoth aircraft carrier in a harbor normally accommodating the smaller ships that SCAP contemplated in its policy statement. I immediately called Yokohama for help. Later that day, the Port facility was alive with Ministry help, but Yokohama sent only its usual complement of guards and a few staff officers (accompanied by Stars & Stripes photographers). At the dock, the Port Officer communicated with the Katsuragi's radio officer and learned that we should come immediately. Therefore, without backup, our two teams of eight boarded the frame Port boat, which slowly chugged out to the leviathan overshadowing the rest of our harbor. Incidentally, none of us, including the Port Officer, had ever been on an aircraft carrier before. As was our practice, we were all unarmed, wearing our fatigues and carried with us only a few boxes of identification cards and a few dictionaries and maps. On other rare occasions, when we went to the ship first, our little putt-putt would pull along side a transport ship, which would lower its side ladder to allow us access to the main deck. In this instance, the Katsuragi lowered climbing rungs to assist our boarding; except for the Port Officer and his assistant, the other eight of us must have appeared rather inept in trying to scale the wall of rungs, but, fortunately, none of us fell back into the harbor. My recall of the rest of the day comes from a detailed letter I later wrote to my parents. Otherwise, the experience was sufficiently traumatic that I would normally have repressed its memory. The main points of my letter were as follows:

Although yesterday was Sunday, we found ourselves quite rushed with work. The "Katsuragi," a 20,000 ton aircraft carrier, arrived in port, and we were to board her at 10 a.m. Before that, we went to Mr. Toyohara's Welfare Ministry Office to get some last-minute details. It seems that three of my men must follow three repatriates, and it's necessary to make certain arrangements with the ministry. As we arrived, we found Toyohara speaking to about 200 of his employees, commemorating the promulgation of the new Constitution as Japan's introduction to Democracy. At the end of his speech, we adjourned to his office. Normally, the men wear business suits; yesterday, they wore formal dress, black coat with tails, starched shirt, vest with pearl buttons, etc. Generally, the office girl serves us tea; yesterday, we were served beer. At the end of our business, we toasted the Constitution and the new Nippon. At 10:30 a.m., we left the port in our so-called Navy launch, and a few moments later, a monstrous aircraft carrier came into full view. Upon boarding, we were guided through a labyrinth of low-ceiling corridors and passageways until we arrived at the Captain's quarters and office. Here, we obtained the vital statistics-close to 9,000 people aboard from Bangkok, Hong Kong, Singapore and Sumatra. Upon completion of preliminary questioning, we told the Captain to have all the former officers on the flight deck at 1 p.m., when we planned to return. We then inspected the ship. The area which was formerly used as a hangar for airplanes was divided into four floors by board partitions. Here, over 8,000 men slept and lived for close to two weeks. We visited engine rooms, latrines, kitchen and control cabins.

That afternoon, we returned to find some 230 officers covered down in ranks and files, standing at attention as we approached. They bowed, the man in charge saluted, and I returned the bow. We called over the officer in charge, who turned out to be former Lt. General Kunomura. Upon interrogation, he informed us that all the officers and men aboard were members of his 2nd Imperial Guard Division. The 2nd Division was in southern China on 7 December 1941, and, at that time, started their march south through Malay to Singapore. Having conquered that area, they went to Sumatra in 1943, where they remained in power until the British took over a year ago. They were all very courteous, and our interviews ran smoothly.

One aspect which I did not mention to my parents was the fact that practically all were still armed. As our team of eight approached the commanding officers, he tendered to me his sword. I accepted it, symbolically, but handed it to the officer behind him, and stated to the General, loudly enough so that all could hear, that our role was not a military acceptance of surrender, which would be processed ashore in Demobilization, but was to assist in an orderly return to civilian life in a new Japan. This was apparently the correct verbal response, because, as we adjourned to the offices of the ship's Captain, we heard applause from the officers on deck, and, for the next three days of processing and interrogations, the repatriates commented on how favorably they were impressed by this act and statement. One element we gleaned was that they were gratified that we did not cause the General under whom most of them had served since 1941, as soldiers and as prisoners, to lose face. The other element seemed to be that we had generated a feeling among most of them that the Americans were a breed far different from the British and Dutch, who had used them in a manner similar to that which we later learned had been employed by the Russians with personnel caught within their jurisdiction. The expressed gratitude to our remaining combined team of five overwhelmed both us and the Welfare Ministry, to the point that the 1st Cavalry liaison officer asked us to go nightly to the railroad station, to ask if all had gone well. As anxious as they were to board the trains on their way home, hundreds took the time to come over to express appreciation for our considerate and thoughtful approach.

One question has bothered me for the past 45 years: why did the British and Dutch allow so many of these repatriates to return with swords or guns, especially in light of SCAP's directive on this point? A few told me that the arms were returned to the Japanese just before departure, lest they fell into the hands of then growing groups of insurgents in those colonial regions controlled by the Dutch. Had we been forewarned, I doubt that we or the Welfare Ministry would have acted differently, because the net impact on these 8,000 (except the three who were earlier removed for War Crimes Trials) was a favorable view of the Occupiers.

The other incident of note, not covered by the SCAP policy, occurred when a ship arrived from Europe, carrying Japanese diplomatic personnel, their families and, in a few instances, their non-Japanese wives or mistresses (who were expelled from the nations where they had been citizens). We were given no advance warning of the nature of its passengers. Upon docking, a call to Yokohama brought forth a large number of upper echelon officers, because this was not the usual cargo to which we were accustomed. The ship was able to dock and process through the warehouse. Unlike the returning service personnel who brought with them the bare necessities, this group, well dressed and healthy, was loaded down with fine luggage, including trunks with safe combination locks. Also, unlike our other encounters, these people considered themselves protected by some form of diplomatic immunity, and their attributes clearly did not include humility.

Initially, they refused to talk to me, wearing only a gold bar, or to my men, wearing only the chevrons of sergeants. We asked the First Cavalry Colonels to give us direct orders, so that those who understood English might comprehend the severity of the situation. We then translated, in even rougher language, but they still refused to open their locked trunks. The First Cavalry personnel were then directed to open the trunks and luggage, forcibly, while the former diplomats hurled their obscenities and threats at our teams. Once opened, the contents disclosed a bonanza of material which was ultimately used in War Crimes Trials.

Our team, later that day, was able to interrogate some lower level members of the diplomatic corps. We asked the reason for the failure of their superiors to destroy much of what they had brought with them, and their response was unexpected. They had been throughout European capitals when Germany fell, and observed the manner in which Americans, British and French had sought out cooperation from people who might serve as a bulwark there against Communism. These diplomats felt that their diaries, correspondence and other documents would be helpful in Japan in gaining the favor of the Americans. The Cold War had not yet reached Japan, and the MacArthur staff was overwhelmed by the treasure trove we confiscated.

Late that afternoon, a group of War Crimes prosecutors and more ATIS translators came from GHQ, and we all adjourned to our small billet in Kurihama. We sent home our Japanese cook and maintenance people, the billet was cordoned off, and we poured over the material into the early hours of the morning. The experts took most of the material back to Tokyo, and left our teams to meet with the verbal abuse of the diplomats a few hours later. When we returned to them only innocuous documents and personal photos, they realized that the MacArthur approach differed from that in Europe, and that they had blundered in their perception of our role in Japan. By this time, they were less surly and more willing to cooperate in supplying information, for, not unlike other diplomats, their posts had been all over the world, and the implications of what they were able to disclose were far more significant that the run-of-the-mill data to which we were accustomed.

Among the contents of their trunks, left untouched but guarded, were gold and jewelry. That morning, one of them offered a bribe to a Nisei member of my team, which he reported immediately. By this time, we were augmented by another dozen interpreters from ATIS, and the warehouse now had small desks at appropriate distances from one another. Luckily, this was the only ship in port, until later that morning, when the Port Officer advised us that a ship was arriving with soldiers from China. We had to ask everyone to leave the warehouse to permit our return to the mundane world of DDT, epidemics and squabbles about the divinity of the Emperor. About a week later, the Japanese radio and newspapers began to report on this fortuitous find and extolled General MacArthur on his perseverance against War Criminals.

While Uraga was a port which processed military and civilian personnel from all over the world, other ports to which we were later assigned dealt exclusively with Soviet-occupied or controlled areas. Uraga was meaningful because it taught us routine and port procedures, but the subsequent locales processed ships from particular regions with which we were called upon to familiarize ourselves rapidly. My main stay in Uraga was from 10 September 1946 to 17 November 1946. On 22 November 1946, I was assigned to the Central Interrogation Center (at ATIS), a euphemism for Cold War interrogations. While there, until late December 1946, I lectured on port procedures and worked on screening linguist officers and men appropriate for the new venture. On 10 December 1946, we commenced an elementary course in Russian, emphasizing military and industrial terms; we learned later that some of the knowledgeable repatriates knew locations, names and titles of individuals, and industrial operations, in Russian only. By

Christmas, most of us left for Kyoto, where the teams were assembled, and, on the 31st, 5 teams were sent to Maizuru, and I, along with 19 other teams, headed toward Sasebo, in west central Kyushu.

Sasebo was then the Headquarters of the 34th Regiment of the 24th Division, and was not then, or later, pleased with our arrival. The irregularity of our hours of free-time, our ability to fraternize freely and the special treatment afforded us by GHQ created a problem for their aura of discipline. Although Sasebo had an excellent port, Colonel Bing, of the 34th, convinced Tokyo a better locale would be on Hario Island to the southeast of Sasebo, reachable only by a small bridge that the 34th could guard - for and against us. At the south end of this small island is Hario Straits, over which rapids a bridge was built in 1955, so that one can now drive from Sasebo to Nagasaki in about two hours, as against the circuitous route of 5-7 hours we had to traverse then. When I visited Sasebo and Hario again in 1984, no one remembered the wharfs or repatriation center; it now contains an amusement park and small inns, and can be traversed in the space of a few minutes on the road to Nagasaki.

When our group of 20 teams arrived at Hario on 5 January 1947, a few teams had already begun to set up for the task ahead. Our lead officer was Captain Malcomb Frehn, a cherub-like civilian type who had been a Missionary in Japan before the War, and whose military background was limited to having been a bugler boy during World War I. He and a few officers from the War Documents Section of the War Department had preceded us by a few weeks, but, by the time of our arrival, all of the small quonset huts where we would live, eat and interrogate had been dropped on a flat bed of clay. As that winter was a wet one, and the clay turned to slush, ends of boxes and boards were used to get to the food, the latrine/shower and to bring the interrogees to us. Our task here was to deal with people returning from Siberia and Manchuria by way of Dairen.

It is not my purpose to deal with what we learned, because that has been considered extensively in Japan, and more recently here by William Nimmo. From the standpoint of procedures and impact, Hario (as well as other ports used later) differed considerably from Uraga. Unlike Uraga, where belligerency was far from the norm, in Hario, it manifested itself daily--against the Russians or Chinese or against their own and, occasionally, against us. A letter from Hario to my parents might explain certain areas of confrontation. Forgive some of the phrasing which sounds like poor translations of the interrogees, but, after extended periods with them, we were thinking in Japanese while writing in English.

The past two nights have been rather wild at the repatriation center. Although the repatriate barracks are only across the road, fortunately we have a tall fence surrounding our area to separate us. Another good feature is the fact that we have GI guards with guns to stand at the entrance for protection. And the last benefit is the fact that the repatriates have no trouble with us, only with their own. Two nights ago, a riot broke out in one of the buildings. It seems that, during the voyage back to Japan, a few of the people with political ideologies different from the majority of the returnees took advantage of the others, and one night, when drunk, threw the ashes of one of the dead soldiers overboard. Back home in Japan, the other people felt free to get even, and raised their nerve to take action. Armed with heavy belt buckles and ropes, five or so younger men attacked two of the voyage trouble-makers and their women-folk. Before the Japanese police broke it up, one of the former "tyrants" was dead, the other was paralyzed, and four of their close relatives were badly beaten. There are always a few people on these ships who have told lies about others to the authorities for their own ends; these are the "tyrants." As a result, when the average Japanese comes home, realizing that the Americans are against tyranny, conspirators and people of certain ideologies, he feels safe in taking the law into his own hands. In fact, he thinks he will be praised for his work by us!

The second incident occurred last night. Weekly, thousands of Koreans who were in Japan during the war are being returned to Korea. Throughout the war, most of these people were nothing more than slave-labor and, as such, consider themselves co-victors in our triumph. The Korean's status in Japan at present is one of co-belligerent awaiting repatriation to Korea. Because of their natural hatred of the Japanese, and the fact that they feel they deserve a share in the profits of victory, they have given the Allied authorities a real problem. Most consider themselves on a par in authority with the American soldier and, therefore, feel immune to both Allied supervision and Japanese police. From this position, they have numerous times taken the law into their own hands. For example, Koreans are the worst black-marketeers in Japan today. Well, with their ship about to depart from port, five dove overboard, swam to shore and were on the loose on Hario island. Within a few hours, police groups were sent from Sasebo and began to comb the area. Our guard was doubled and, throughout the island and at the bridges, swarms of police could be found. I've heard they were captured earlier today. Naturally, their objective in wanting to remain in Japan is obvious...here, they are conquerors, while in Korea, they are apt to be peasants.

Those are only sidelines in our work here; in fact, that sort of thing doesn't even concern us. What does concern us is our safety and, since I did not want to tell you this to frighten you, I must say we use every precaution for safety. We have our own guards, in addition to protection from the Japanese police; no one is allowed on the island carrying weapons of any sort; our tall wire fence serves as ample protection. Lastly, they have only respect and admiration for and fear of the Allied forces; it is their own they hate.

Our Captain returned from Tokyo today with the news that possible replacements will be coming through shortly--possibly within two weeks--more likely, longer. At any rate, I will not look forward to my last five months in Japan on this island.

Rereading this letter caused a bit of shock at the racism expressed, but the Japanese media at the time were citing the same concerns.

Our little camp on Hario did not lend itself to the best conditions for interrogation. We were ill-prepared for the task, because we needed maps in Chinese and Russian, as well as Japanese, and had very little knowledge about the Siberia from which these people were returning. Fortunately, most repatriates sensed correctly the reason for our being there and cooperated. Those who did not had undergone indoctrination that took hold, and our task with them was to center on them personally, while, from those who were cooperative, we were able to gather significant data of a military or industrial nature, or about those who had been successfully indoctrinated.

The deficiency in knowledge of the area was cured the first week. As these people were returning through Dairen, and Dairen was the commercial city for its neighbor, Port Arthur, the formidable naval base about which we knew almost nothing, one of the repatriates sneaked to me a 1931 Guide Book of Dairen, covering it street by street in detail, which I have not seen since for a city that size. People were sent down from Tokyo to photograph each page, but, until they got us all copies, I found myself in great demand in all of the cubicles in the few quonset huts where interrogations were being performed. I was then collating all we learned on Dairen, and what little we learned about Port Arthur, and found myself lecturing almost nightly in the quonset hut mess hall.

Another find a few weeks later was a returning Major who spent the war in Harbin, listening to Russian radio transmissions to Vladivostok. He had been both a linguist and cryptoanalyst, but, because almost no one knew what he was doing, there was no one to inform on him to the Russians or to the Hachi-Ro-Gun [Eighth Route

Army of the Chinese Communist Forces], and he spent his 16-month internment period as a forester in southern Siberia. He not only gave me his Russian-Japanese-Russian dictionary, but offered to stay with us until specialists came down from Tokyo. He was less surprised to find me, a Caucasian, speaking in his native tongue (because he had encountered in Manchuria many White Russians who knew his language, and were supportive of Japan) than to find the large number of Nisei who were members of our Army; in his pre-1945 experience, one could find, or learn of, very few people of Japanese ancestry who worked for, or in, the Soviet armed forces structure.

Our inquiries were not limited to the peninsula, because many of the repatriates came from as far as Irkutsk. Very few had not been used as manual labor, initially, in disassembling Manchurian industry and moving with it into Siberia for reassembly. During the balance of their 16 months, their labor was employed in all types of construction, except in the case of those used in forestry. One area of intensive forestry was that of Birobidzhan, bordering on the Amur River. The Army worked them long hours, and gave them little food or clothing, but the natives supplied them with supplements, even though they were often treated as badly as the prisoners. The repatriates knew their benefactors only as To. I had learned earlier that this was the code word developed by White Russians for the alternate reading of the kanji for 10, Ju, which sounded like the pejorative in Russian for Jew. Not unlike my translation team at ATIS early in the Occupation, these people had never encountered Yudaijin.

In a lighter vein, the anecdotes about our few months in Hario will remain with most of us as memories of a strange era. While the Army was becoming one of Regular Army and enlistees, and the personnel of the 34th Regiment were coming to take themselves quite seriously about discipline, our little army on Hario seemed to be a counter-productive thorn in their sides. They didn't want us initially, and Sasebo was an uncomfortable place for time off. Officers were welcome at their BOQ, which we used because they had hot meals and warm-water showers, but, once we sensed that Nisei officers did not fit into their pattern, other sites were sought beyond Colonel Bing's jurisdiction (even though we had to pass through Sasebo to get there). We might find ourselves working, collating what we found, and preparing reports for 3-4 days almost without rest, and then we might have a few days off until the next ship arrived. Our Missionary leader sensed our need to go to Nagasaki, Beppu, Fukuoka, or as far as Kagoshima, but, to get into and through Sasebo, we needed jeeps. Inasmuch as each team was an independent unit--I believe mine was the 343rd Interrogation Team--each was entitled to certain equipment. Once our reports, in detail about areas unknown to Washington, began to flow into Yokohama and Tokyo, our wily leader requested one jeep for each team. To the surprise of Colonel Bing, who was suffering a shortage of gasoline for his own vehicles, the train stopped in Sasebo, unloading about 25 jeeps, which were being driven by GHQ personnel through Sasebo in a cavalcade toward the bridge to Hario. A call to Captain Frehn disclosed that each of our teams of four men was entitled to one jeep. Nonplussed, Colonel Bing informed our leader that we would get no gasoline from Sasebo. We, however, had some secret weapons gained through common ancestry with those living in the area. The first to land in Kyushu in October 1945 were Marines, who brought with them gasoline sufficient to supply a full-fledged invasion. These barrels were initially stored in a few large warehouses about 10 miles south of Sasebo. When the Marines left, they were never told what to do with the gasoline. Assuming that some other group would come there to replace them, they asked an elderly farmer if he would guard the reserve until someone else came to take charge. This story was well known in the rural areas, but not in Sasebo. One of our more creative linguists heard the tale, visited the site and found the farmer still protecting the untouched reservoirs 12 months after the Marines left him in charge. When this sergeant thanked him, and told him he was relieved of his duty, the farmer thanked the sergeant for the opportunity to help. This solved our problem with fuel for the few months we lived at Hario, and we often wondered at the consternation of the minions of Colonel Bing, as they saw our linguists driving through Sasebo for ports and missions unknown.

113

Colonel Bing invited our leader into Sasebo, suggesting that they get together for a drink. Captain Frehn respectfully declined, as his Missionary zeal had led him to the life of a teetotaler. In pursuit, Colonel Bing sent his officers to make two surprise inspections of us in one week. On both occasions, we were all in our cubicles doing interrogations or translations. As one of our men came out of the hut for a breath of air, disheveled and exhausted from a session, one of Colonel Bing's 2nd Lieutenants approached him and told him that he looked sloppy and needed a haircut. He happened to be addressing a 1st Lieutenant linguist from Hawaii, where long hair is an object of beauty among the Polynesians. After showing his silver bar, he asked him to follow him into the quonset hut. In addition to the stench of unbathed returnees, coupled with smoke from extra cigarettes GHQ had sent us, both the repatriates and the interrogators in each cubicle were wearing stocking hats, because the small space heaters provided for every third or fourth cubicle did not furnish heat sufficient to allow for leisurely conversations. This applied equally to the barracks used by the repatriates and to the quonset huts where we slept. In fact, some of our men purchased tatami and futon, so they could sleep closer to the space heaters.

The inspectors left without further comment, but a few days later, Captain Frehn received a written request that all personnel should have regulation haircuts. Our leader discussed it with the officers after breakfast, and this resulted in taking it under advisement. In the absence of a response, Colonel Bing sent a new crew of officers for an unannounced inspection. Between the bridge and our area, a group of Japanese had almost completed construction of a simple stockade to protect our 25 or so jeeps and barrels of gasoline stacked upright three to four high. Their eyes having been assaulted by this form of insult, as they descended upon us, a number of people were called out for uniform inspections, in the slushy clay, and their leader asked us about the haircuts. Fortunately, Captain Frehn had gone to Yokohama to make personal delivery of important data and was not present for reprimand. They then asked to inspect the so-called barracks, and were shown tatami, with futon--at which point they left without comment. The ongoing battle with Colonel Bing seemed to end at that point, but the Japanese who worked for the Welfare Ministry spread the story throughout the area: the mild Missionary and his little army had prevailed.

When we closed down in April, after the Russians stopped exit through Dairen, an anonymous call to 34th Headquarters advised them of the gasoline warehouse. I have been told that Hario was revived the following year, but never with the intensity of effort that was exerted in that initial exploration of indoctrination tactics.

In early April, some of our teams were sent to Hakodate. The port in Karafuto had been opened, and the Soviets were releasing almost anyone who wanted to return. Due to the broad unwatched beaches of northwest and northeast Hokkaido, many had escaped earlier on fishing boats, and they supplied the authorities with names of persons then remaining behind who were indoctrinated. Our job was to identify them, because they had a tendency to change their names. We lived in the Monopoly Building, and an adjacent office building, and ate and worked within a few blocks of our residence. By this time, the Welfare Ministry had it down to a science, and our discoveries were less exciting, especially in light of the trickle coming from Karafuto.

This lasted into June, when some teams were sent to Maizuru, where we dealt with people coming through ports in North Korea, and one small ship actually came from Vladivostok. After two months, I also left for demobilization.

What I have discussed covered only the first two years of the Occupation--a learning process for both Japan and its Occupiers. Subsequent events and their national development may have altered what we, as neophytes in the business of Occupation, observed and did. Later writers may have come to characterize those early years as one of "manifest destiny," but we, as interpreters and translators, never viewed our roles as much more than a liaison between two groups who could not otherwise communicate well without us. By mid-1947, the civilian soldier had been replaced by the professional, the Occupied had come to learn better how to communicate in the language of the Occupier, and the need for our limited skills had diminished. Our impact, at the grass

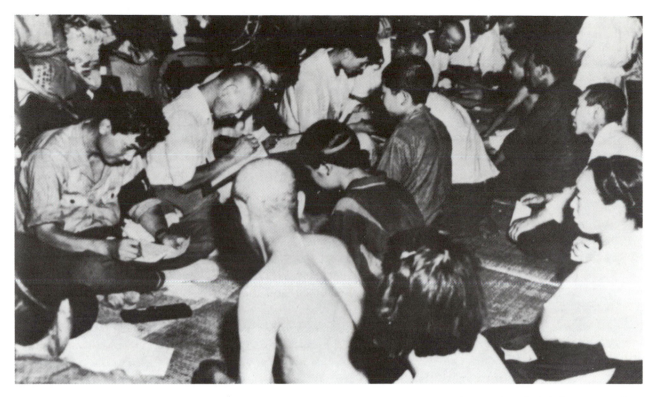

Repatriates are interrogated aboard the *Tokugu Maru* at Hakodate, the initial processing phase.

roots, is not capable of definitive recognition, but, for its time, we would like to feel that it helped to bridge the gap between two completely alien cultures and societies.

During this earlier part of the Occupation, the Americans were admired and respected by most Japanese. It might have been the acknowledgment of having done wrong, with mixed signals coming from the oddly benevolent, yet strong, victor. Another element may have been the recognition of a future confrontation with the Soviets, in which Japan would need U.S. protection. The Russian declaration of war against Japan was a stab in the back, more despicable than the use of the A-Bombs. Within that framework, our role as communicators was simplified.

Democratization and freedom were key phrases, and, once the Occupied discovered good will on the part of the Occupiers, reciprocity came easily. Wherever possible, these values had to be conveyed in language as well as deeds; to the extent that civilian soldiers set the early tone of the Occupation, the use of linguists in uniform, but with a civilian mind-frame, coupled with an affinity for the culture and society of the subdued, resulted in what all agreed was a masterful success at the grass roots during its first two years.

HOMECOMING OF JAPANESE POWs FROM THE USSR

William F. Nimmo

WILLIAM F. NIMMO is Lecturer of History at Old Dominion University, Norfolk, Virginia, and at the College of William and Mary, Williamsburg, Virginia. His career with the United States Army, in both military and civilian positions, involved extensive periods of residence in and travel to Japan. He received the B.A. degree from the University of Oklahoma in 1979 and the M.A. in International Studies from Old Dominion University in 1985. Mr. Nimmo earlier studied at Sophia University in Tokyo. William Nimmo is the author of *Behind A Curtain of Silence: Japanese in Soviet Custody, 1945-1956*, (Westport, CT, Greenwood Press, 1988), translated as *Kensho Shiberiya Yokuryu* [Examination of Siberian Detention] and published by Jiji Press, Tokyo, in 1991. His forthcoming book, *Japan and Post-Soviet Russia* is scheduled for publication by Greenwood Press in 1993.

I'm going to discuss the 1949 return of Soviet-held Japanese war prisoners and their disruptive activities in the period just after repatriation. First, I'd like to present a brief analysis of the Soviet attack on Manchuria and other Northeast Asia locations in 1945 that led to the capture of a large number of Japanese civilians and military troops.

The Soviet Union, as a result of agreements made at the Yalta Conference in February 1945, declared war on Japan and began hostilities against Japanese forces on August 9, 1945. Japan was already at the brink of surrender--its military capabilities were seriously diminished, Hiroshima had been the target of the first atomic bomb, the Supreme War Council and the Cabinet were meeting on that Thursday morning to find a way to bring the war to the speediest possible conclusion, and Nagasaki became Japan's second city to be the victim of nuclear firepower while the meeting was in progress-- when Soviet Forces in the Far East, about 1,500,000 troops, initiated massive strikes against Japan's Kwantung Army in Manchuria and northern Korea. A few days later, Soviet military units invaded Southern Sakhalin and the Kurile Islands.

The Japanese defenders were overwhelmed in less than a month, and Soviet forces gained control of approximately 570,000 square miles of territory in Northeast Asia, an area four times the size of Japan. Large numbers of Japanese were in this region: almost 2,000,000 civilian residents and about 800,000 soldiers.

Virtually all Japanese in Soviet-controlled areas encountered difficulty in returning to Japan. Repatriation from non-Soviet areas was almost completed before the first group of Japanese began to leave locations under control of the Red Army. Civilians experienced severe hardships in the first winter after the war--about 250,000 Japanese civilians died in Manchuria and North Korea due to starvation and exposure to extreme cold--but another group suffered even harsher treatment. More than a half million Japanese--450,000 soldiers and 125,000 civilians--were removed to the Soviet Union where they were subjected to forced labor and intensive communist indoctrination for two to four years at Ministry of Internal Affairs (MVD) camps.

Some POWs returned in 1947 and 1948, but my comments will address the more volatile actions of the 1949 repatriates. The deportation of Japanese to the USSR, their experiences in labor camps, attempts by the Supreme Commander for the Allied Powers (SCAP) to obtain their release, and the personal reminiscences of prisoners--widely published in Japan--are all matters of interest. However, for the purposes of this symposium, I will concentrate on two areas: 1) Marxist-Leninist indoctrination, and, 2) Return to Japan.

THE INDOCTRINATION PROGRAM

Most Japanese in the Soviet *lagers*, or labor camps, were subjected to extensive communist indoctrination. Some POWs became proponents of the Soviet line, often displaying even greater enthusiasm for communism than political indoctrination officers, and were dubbed by other POWs as *akuchibu*, a Japanese phonetic variation of the Russian *aktiv*, or activist. The political indoctrination programs centered around community life in the 600 labor camps for Japanese prisoners, usually taking place in the evenings after an exhausting day of work. Although Soviet officials exercised general supervision, most of the political education in the camps was conducted by Japanese *aktivs*, some of whom were excused from hard labor in order to spend all their time on development and implementation of training programs.

MVD officials sent promising Japanese POWs to political schools for periods varying from one week to three months, and graduates returned to POW camps where they served as instructors and group leaders. Most courses were held in Khabarovsk, but MVD officials and Japanese *aktivs* also conducted long-term schools in Vladivostok and Moscow. Since political school students were excused from hard labor and even received pay, thousands of willing applicants clamored to sign up. Political school graduates became the keystone of the Soviet program to educate Japanese in pro-Communist theories and were influential in preparing POWs for an activist role in the

Japan Communist Party upon their return to Japan.[1]

The basic organization for indoctrination at the *lagers* was the Friendship Society, or *Tomo no kai*, established in the nature of an informal club, but exploited by MVD political officials to serve the needs of education in Marxist-Leninist principles. The Friendship Society served as a basic forum for political discussions, lectures, songfests, amateur plays, film showings, and rallies.[2] A Japanese-language newspaper, the *Nihon Shimbun*, published in Khabarovsk, was distributed throughout the *lager* system and used extensively in Friendship Society meetings. Often the only printed news available to POWs, it was a principal source of material for the indoctrination program.

MVD political officers, assisted by Japanese POWs with previous journalistic experience, staffed the *Nihon Shimbun*, using *Tass* dispatches and radio broadcasts from Japan as a major source of news. Japanese staff members wrote articles based on the monitored broadcasts from Japan, playing up negative aspects of American occupation policies. Friendship Society meetings often centered around *Nihon Shinbun* articles, such as:

> GHQ has made warning to the Japanese people concerning public meetings and demonstrations in order to hold in check the labor class and to prosecute democratic organs.

> ...US Occupation Forces have employed former Japanese officers in government posts and positions. These men, at present wearing civilian clothes, are to fight in the coming war in US uniform.

> ...The Americans are murdering Japanese. The Japanese who even slightly oppose the looters have to expect great sacrifice. The drunken American soldier looks upon Japan as a conquered nation and regards Japanese people as his slaves. The laborers and farmers of Japan are gasping for breath under the colonial slave system created by American reactionaries.[3]

The Friendship Society, coupled with the *Nihon Shimbun*, served as an important element in the program to inculcate Japanese POWs with attitudes favoring the Soviet Union and the JCP while fostering hatred for the Emperor System supposedly backed by the United States. Japanese POWs received no information concerning the new 1947 Constitution of Japan under which sovereignty was vested in the people and the Emperor was made a symbol of the state.

Daily routine in the POW camp milieu was ideally suited to an indoctrination program. Soviet political officers and Japanese *aktivs* were able to control all news, discussions, recreational activities, work, and *lager* residents never had an opportunity to hear opposing arguments. POWs were kept so busy that they rarely had an opportunity to reflect on their situation. Imadate Tetsuo explained:

> Every POW was just trying to do his own work, and did not have a second to think on his own. He did not have any chance to have his own ideas or thoughts. Also, he was not allowed to possess an individual identity. . . .

> The POWs' constant hunger also did not help them. If anyone could manage to think on his own, it was usually about food. The Soviet method of keeping Japanese prisoners under control consisted of providing miserable living conditions and making them work. Keeping the Japanese prisoners so busy that they were not able to think on their own was part of the Soviet plan. Group activities were the basis for the Japanese POWs' daily life.[4]

After four years of indoctrination, most of the 105,000 Japanese prisoners remaining in the USSR were thoroughly brainwashed. In the spring of 1949, preparations were begun to repatriate all POWs--except for 10,000 charged as war criminals--to Japan. The pace of indoctrination was stepped up to a feverish activity.

Initial repatriation was reserved for the most ardent converts, and POWs spent several weeks at Nakhodka, in the Soviet Far East, rehearsing communist slogans, songs, and chants. *Aktivs* drilled repatriates intensively to prepare them for a program of activity upon arrival in Japan "to counter the colonial slave system created by American reactionaries."[5]

RETURN TO JAPAN

Highly indoctrinated repatriates began to leave Nakhodka in June 1949 for the two-day voyage to Maizuru, a port on the Sea of Japan 45 miles west of Kyoto City. Four Japanese ships made voyages between the two ports, with a ship leaving Nakhodka every two or three days. Passengers on many of the trips were unruly, and the ships' crews often faced hazardous situations. Shipowners charged repatriates after one voyage with "intimidation, obstruction of performance of official duties, and robbery." Activists on that trip had conducted a People's Court on the high seas and tried ship officers for "undemocratic behavior."

Highly indoctrinated repatriates on an August 1949 voyage accused three Japanese Army officers of being traitors because they refused to participate in political meetings. Activists wanted to hang one of the three as a "first class war criminal" but were stopped by the ship's captain and crew. Although ship regulations prohibited loud singing and chanting of slogans, many did so anyway. This activity led to an unusual problem, as noted in one report:

> Because of heat and dancing of the repatriates on 12 August 1949, a number of repatriates have stomach trouble from drinking too much water. One source said: "Apparently their dancing dislodged dirt and scales in the water tank." The repatriates demand that the ship's captain accept responsibility for their stomach trouble.[6]

Difficulties with repatriates on shipboard were attributed to *aktivs* who held a tight grip over most of the others. However, some anti-Communist NCOs and officers, venting long-repressed indignation over "turncoat" activities of younger repatriates, sought revenge. A few passengers were lost at sea in the ensuing brawls. On one voyage: "Fights broke out on the ship 20 minutes after departure. Anti-Communists took the offensive and their number had suddenly grown larger. The Communist contingents were beaten with fists and thrown down a flight of stairs to the deck below."[7]

"We are entering enemy territory!" screamed passengers aboard the Takasago Maru as the ship approached Maizuru in late June 1949. Then, lining the ship's deck, the ex-POWs robustly sang the *Internationale* and the *Communist Youth Song*. Chants replete with Marxist slogans filled the air, followed by the *Song of the Red Flag* and other singing. One refrain expressed opposition to the Japanese Government and called for abolition of the Emperor System. These were the voices of young Japanese men, many of whom were only 17 or 18 when captured, who were the product of several years of intensive indoctrination.

Repatriation Relief Agency officials required ex-POWs, before disembarking, to fill out information cards providing name, age, former military unit, and place of internment. *Aktiv* leaders, however, ordered repatriates to withhold the requested data, explaining that compliance would be considered "anti-democratic behavior." A standoff ensued when SCAP officials insisted the information be provided. Officials soon discovered a solution; they isolated the *aktivs*--identified by ship officers--immediately upon arrival and herded them into a quarantine area in the port. With their leaders gone, repatriates readily cooperated, and this system was used for the remainder of 1949.

Repatriates, distrustful at first, began to change after two or three days at Maizuru. Some began to hum long-forgotten Japanese songs in place of revolutionary songs they had learned. Fear of the *aktivs* was still evident, but when safely out of their former tormentors' presence, repatriates expressed frank comments critical of their sojourn in Siberia. A "Welcoming Center" at the port was designed to show changes in the "New Japan," and to refute negative propaganda about the Allied Occupation of Japan. The Center was adorned with welcoming placards, and pictures and letters from schoolchildren were displayed in the Home Prefectures Room. Nevertheless, the hard-liners--about ten percent of the repatriates--clung to their leadership positions and were cynical in their view of the welcoming efforts.[8]

Attempts to wean veterans of the four-year Soviet indoctrination program were not always successful, as evidenced by a July 1949 news report:

> This summer's repatriates are unruly. Their brusqueness, bordering on sheer rudeness, toward attendants at the Maizuru Repatriation Center and the throngs that turned out to welcome them, caused unnecessary tears to flow and hearts to break. To add insult to injury, they derided their welcomers, flaying the reception as being *shimeppoi* [gushy and sentimental], accusing them of sabotaging the repatriation by not sending ships and criticizing their lack of fervor towards the "creation of a new Japan."[9]

Anxiety mounted among Japanese and American officials as ships from Nakhodka continued to ply their way across the Sea of Japan with cargoes of recruits for the Japan Communist Party. Would the repatriates wreak havoc on a Japan that was just beginning to recover from a devastating war? Did Stalin have some plot to place "Manchurian candidates" in strategic locations to aid the Red Army in some forthcoming war against imperialism?

Yomiuri Shimbun editorialized:

> One repatriate is quoted as saying that of the 2,000 repatriates on the Takasago Maru, 20 percent are ardent believers in communism, 60 percent are pinkish sympathizers, and the rest are as yet uncontaminated. Companions forced communism on most repatriates.

> If they are the victims of forced indoctrination, it would do well for us to accept the incoming repatriates with a completely unbiased attitude. It behooves us to warm up their clammed minds with sympathy and consideration and exert our utmost to get them jobs and help them into stable livelihood.

> The repatriates, on their part, would do well to observe the prevailing conditions in Japan coolly and critically comparing them with the news which they read in the Nihon Shimbun while in POW camps. It is to be hoped that they will learn what democracy really means on the basis of their own judgement and start anew on their new road of life.

> The JCP is obviously awaiting you to join its ranks. It would do well for the repatriates to realize that once they fall into the trap, they would once more be plunging themselves into a pit--a pit exactly like the one into which Japanese militarists once drove them.[10]

LAST TRAIN HOME

After completion of processing at the reception center, repatriates boarded trains at Maizuru Station bound for various parts of Japan. Once again, as *aktivs* rejoined other returnees, the tumultuous sounds of chanting, shouting, and singing were heard, especially when trains approached larger cities. Repatriates staged loud demonstrations in busy sections of urban areas, causing consternation among police and railway officials. The JCP Secretariat issued instructions to regional and local organizations specifying welcoming procedures, such as: waving red flags, distributing copies of *Akahata* (the JCP newspaper), recruiting party members from among repatriates, and arranging for continuing education of repatriates.[11]

Views of the Japanese countryside kindled sentimental memories leading to ambivalent feelings, but JCP members were on hand at train stations all along the route home to reinforce the *aktivs* in maintaining "democratic attitudes." Party members told repatriates at Tokyo's Shinagawa Station: "You were detained in Siberia for a long time because the Japanese government did nothing to hasten your repatriation. We Communists are the ones who have enabled you to return to your homeland."[12]

Japanese repatriates--indoctrinated with Communist propaganda--demonstrate at Railroad Station.

Before continuing on to other parts of Japan, most repatriation trains initially went from Maizuru to Kyoto, where a serious confrontation occurred on the night of 5 July 1949. More than 100 repatriates left their train and joined leftist union members at a rally in front of Kyoto Station. Police attempted to stop the demonstration, but just then a second train carrying more than 700 repatriates arrived. When this group learned of the rally, they overwhelmed police and poured off the train. Police reinforcements arrived, but before order could be restored a third train with 900 repatriates pulled into the station. This group soon joined the demonstration, and turmoil followed. Repatriates and unionists engaged in riotous behavior throughout the night with much singing and shouting, along with pledges to overthrow the "imperialist" government. Injuries and arrests were numerous, and it was late the next day before police broke up the demonstration and persuaded the repatriates to resume their homeward journey.[13]

As trains arrived in home prefectures, singing and chanting burst forth to the amazement of local residents. At Mito, in Ibaraki Prefecture, 60 repatriates pushed away from the crowd of family members and friends struggling to buttonhole them, stalked out from the station, and then proceeded as a group to the local JCP office. But one former POW explained: "Most joined the Communist Party in Siberia in order to be sent

122

home.   Those refusing to join were sent back to the hinterlands of Siberia from Nakhodka."[14]

Repatriates from Siberia were making a general nuisance of themselves in various parts of Japan throughout the summer of 1949.   About 300 former prisoners got off their special train in Okayama and staged a sitdown strike in front of the station. Joined by a local mob, repatriates went to the police station and presented a three-point demand, including the release of three men arrested during a riot of repatriates a week earlier.[15]   In another instance, about 50 returnees demonstrated in Sapporo station against the Japanese government and the U.S. Occupation forces.   Many similar disorders took place throughout Japan, leading the Ministry of Justice to issue an ordinance in August 1949 "binding repatriates to return peacefully to their homes."

As repatriates continued to flow back to Japan, confusion at Maizuru and train stations gradually subsided.   Enforcement of the cabinet order and intervention of family members were major factors in the decline of radical behavior.   Anxiety over repatriates' health led Kyoto University to study their physical and mental condition.   There were some health problems according to the investigation, most not too serious, but "the mental fatigue of the repatriates was found extremely marked in adverse proportion to their physical health.[16]   Even so, troublesome activity disappeared by the end of 1949, and most repatriates faded into the towns and countryside of Japan.

Villagers turn out to welcome repatriates to their home town.

PUBLIC REACTION IN JAPAN

Public interest in the forced detention of Japanese in the Soviet Union was high in 1949, as evidenced by the great number of books, magazine articles, films, and songs about the issue. There was a "*Shiberiya 'Mono'* [Siberia *Monogatari* (Narration)] boom with more than twenty such works published, falling into two basic categories: pro-Soviet and anti-Communist. Magazine articles described the tracking down of the notorious Corporal Yoshimura, of the *Prayer at Dawn Case* in which Japanese prisoners in Mongolia received brutal treatment at the hands of one of their own comrades. Investigators found Yoshimura on remote Fukae Shima, an island 70 miles west of Nagasaki, and learned that his real name was Shigeyoshi Ikeda. He was brought to trial in Japan and sentenced to imprisonment for five years.[17]

A song of the repatriates, *Ikoku-no-Oka* (Hills of a Foreign Land), was popularized by a former soldier, Tadashi Yoshida, on the Radio Amateur Hour. Shin Toho Studios produced a full-length feature film, narrated by Yoshida, to portray conditions experienced by Japanese prisoners in the USSR.

Within a year of their return, most repatriates had readjusted to life in Japan without major difficulty, but there were psychological and medical problems for some returnees. Illnesses contacted while in Soviet custody, especially tuberculosis, led to early deaths for some civilians and former soldiers. Others were to be tormented by long-term stress and psychiatric problems for many years after return to Japan.

Concerns that the repatriates would form the nucleus of a militant Red Army in support of the JCP proved to be unfounded. Although repatriates showed support for the Communist Party upon arrival in Japan--about 60 percent favored Communism--enthusiasm had evaporated by the end of 1949, with only 10 percent of the returnees still engaged in Communism. Sawayoshi Mayama, 27, of Saitama Prefecture, was typical of those who decided to renounce their Marxist views after "having seen a real working democracy here in new Japan."[18]

While the disruptive tactics of the 1949 repatriates were a cause for concern, an even more distressing issue was the matter of accounting for missing Japanese believed to be in Soviet hands. Japanese and American records indicated that about 400,000 Japanese remained to be accounted for by the Soviets in May 1949, but a *Tass* press release that month claimed there were only 95,000 POWs plus about 10,000 "war criminals" left in the USSR. SCAP accused Soviet officials of holding large numbers of unrepatriated Japanese, with implications that the Kremlin had sinister motives in its plans for use of the "missing 300,000," and rallies throughout Japan were held to demand their return. William Sebald, Chairman of the Allied Council for Japan, declared: "We can only guess at what may have happened behind the curtain of silence that has shut off these hapless Japanese from their homeland and people for the past four years."[19]

In fact, however, most of the missing Japanese were dead. Civilian deaths among Japanese in Manchuria accounted for the largest number of casualties. Furthermore, SCAP and Japanese government estimates that 700,000 prisoners had been taken to the USSR in 1945 were overstated; it was later determined that the correct number was 575,000 and that about 10 percent had died in Siberia. SCAP records had not been revised to show deceased POWs and civilians even though repatriates told of extensive deaths in Soviet-occupied areas. Soviet officials had provided no accounting of postwar deaths, and American, British, and Chinese members of the Allied Council for Japan wanted an explanation from the Soviet representative. Had SCAP reduced the number of unrepatriated Japanese to reflect estimated deaths, it would have lessened pressure on Soviet officials to provide information.

For the remainder of the Occupation era, Soviet officials stubbornly refused to provide any accounting of Japanese deaths in the Soviet *lagers*. In the late 1950s, a more cooperative Soviet government provided the names of 2,776 deceased Japanese. The Japanese Ministry of Welfare, through painstaking investigation, was able to determine the names of most of the dead. It was not until 1991, however, that Soviet President Mikhail Gorbachev, during a visit to Japan, presented Prime Minister Toshiki Kaifu with a list of names and burial locations of 60,000 Japanese prisoners who died in Siberia.[20] After more than four decades of denials that Moscow had any information on the subject, the facts behind the "Curtain of Silence" were finally divulged.

NOTES

1.   Military Intelligence Section, (MIS, GHQ, SCAP) "Communist Indoctrination of Japanese Repatriates from Soviet Territory," 2 February 1949 (SECRET, declassified 20 August 1975), Record Group 6, MacArthur Archives, Norfolk, Virginia.

2.   Imai Genji, *Shiberiya no Uta* [Song of Siberia], (Tokyo: Sanichi Shobo Ltd., 1980), pp. 279-80.

3.   MIS, "Communist Indoctrination," pp. 10-11.

4.   Imadate Tetsuo, *Rageri no Naka no Nihonjintachi* [Japanese Inside the *Lager*], (Tokyo: Niji Isseiki Shobo, Ltd., 1974), pp. 211-12.

5.   MIS, "Communist Indoctrination," Tab 2.

6.   MIS, Spot Intelligence Report, 13 August 1949.

7.   Edward Norbeck, "Edokko, A Narrative of Japanese Prisoners of War in Russia," *Rice University Studies* 57, No. 1 (Winter 1971): 65.

8.   Nippon Times, 30 June 1949, p. 1.

9.   Ibid., 3 July 1949, p. 4.

10.   Yomiuri Shimbun, Editorial, 29 June 1949.

11.   Government Section, "Review of Government and Politics in Japan," March 1949, 153, Record Group 5, MacArthur Archives.

12.   MIS, Spot Intelligence Report, 15 May 1948.

13.   MIS, Daily Intelligence Summary, 16 July 1949, p. 1.

14.   Nippon Times, 26 July 1949, p. 3.

15.   Ibid., 3 August 1949, p. 1.

16.   Ibid., 30 August 1949, p. 3.

17.   "Yoshimura Tai wo Sabake" (Judgement of the Yoshimura Unit), *Shukan Asahi*, 13 March 1949, pp. 3-9.

18.   Nippon Times, 23 August 1949, p. 3.

19.   Allied Council for Japan, Minutes of 26 December 1949 meeting, Box 18, Record Group 5, MacArthur Archives.

20.   Wall Street Journal, 19 April 1991, A12.

WHEN THE TWAIN MET

Robert C. Christopher

ROBERT C. CHRISTOPHER is Administrator of the Pulitzer Prizes, Adjunct Professor of Writing at the Graduate School of Journalism, Columbia University. He was writer, foreign correspondent, and senior editor for business at *Time* magazine from 1950 to 1964, and later served as foreign editor and executive editor of *Newsweek* and was Managing Editor of *Geo* magazine in 1980-81. He was educated at the Hopkins Grammar School in New Haven, Connecticut, and Yale University where he received the B.A. degree with exceptional distinction in Oriental Studies in 1948. Robert Christopher is author of *The Japanese Mind: The Goliath Explained*, Linden Press, 1983; *Second to None: American Companies in Japan*, Crown Publishers, 1986; and, *Crashing the Gates: The de-WASPing of America's Power Elite*, Simon & Schuster, 1989. He enlisted in the United States Army as a private in 1942, attained the rank of captain, and served as a Japanese Language officer in World War II and as an intelligence officer in the Korean War. Mr. Christopher is currently at work on a book about the Occupation from which some of the material in this paper is taken.

There was--or so it seems to me in hindsight--a special quality to the very first contacts between Americans and Japanese in the period immediately following the initial landings of U.S. personnel at Atsugi Naval Air Station in the final days of August 1945. After nearly four years of bitter hostility both sides approached these encounters with understandable apprehensions and both, in my experience, found the reality quite different from anything that they had envisaged.

In my own case, the first surprise was to find myself in Japan at all. As a language officer with the signal intelligence service, I had unthinkingly assumed that demand for my particular skill--which consisted of the ability to translate the archaic variety of the Japanese language then employed in Japanese Army communications-- would vanish with Japan's surrender. Instead, toward the middle of the war's final month, I was summarily pulled out of my unit's base in Central Luzon and attached to something called TAICOM (for Target Investigation Committee). Ambiguously named, no doubt with deliberation, TAICOM was a hastily organized inter-service task force charged with sweeping down upon military message centers in Japan and seizing all available codebooks, cipher machines and other cryptographic materials before our erstwhile enemies got around to destroying them. Such was the importance attached to this mission--which in the end proved pretty much of a wild goose chase--that my teammates and I were furnished with a document that directed the commanders of all Eighth Army units to give us any assistance that we required "including the use of combat troops if necessary." More to the point, we also had thrust upon us priority travel orders from Manila to Japan.

As a result, I arrived in Japan only two days after General MacArthur himself, but even in that short time certain familiar patterns of American military behavior had already begun to assert themselves at Atsugi. On the wall of the field's main building somebody had chalked up the front line G.I.'s derisive assertion of one-upmanship "Kilroy was here." And the ineffable boredom characteristically affected by U.S. military policemen was plainly visible on the visage of the M.P. sergeant who directed incoming personnel to the small fleet of ramshackle Japanese trucks that was serving as a ground shuttle to Yokohama, where MacArthur had temporarily established his headquarters.

Already sprawled about in the rear of the truck that I boarded was a motley assortment of officers and men that included two Naval lieutenants and, rather mysteriously, a mustachioed British major sporting the red beret of the Parachute Regiment. Though MacArthur had expressly ordered his travelling companions aboard the *Bataan* to refrain from carrying weapons, every man in the group that I joined either had a pistol at his hip or a carbine slung over his shoulder. Yet all the same I found myself in unhappy agreement with the British major when he crisply observed that if we were to run into a Japanese ambush "this lot wouldn't be much use, I fear."

The thought that prompted this comment--the possibility that one of the more intransigent units of the Japanese Army might decide to go out in a murderous burst of glory--did not seem at all improbable to any of us that morning. But as our little convoy lumbered down the dusty road to Yokohama, we scarcely encountered any Japanese at all. The only people I can recall seeing, in fact, were a lone farmer and his wife who were working in a rice field with a two- or three-year-old child by their side. As we rolled past them, the two adults carefully kept their backs to us, but the child, to whom one distant Japanese Army truck full of soldiers doubtless looked like any other, began to wave enthusiastically. At that, his mother, still without glancing in our direction, reached out and hit him alongside the head--which, although I could not know it then, was to be the only time in my life that I would ever see a Japanese parent strike a child.

In retrospect, I find I cannot be sure just what emotion drove that peasant woman to an act so uncharacteristic of customary Japanese behavior. At the time, however, all of us in the truck took it for granted that she was expressing hostility toward her country's conquerors and that only served to magnify the uneasiness that I felt as I settled into the building in Yokohama that had been commandeered as an officers' billet by XI Corps headquarters, the unit which my particular TAICOM teammates and I had been ordered to join.

There, looming conspicuously in the middle of a handsome, marble-floored reception hall was a Lister bag, the huge, ungainly device for water purification that the U.S. Army customarily used in the field in those days. It was a sight that somehow reminded me of an illustration in one of my grandfather's 19th century history books--a woodcut that showed Gothic invaders camping out in the looted mansion of a patrician family following Alaric's sack of Rome. But it also served, however inadvertently, to symbolize a distrust of all things Japanese. And just how intense that distrust was became even clearer an hour or so after my arrival when a careless XI Corps major reported that his revolver had disappeared. Though it eventually turned out that the missing weapon had been appropriated by another U.S. officer, the first reaction of all the Americans present was to subject the handful of Japanese maintenance men still in the building to a thorough body search.

The most memorable moment of my few days in Yokohama, however, occurred the morning following my arrival. Suddenly, from the street outside our billet, I heard martial music. Hurrying to a window, I saw the band of the 11th Airborne Division marching toward me along a board boulevard that ran alongside the Yokohama waterfront. As I watched, the paratroopers swung into a small park opposite my perch, came to a halt and then, to the strains of "The Stars and Stripes Forever," proceeded to run Old Glory up a flagpole at the water's edge. Suddenly, to my astonishment, I heard myself screaming out at the people of Japan--none of whom were, in fact, in sight--"Look at that, you little bastards! Just look at that!"

To recall that outburst today causes me embarrassment, but in the context of the time it was, I think, understandable. Driven home by the sneak attack on Pearl Harbor and tirelessly stressed by Washington's wartime propagandists, the fanaticism and brutality repeatedly displayed by Japanese forces in their conquest of most of East Asia had aroused an indiscriminate loathing in nearly all Americans. Even as humane and judicious a statesman as Secretary of War Henry Stimson had no hesitation about suggesting that there were "racial characteristics" that rendered even American citizens of Japanese ancestry "untrustworthy." While the war was still on, Senator Lister Hill of Alabama, with what proved a high degree of prescience, voiced the hope that the United States would employ its might to "gut the heart of Japan with fire." And shortly after the surrender, Senator Theodore Bilbo of Mississippi with his customary moderation urged upon General MacArthur the sterilization of the entire Japanese population.

That kind of bellicosity, however, proved hard to sustain when one actually began to come in contact with individual Japanese--or so at least it proved in my case. A day after the flag-raising episode, I visited the Yokohama docks with a naval lieutenant attached to my TAICOM team and there we struck up a conversation with a Japanese major in command of a guard detail. At a certain point, my colleague, whose Japanese was more colloquial than the somewhat antique brand I had been taught, asked the Japanese officer what he intended to do after he was demobilized. "*Rumpen desho* (I suppose I'll be a bum)," was the despondent reply--and to my astonishment I suddenly realized that I had been sideswiped by a sense of sympathy for someone whose termination with extreme prejudice I would have regarded as eminently desirable only a couple of weeks earlier.

My re-education was advanced a bit more a day or two later when in company with three or four other young officers I decided to make an unauthorized trip into Tokyo where GHQ had yet to move. Soon after we boarded the inter-city train from Yokohama, our party was approached by a conductor who firmly declared that we must pay the regular fare and refused to be deterred either by the fact that we had no Japanese currency or by the more ominous reality that we did have both sidearms and an extremely hostile reaction to the thought of being ordered about by any Japanese regardless of his function. Regulations, the conductor stubbornly insisted, were regulations and nothing budged him from that position until in a moment of inspired invention one of our number assured him that General MacArthur had just that morning decreed that Occupation personnel were entitled to free passage on public transportation.

Only then, his bureaucratic honor preserved, did the conductor move away and while all of the Americans present proceeded to chortle at his gullibility, all of them, I suspect, shared a sneaking sense of admiration for his gutsiness.

If Americans initially approached the Occupation in vengeful spirit, the attitudes displayed by the Japanese were, as the conductor's behavior demonstrated, both more complex and more diverse. On the most obvious level, the end of hostilities offered the ordinary people of Japan desperately needed respite from a national ordeal of almost incomprehensible magnitude. Though it was the atomic destruction visited upon Hiroshima and Nagasaki that epitomized that ordeal in the eyes of the world, far more suffering had actually been inflicted on the Japanese people by the age-old weapon prescribed by Lister Hill: fire. In Hiroshima and Nagasaki between them, an estimated 110,000 people had been killed, but the firebombs showered down by 130 B-29s in just one of scores of raids on Tokyo had caused the deaths of more than 199,000 people and reduced four square miles of the capital to rubble and ashes. Similarly, in neighboring Yokohama a single raid lasting less than an hour had left nearly half the city's buildings ablaze.

All told, more than two million Japanese had been killed in the war, nearly a third of them civilians. Of those who survived, roughly one-fifth--some fifteen million people--had been rendered homeless by war's end. Yet strangely enough by American lights the most notable emotion displayed by many Japanese when the bombs ceased to rain down was not relief but trepidation. Despite the best efforts of wartime censors and the dreaded Thought Police, ordinary Japanese were for the most part aware of how their own troops had behaved in conquered lands and saw no reason to assume that Americans in a similar situation would prove any more benign.

Semi-official support for this pessimistic assessment, moreover, was readily forthcoming. In the week before the arrival of the first U.S. forces, Japanese radio broadcasters repeatedly urged any women left in the nation's cities to seek refuge with rural relatives. Girls who were unable to do that were instructed to clothe themselves in the bulky, distinctly anti-erotic coveralls customarily worn by female workers or to crop their hair and dress as boys. And on August 29th, with American troops about to pour into Atsugi in strength, men with megaphones appeared on those streets of Yokohama where there were still inhabited homes and bellowed warnings to all women to get indoors and stay there.

The effect of all this sounding of the alarms was dramatic. At the end of a full week in Japan I had, to the best of my recollection, laid eyes on only one Japanese female who could conceivably be described as nubile. The first opportunity for "fraternization" that I encountered came when, early in that illicit visit to Tokyo I referred to earlier, a painfully respectable-looking woman in middle age determinedly tried to press her sexual services upon the members of our party. Only after we convinced her that our interests were for the time being at least confined to sight-seeing did the lady reveal that she was one of a corps of patriotic matrons who had volunteered to sacrifice themselves to the lust of the brutal Yankee soldiery in the hope of forestalling mass ravishment of innocent Japanese maidens.

My first reaction to this incident was to marvel that anyone could seriously think that American soldiers would engage in unprovoked mistreatment of civilians on any large scale. That fear began to seem slightly less mysterious, however, an hour or so later when my buddies and I were strolling through the Ginza area and found ourselves being followed by a silent throng of perhaps fifty Japanese adults and youngsters. Though there was nothing ostensibly threatening in the situation, it clearly irritated and/or rendered nervous one member of our group who finally whirled and snarled at the crowd: "What am I? Jo-jo the Dog-Faced Boy? Get outta here! G'wan, beat it!"

With that, most of our uninvited followers fell back a few paces, but one of them--a woman whom I judged to be in her twenties--chose instead to come forward and to attempt in quite passable English to strike up a conversation with us. "Is this your first visit to Tokyo?" she inquired for all the world like a hostess making polite small talk. "Naw," the officer who had just shouted at the crowd prevaricated. "We've flown

130

over the place a whole lotta times."

Without a word, the woman dropped back into the ranks of her countrymen, leaving me with some concern that once she reported my buddy's comments to them we might all be lynched. But that, of course, proved as unrealistic a fear as the Japanese housewife's expectation of mass ravishment.

Perhaps a week after that, Captain Sid Haken, my immediate superior on our TAICOM team, commandeered a weapons carrier from XI Corps motor pool and with me as interpreter set off into as yet unoccupied reaches of north-central Honshu to search for cryptographic materials at what we thought might prove likely sites. At my suggestion we followed what was billed on our maps as National Highway No. 1 but which after a couple of hours' drive turned into a meandering narrow road without even a macadam surface--a turn of events that prompted Sid Haken to snort contemptuously: "If this is National Highway No. 1, I'd sure hate to see No. 2."

So poor was the road that we found it hard to believe we had not lost our way and repeatedly stopped to question peasants as to our whereabouts. When we did so, the target of our questions would as often as not wave his hand in front of his face to signify total incomprehension and more than once I had to say very slowly "Listen to me; I am speaking Japanese" before the light of understanding finally appeared in his eyes. The unkind might suggest that this was because my Japanese was deficient, but I believed then and still do that the real reason was that the rural folk to whom I was talking simply were not prepared to have an alien intruder like me speak to them in their own language.

There was, however, no sign of hostility or refusal to be helpful once they finally accepted that it was, after all, possible to have communication with this particular alien in a sensible language. The contrary, in fact, was the case. Not too long after Captain Haken and I set out we came to a spot where National Highway No. 1 intersected what was obviously the main street of a small town whose name I have long since forgotten. Just about to move into the intersection as we approached it was a procession of some 30 or 40 solemn-faced souls whose leader carried a staff bearing a much-enlarged photograph of a plump and rather bewildered-looking young man. Though I knew nothing about Japanese funerals it occurred to me that this was quite possibly some kind of memorial to one of the last Japanese casualties of the war and that, outnumbered as Sid and I were, it would probably not be a wise time--much less an appropriate one-- for a display of victors' arrogance. Accordingly, we cut the engine on our weapons carrier and removed our caps. As we sat there, the forlorn little cortege plodded past us, its members evincing no awareness of our presence--until, at the very last moment, one of them turned toward us and bowed in what I look to be a gesture of appreciation.

Later that day when a heavy storm struck, Sid Haken and I found ourselves confronted with a narrow creek which had risen so much so fast that it had washed away the rickety little bridge which normally spanned it. By enormous good fortune, there was some kind of road crew working in the area and when I explained to its boss that Haken and I were determined to keep pushing north, all hands cheerfully turned to and proceeded to lay across the stream a makeshift bridge of long heavy timbers over which, with considerable nervousness, we succeeded in inching our vehicle.

From then on, the rest of that day's journey was all uphill in the literal sense and mostly downhill in a figurative one. Instead of abating, the storm sweeping over that part of Honshu intensified and the road on which we were travelling began to wind ever more steeply up into the mountains. As we came around one narrow bend where the ground fell off precipitously on one side and rose equally sharply on the other we abruptly came face to face with an aged fire truck headed down the mountain on some mysterious errand. Happily, its driver like Sid Haken was proceeding very cautiously and with a reassuring wave of his hand he proceeded to back uphill for perhaps 75 yards until the road widened sufficiently to permit our vehicles to pass each other. Fortunate as its outcome was, however, this incident left Haken and me distinctly disinclined to push our luck much further and, upon consulting my map, I discovered that we were not far from Karuizawa which I vaguely remembered hearing fellow officers who had

131

been raised in Japan describe as a summer resort favored by foreign residents of Tokyo.

On the strength of this rather hazy intelligence, Captain Haken and I decided that Karuizawa might be a good place to break our trip and, in fact, when we arrived there we quickly located a handsome old Western-style hotel which, it turned out, was serving as a refuge for European residents of Tokyo who had fled the city to escape U.S. bombing raids. There, a reluctant German desk clerk, decked out so I seem to remember in a morning coat and striped pants, officiously informed us that the hotel was not open to the general public. A brisk reminder concerning the outcome of the war in Europe quickly brought him into line, however, and while we were waiting in the lobby for our duffel bags to be carried in we were approached by a Swedish lady whose brother-in-law, it transpired, was the U.S. Navy commander in charge of TAICOM's Tokyo headquarters.

That happy encounter not only got us an invitation to dinner at the lady's family cottage but an introduction to a Japanese diplomat's daughter of half French ancestry with whom I immediately fell desperately in love. As things eventually developed, my affections were not reciprocated but the young lady nonetheless left me with a memory that has intrigued me ever since. Some time after our initial encounter in Karuizawa, she and I attended a party given by some members of the Mitsui family at which one of our fellow guests proved to be a young Canadian-born Japanese who had been attached to a kamikaze squadron and who made a point of informing me how much he regretted not having had the opportunity to make that final dive. When I mentioned this to my seemingly thoroughly Westernized date after the party, her impatient response was: "That Billy Y... makes me so tired. Nobody's making him stay alive, after all."

From Karuizawa Sid Haken and I in due course made our way to Takada, a small city just inland from the Sea of Japan near which we believed--mistakenly as it turned out--we might find a Japanese Army communications center still in operation. There we spent the night in a small *ryokan* (hotel) run by a couple with several children, the youngest of whom may have been three or four. The innkeeper and his wife received us with great courtesy but a certain uneasiness--which, however, diminished visibly when we presented them with a selection of K-rations and suggested that these be made the basis of our dinner. In the end, as a matter of pride I suppose, our hosts insisted on depleting their own meager supplies of food by serving us a clear soup and some small whole fish whose cold-eyed stares seemed to me to have a distinctly reproachful quality. But the bulk of our meal--and, with our encouragement of the family's as well--did, in fact, come out of U.S. Army ration boxes.

After dinner, Captain Haken and I joined the family in huddling around a charcoal brazier. As their father and I chatted the children sat in wide-eyed silence--at least until I remarked that their town had apparently escaped any bomb damage and the innkeeper replied that while that was true they had from time to time been overflown by U.S. bombers presumably en route to or returning from more lucrative targets. At that, the youngest child's reserve abruptly vanished. "B-29, B-29," he intoned in Japanese, extending his arms like wings as he spoke.

After that, my memories of this excursion into unoccupied Honshu become kaleidoscopic. Some of the scenes that flash past in memory:

The solitary sergeant left in a rural armory who unhesitatingly turned over to us two Japanese officers' swords in exchange for chits signed "Theodore Roosevelt" and "Benjamin Franklin"--signatures whose spuriousness was, I later came to suspect, as apparent to him as it would have been to an American supply sergeant.

The confusion of the housewife in a small country town when she suddenly realized that in her eagerness to catch sight of the first Americans to reach the area she had rushed out her door uncovered to the waist.

The expressionless face of a young man who, out of what I took to be a mixture of helpfulness and uncontrollable curiosity, voluntarily climbed aboard our vehicle, showed us the way to the Japanese Signal Corps installation we were seeking, then climbed out and uncomplainingly set off on foot back to the point three or four miles away where we had picked him up.

In all of this lengthy hegira, as I noted earlier, Captain Haken and I uncovered nothing whatever of any great intelligence value. That so frustrated us that upon our return we decided to visit the communications center of the area army headquarters then located in the Imperial Palace grounds. Though deeply skeptical, the Australian troops standing guard at the Palace at that time finally decided that they had no choice but to honor our laissez passer from General Eichelberger and escorted us to the office of an elderly Japanese lieutenant general. When I began to question him, he politely explained that he himself knew nothing about codes and summoned in a young captain who did. As the captain was explaining to us how he would go about enciphering a message, he inadvertently--or so I assume--got one step in the Japanese Army's normal procedure wrong. When I unthinkingly corrected him he threw me a brief sharp glance and then became considerably more technical and professional in his explanations. Once again, I learned nothing of any military value but on a purely personal level the visit was a gratifying one. As Captain Haken and I took our leave, the general rose from behind his desk and threw us a snappy salute--which marked the sole occasion in my military career when a general saluted me first.

Shortly thereafter, I was, understandably enough, released by TAICOM and assigned to other duties at GHQ. As a result, I had less opportunity to explore rural Japan, but one trip that I made shortly before my return to the United States further challenged some of my preconceptions.

On this occasion, my destination was an Imperial *bokujo* (country estate) in Chiba to which I and two other American officers had been invited by a gentleman named Kimura. In addition to occupying a top position in the Imperial stables--he was one of the most accomplished horsemen I have ever met--Kimura-san was an engaging and remarkably direct person. At one point, however, I was seized with the suspicion that he was not being entirely honest with me.

This suspicion arose in my mind when, as he was showing us around the *bokujo* stables, he pointed out one of the famed Imperial white horses and I announced that I wanted to ride it. When Kimura replied that the animal was not fit to be ridden, I at first assumed that his real motive was to avoid anything that might conceivably be interpreted as a show of disrespect for the Emperor. But that, it turned out, was not the case. Because the Emperor was not fond of horses, Kimura explained, those designated for his Majesty's personal use were especially chosen for utter lack of spirit. "You can ride him if you want," Kimura shrugged, "but you won't have much fun."

As it transpired, I did not have all that much fun anyway. The horse that I finally did choose to ride proved so spirited that he threw me twice within the space of ten minutes. And to top things off, when evening came around Kimura insisted that we pay a call upon the mayor of the nearest town--who proudly led us into a room full of uncomfortable Victorian furniture and sat us down to listen to his twelve- or thirteen-year-old daughter perform upon the piano.

At that point, recalling a number of similarly painful experiences during the considerable part of my childhood I had spent in a small town in Connecticut, it occurred to me quite forcibly that while it might be true that East was East and West was West, it seemed something of an overstatement to assert flatly that the twain could never meet.

And that, I strongly suspect, was the most important lesson that most Occupation personnel who were exposed to grass roots Japan consciously or unconsciously carried away with them.

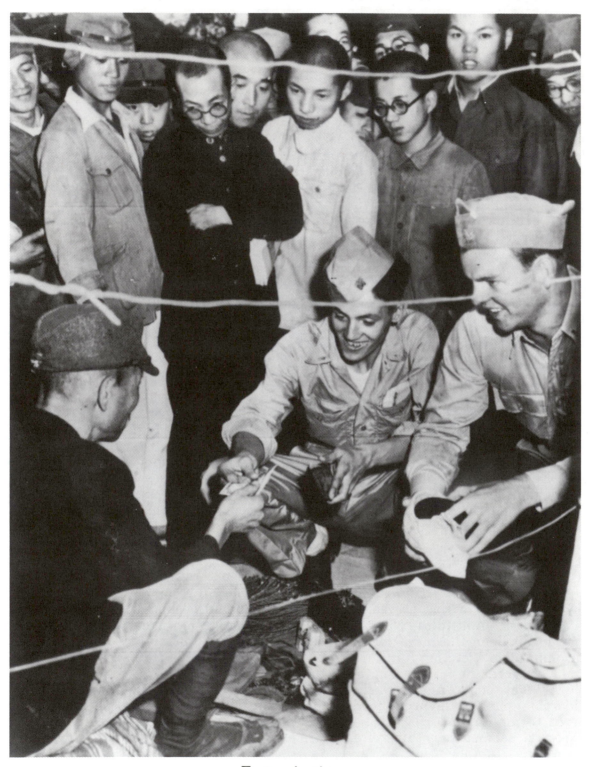

Fraternization

JAPANESE AND G.I. RAPPORT

Edwin L. Neville, Jr.

EDWIN L. NEVILLE, JR. is Associate Professor of History, Canisius College, Buffalo, New York. In 1945-46 he served as a Japanese Language Officer in the U.S. Marine Corps in the Allied Occupation of Japan. Edwin Neville received his undergraduate education at Harvard University, receiving the A.B. degree in Oriental Language and Literature in 1948. His graduate study was conducted at the University of Michigan where he received a M.A. in Far Eastern Studies in 1949 and the Ph.D. in History in 1959. He is the author of "The Japan Self-Defense Force and Foreign Policy," *Journal of Asian Affairs*, Vol. IV, No. 1 (Spring 1979), pp. 41-47; editor of *The NASILP Bulletin*, The Journal of Self-Instructional Language Programs (1975-78); and, "The Diary of Private Sullivan," Marine Corps Gazette, November, 1968.

This paper is anecdotal and personal. I did not see the big picture at the time. And yet, this paper presents a theme that runs very deep and is true, and it needs to be stated.

I believe that if you treat people right, they will treat you right, and vice versa. Very simply, this is the story of the relationship between the Japanese and G.I.s during the Occupation.

I was born in St. Luke's Hospital, Tokyo, Japan on 8 May 1926. My father, Edwin L. Neville, was Consul General in Tokyo and shortly after became Counselor of the American Embassy from 1926 to 1936 during which time he was thrice Charge d'Affair in critical times in United States-Japan relations. I attended the American School in Japan (ASIJ) until I was ten at which time my father was assigned as Minister to Siam (Thailand after 1938) and I was sent to boarding school in the United States.

I studied Japanese in my freshman year at Harvard and enlisted in the U.S. Navy as a Yeoman 2nd class prior to my 18th birthday to attend the 14-month Japanese language program at the Naval Japanese Language School at the University of Colorado in Boulder. I took a commission in the Marine Corps as a 2nd Lt. (040175) at the age of 18 years and 5 months in August 1944. Upon completion of the course in June 1945, I was assigned to Camp Lejeune, North Carolina.

My whole time in the Occupation was spent with the Marines in Kyushu in 1945 and 1946. Different tasks I undertook and actions that occurred during this period in Kyushu which come to mind include: numerous stories, vignettes, both humorous and sad, and people. But the main impression that will always stay with me is the excellent rapport that existed between the Japanese citizens and American soldiers. There was good feeling on both sides. It was marvelous to behold.

INITIAL INTERFACE

However, good feelings on both sides did not begin instantly when Japan surrendered to the Allies. The Japanese people were frightened and the American G.I. did not know what to expect. I was not involved in the initial landing of Marines at the huge Japanese naval base at Sasebo. I came later from Guam after the Marines had secured it. But the stories all gibed with those that told of landings elsewhere in Japan. Sasebo was deserted, and the stench of the refuse piled high throughout the city was unbearable. As the Marines began the cleanup of the city, gradually young children would appear as scouts to see what the Americans were up to. Tremendous propaganda by the Japanese government about the treacherous Americans who would kill, mutilate, torture and rape the Japanese population if they ever won the war had instilled fear in the Japanese who were petrified. What happened blew away these fears. The Marines gave the kids candy, chewing gum, food, whatever they had instantly at hand. They showered them with love and attention. The kids went back and told their folks that these were the good guys. Gradually, the citizens of Sasebo returned from the countryside or from behind their shutters of the houses that still stood, since Sasebo had been under major attack during the war by American bombers. Moreover, many Japanese were starving, and the Marines fed them and gave them food to prepare at home. The change in attitude in a short period of time was startling. Good feelings bubbled up on both sides.

A major job of the language section at I Corps in Sasebo was the translation of daily newspapers and documents when I first arrived. Two vignettes stand out in my mind which took me away from the translation grind. One experience was the excursion by car of the commanding general of I Corps who took me along as interpreter to buy pearls to try out my skills, as I reflect on it now. However, he bought the best pearls, and this was an example of a fact of Occupation life. Americans bought a great deal of Japanese merchandise and put many Japanese to work. The input of the armed forces into the Japanese economy was considerable at a time when Japanese living standards had fallen to their lowest level.

The second experience was my assignment to a team whose purpose was to blow up military equipment and munitions on the Tsushima Islands. Time has blurred much of what took place, but we were operating off LSTs during the day and blowing up guns and destroying ammunition, and I particularly remember the Japanese who did the job. After one spectacular blow-up, they pulled out bottles of potato whiskey. That is all the booze they had, but they shared them with the Americans. They did not have much to look forward to except mustering out, but that was okay, and we were okay.

NAGASAKI

Shortly thereafter, I was shipped off by train to Nagasaki enroute to my assignment with the 2nd Marines in Miyazaki to replace Jerry Downs who was returning to the United States. We had gone to school together in Tokyo. He was a grade ahead of me, and he was shipped overseas shortly after I arrived in the Naval Language School in Boulder. In fact, I bought his car for $75.00, which enhanced my enjoyment at the University of Colorado.

The train to Nagasaki was packed with standing room only. As we neared Nagasaki I could see through the window a ridge line to the east coming closer to the train, but there was nothing else in view except agricultural plots growing truck farming items. There were no rice fields. At that time, it did not dawn on me that anything was unusual until the conductor in his usual fashion just before a station called out, "Nagasaki! Nagasaki!" I thought he must be kidding because I did not see any houses which one would expect coming into a city of this size. And then, there was a sudden rude jolt, and the train came to a stop. I could not believe that we were already there. There was no platform. But we filed out through several cars ahead of us before finally reaching a truncated platform whose steel girders overhead were twisted and gnarled in a weird design. I saw an opening ahead with sunlight streaming through and the bay in the distance. When I walked out of the station and turned left, suddenly the whole city burst into view. The atom bomb on 9 August 1945 had dropped below the ridge line splitting the city before it blew. One part of the city was annihilated. The rest was untouched, except for the fact that in 1944 and 1945 Nagasaki had been repeatedly carpet bombed as every other city in Japan had except for Kanazawa, Kyoto and Nara. Nagasaki, or at least the part that remained, had been pretty well bombed out.

One particular event happened in Nagasaki that occurred repeatedly to me in Japan, and still amazes me. When I was kid, I rode my bicycle all over Tokyo. As an interpreter in the Marine Corps I walked all over every city that I was assigned to, usually at night because of being on duty during the day. If there were streetcars, I would ride the streetcars. If a jeep were available and I could sign one out, I would drive into the countryside. Never once during my tour of duty in Kyushu during 1945-46 did anything untoward happen. I was respectful to the Japanese and the Japanese treated me well. Where possible they rolled out the red carpet. The second night in Nagasaki, I cut through what appeared to be a long dark alley or side street. Not until I was well down the alley did I begin to wonder, "What happens if someone attacks me?" Of course, no one did, but on thinking back in hindsight, it was a pretty risky business when compared to the urban society we have now in the United States. It was, however, very safe in Japan for which I was grateful.

MIYAZAKI

I was transferred shortly thereafter to Miyazaki as Language Officer Interpreter for the 2nd Marines. It was another bombed out city. One comment from an English teacher in the school system has stuck with me all these years. He said that he could understand the bombing that took place that destroyed the cities of Japan. Japan deserved it, but what he could not understand was: "Why, oh why did you have to drop the atom bomb?" Of course, this question will probably always remain a controversial topic in academic circles for centuries to come.

I was not involved in the daily platoon forays into the countryside looking for caches of munitions that were hidden or overlooked in the initial pinpointing of official weapons and munition sites to be blown up. My predecessor as Language Officer for the regiment, Jerry Downs, had interrogated Japanese officers from generals on down before their demobilization to find these caches, which had been disposed of. Over the next three months Marine units were scouring the countryside in three successive waves into every nook and cranny of the sector under our jurisdiction. Daily on the huge map of Miyazaki Prefecture which was on the wall of the Regimental headquarters was charted the movement of patrols on these reconnaissances. It was interesting to watch their progress. Nothing was left to chance.

I did some document translations and interpreting for superior officers, but by and large I was assigned to special projects. For instance, one of the concerns of the Occupation was to ensure the freedom of speech and assembly of all Japanese regardless of political persuasion. One result was my being assigned to interviewing the prefectural chairman of the Japanese Communist Party to get his views of the openness of society under the Occupation. Another was that when political rallies took place, I was to attend to view how police reacted, particularly when socialists or groups further to the left had scheduled open meetings which were being advertised.

Naturally, I found everything normal. The rallies were not large, and the police were hardly noticeable. The communist party chief was affable, although I had to listen to a forty-five minute exposition of the Marxist view of society since I was a guest in his home. My appearance seemed to be accepted by all parties concerned. During my tour of duty in Japan, I never heard negative responses from the Japanese nor felt a negative attitude. However, I heard through the grapevine that some Marines were calling me "chicken". This had to do with fraternization with women, a major problem in maintaining marine discipline.

The first assignment I received upon arriving in Miyazaki was to interview the madam of a brothel who was about to be operated on for a gunshot wound in her stomach. She died later on the operating table. Her story was that a young marine assigned to guard her house so that other Marines would not become clients was playing around with his rifle in the *genkan* (entrance to the house), and it accidentally went off. The rifle at that moment was pointing right at her and the bullets penetrated her abdomen. She said that it was not really his fault. He admitted the shooting and was immediately court-martialed and sentenced. Her testimony was used in the form of a sworn statement by me although I did not appear at the court-martial.

In another case, I recall, I was asked to participate in a raid on a brothel to interpret. I did. All the women had something on, but the Marines who had not escaped from the house were found in the nude when the closet doors were slid open. They were reprimanded but not court-martialed. How could they be? When I arrived in Nagasaki, I was surprised to find in the lot next to the officers' quarters a brothel under the auspices of Occupation forces. I was surprised because I had never kissed a girl until I went to college, and it did not seem to be in line with American morals or moraes. General MacArthur did not think so either, because shortly after that the whole brothel system was shut down.

However, that was not going to stop anything. The Marines were girl crazy and the Japanese girls loved the attention. Fraternization was rampant. Some of the respectable citizens of Miyazaki opened their doors to the Marines and invited them to their homes on special occasions, particularly if they had daughters who might be able to establish legitimate relations with the Marines. It was an interesting time.

OITA

As the number of Occupation forces wound down in early 1946, the 2nd Marine headquarters was transferred to Oita. All Japan had been completely covered by military patrols three different times. There were not any armaments hidden. There was no place to hide them that had not been covered by the military patrols, except possibly in the Buddhist temples or Shinto shrines. Consequently, one last sweep of all religious property was undertaken. I was assigned to a unit commanded by Lt. John Weinberg, a classmate of mine at Deerfield Academy. We had a wonderful ten day excursion of Oita Prefecture by jeep.

We stopped at every shrine or temple no matter how small or large. There were post box size shrines and there were huge temples. We looked into every small shrine and entered and searched every large temple. Local Japanese officials had been alerted all along our route to guide or direct us to predetermined locations which we already knew we were going to visit. There was no guesswork in this, but it was surprising how many small Shinto shrines we stumbled on. Most of them were not being kept up. At night, inns were provided for sleeping quarters and an evening meal. It is surprising how often local officials also provided young girls, presumably from brothels, to be with us, and they slept on the premises, but there was absolutely no physical contact between the sexes. There was a great deal of animated conversation, but there was no thought of anything else, particularly since we were acting under orders.

The visit of most note on this excursion was to the Usa Shrine, one of the five major Shinto shrines in Japan. Not only was it a religious institution, but it was also a productive business operation. At the entrance to the shrine were a whole series of shops which produced and sold objects that one would find in a 5 and 10 cent store in the United States. My roommate in Miyazaki and Oita was Lt. Thomas O'Connor, whose father had represented Kresge's before the war and bought these type of objects for sale in Kresge's stores in the United States. I visited O'Connor and his family in Kobe in 1952 where he was also carrying on his father's business in the same way. What made Usa interesting was that all the objects in Usa were stamped on the back or base: "MADE IN USA." This helped Japan, particularly in the years 1936-1941 when sentiment in the United States was running strongly against Japan, and after the war when Japan needed to trade abroad. It was not until long after World War II that the Congress of the United States passed legislation forcing all imported production items to be labeled with the nation of origin.

Beyond the shops lay buildings connected to the shrine with the shrine itself on the top of the hill further inside the grounds. We searched all the buildings and the shrine itself. When we reached the inmost part of the shrine, there was what appeared to be a bedroom with a king size bed, kind of messy, with two beautiful heirloom swords lying on the floor. These were the only possible weapons we found in our foray sweep. I talked Weinberg out of confiscating them because, I felt these were more identifiable with religious art and culture than military equipment. However, this decision turned out to be wrong. The battalion executive officer ordered us to return to Usa and pick up the swords. The fastest way was by train and the two of us went alone. The Japanese officials of the Usa Shrine were not distressed at all by this. They expected it. However, I was bothered, and when I went to Tokyo on an R & R, I dropped in to see Langdon Warner who had been brought over by MacArthur to head up SCAP's Arts and Monument Section to preserve Japan's heritage. He was an old friend of the family, and I took a Fine Arts of the Far East course from him at Harvard. I mentioned this episode to him. He was interested but indicated that unless art treasures that were well known or massive transfers of cultural items were involved, there was no way to investigate the propriety of an action. I have often wondered what happened to the swords. When the Japanese began on an intensive scale to buy back swords from Americans, who took them home, were these swords returned to Japan?

Oita was a greater attraction than Miyazaki due to the famous hot springs of Beppu nearby. The Marine barracks were in Oita but the officer quarters were lodged in an inn over one of the hot springs in Beppu. We had first class service and fabulous living conditions when not on the road. Down the street was a CIC unit which I would ordinarily have visited to fraternize. Officers of our unit talked me out of it, because they claimed the CIC was similar to our internal affairs unit in a police department. Their job was to investigate the efficacy of Occupation forces, and my name did not need to be in their raw files.

Oita was a port city. On one occasion a medical officer and I toured the port facilities to assess whether they were capable of serving ocean going steamers carrying civilian Japanese returning from Manchuria who would be processed in Oita, interrogated, and released to their home districts in Japan. Already Fukuoka was a major port for the disembarkation for Japanese civilians. The Occupation felt that another port in Kyushu might be necessary to speed up this processing. We came to the logical conclusion regretfully that not only the port facilities but also the interrogation and housing facilities for the returnees as well as the transportation capabilities were inadequate for the scale of movement of Japanese civilians envisaged through Oita from Manchuria. This was merely a forecast of what was to come.

FUKUOKA

The 2nd Marines were returned stateside and I was transferred to the 6th Marines in Fukuoka to head up the team interrogating the civilian Japanese returning from Manchuria, where the Russians had held up withdrawing their troops in contravention of various Allied agreements. The team was already a functioning unit with well established procedures that worked. The civilian Japanese disembarking off the boats in units of 200 to 300 each were first doused with DDT then brought into a warehouse which they filled to capacity. Then the interrogating team would, starting from the rear, ask questions of each returnee in order to find those who had had contact with Russians. We looked at any papers or photographs they had to ascertain if any had been in locations where the Russian army presence was known to have been. When we found any, we immediately assigned them to be interviewed. Those selected were brought back into another connecting building in which each member of the interrogating team had a stall to interview the returnees. A long form was filled out on each interview, and at the end of the day, I wrote an analysis and summary of the interviews to which were attached the raw interview forms and forwarded them to the executive officer of the 6th Marines.

The only question in my mind centered on the fact that the Russians had pulled out of Manchuria before I arrived in Fukuoka to head up the interrogation team. Consequently, the answers to the questions we asked turned out to be what the Russians were doing before they left. No updated questions were given us. We could only fill out answers to questions the Occupation gave us.

Nevertheless, through these interviews it became plain that the Russians gutted Mauchuria. Anything moveable was taken that would help in the industrial reconstruction of Russia including whole factories, machinery, and mining equipment. The Russians did not destroy Japanese armaments and ammunition. They piled them on the outskirts of the major cities of Manchuria and let those who were organized utilize them, meaning the Chinese Communists.

The returnees from Manchuria did not know what was going to happen to them. They were being returned to their former home districts, but they were not sure how they would be received, for they had settled in Manchuria and dug in their roots. They were friendly and cooperative and appreciated any help they might receive.

However, when they were doused with DDT, whatever insects or bugs they had fled. When I and the others of the interrogation team went through their possessions and talked to them, whatever they had jumped on us. The most prevalent bug was scabies which lodged under the skin and over time produced small welts. It was a gradual accumulation, which although unnoticeable at first eventually became a first class problem. At this point I had to be painted on spots all over my body and face with a medicine that drew the scabies out and destroyed them. It was embarrassing to walk around looking like I had been creosoted, but by this time I was in Sasebo, awaiting orders to return to the United States. The Fukuoka operation was shut down and the remnants of the 6th Marines prepared for departure which occurred in June 1946 on the troopship, S.S. General Grant.

KARUIZAWA

Recognizing that there was now nothing to do and time on my hands until the ship arrived, I requested permission to go to Tokyo and Karuizawa to handle the business of a house in Karuizawa which my family owned and which had been confiscated by the Japanese government and given to the famous writer Mushakoji. Orders were cut that allowed me to go to Karuizawa. In Tokyo I started the ball rolling by filing papers for the return of the property and arranging for someone to follow through on this. Karuizawa before the war was a summer resort for the foreign community that worked in Tokyo as well as a retirement community for Japanese intellectuals who associated with foreigners. Karuizawa turned out to be a serendipity experience. A Ranger outfit was stationed in Karuizawa to which I reported, and I found old friends of various nationalities who had been confined to Karuizawa during the course of the war. It was extraordinary to find Americans of partial Japanese ancestry who had lived through the war in perfect safety in Karuizawa. I saw our house on the side of Atago Mountain. It was in good shape, and the caretaker who lived and worked just below the house was still looking after it. Old memories flooded through my mind. It was a great experience to be back.

OKAYAMA

At the end of the Occupation, after the Peace Treaty was signed in 1951, when I had completed all my work towards a Ph.D. in History at the University of Michigan except for the dissertation, I ended up in the Field Station of the University of Michigan in Okayama, Japan to write my dissertation and participate in the interdisciplinary study of a Japanese village, Niike. The Field Station had been requisitioned under Occupation authorization. What a difference! The Japanese still had excellent relations with Americans and vice-versa, but this area had been occupied by the British and Australians and there were not many good words that the Japanese had to say about the British and Australians.

I have to repeat the refrain that continues to stay with me. The rapport between the Japanese and Americans in the Occupation was a wonder to behold.

GENERAL DISCUSSION

Peter Bates. I am a former language officer with the British Commonwealth Occupation Forces in Japan. Could not really let those remarks about the Japanese reaction to the British and Australians in Okayama pass without comment. I'm sure that was a correct verdict, but I would also add that it may very well stem from the fact that there was a very strict non-fraternization order in existence in BCOF issued by General Northcott the first commanding general, which, amongst other things, forbade entry into Japanese homes and made the behavior of Occupation troops under very strict surveillance. I think that contrasted quite sharply with the American behavior. I could just add that a former officer in the Cameron Highlanders who was there at the time, a very professional and regular bunch of troops, gave it as his opinion that the Americans had given up soldiering by that time. (Laughter)

Edwin Neville. Thank you very much for your comments. (Laughter)

Allen Meyer. There is a book that came out a few years ago by Theodore Cohen who was the Labor Department head and there is a section (it was translated, it was written originally in Japanese and translated into English) and there is a whole section on fraternization. I'm sorry I didn't bring it with me. It seems that when the Americans first came to Japan, many division and regiment heads said we should adopt a no-fraternization policy for the same reasons perhaps that the British--who were more familiar with not colonization, but with surviving in someone else's land--in any event, an interesting comment was made that when the matter was brought to General MacArthur's attention--he was--he vacillated for a few weeks on the subject and finally he told one of his generals, "I will never promulgate an order that cannot be enforced." And that was the position of the Americans on fraternization. (Laughter)

Bernard Muehlbauer. I was in the Occupation as a young soldier. I first got there in July of 1947 right out of basic training. When we landed, we had about 175 enlisted men, no officers; they were somewhere else. We had our orientation as to our conduct in Japan. We were first greeted by the Major from the 8th Army Provost Marshall's office and he strode out on the stage very self-importantly and launched into a tirade. He referred to us by all kinds of names--referring to our ancestry among other things--we were sitting there wondering: "What happened, we just got here, we haven't done anything yet." But, he was saying that "I am here to warn you not to mess with the Japanese women or the booze. I've got stockades full of guys like you who tangled up with the two. So, leave 'em alone." And he said, "Also, as to your relation with the Japanese. If you lay a hand on your Japanese brother, we'll put you so far in jail, they'll pack daylight to you. If your Japanese brother lays a hand on your uniform in anger, he won't live to be able to get to the nearest police station. Now, start something." We were looking around at each other and saying, "What is this, what have we run into?"

Then a medical officer came out and he also gave us orientation and he described very graphically all the various forms of VD that you can get by even walking through some of these places. And then a Chaplain came out and he said essentially the same thing, but in much better language and our orientation was over. It didn't have much effect because the men were immediately planning how they could jump over the fence at Camp Zama and get down into the village. They had no money and no time, but they were going ... but then I was assigned down to Osaka with the 25th Infantry Division and they had that town sewed up very tight. They had large sections that were absolutely off limits and if you were caught even driving through there, you got arrested by the MPs. They had, they attempted to keep us apart and, of course, it didn't work.

However, though, if you were caught off-limits for fraternization, it could be quite severe. As the months went on, it got more lax and more lax and finally the, unless you really got involved in an incident, nothing was done. But the Army, though, was, I don't know, they used this, I guess, as a scare tactic. It didn't work on us very well. I know, I as a young soldier of 17, I was going to be a good soldier. I was not going to drink the booze; I was not going to mess with the women. I was going to be a very fine model of an American citizen. It took me two weeks to fall off the wagon--when I got my first pass. (Laughter)

W. Soren Egekvist. I came into Atsugi--I could speak Japanese--and I was an unattached officer so I got on the train, went into Tokyo. I knew where the NYK building was so I went to the NYK building for the first night. They had a barbershop in the basement, so I thought well I'd get a shave. As the barber ran his razor over my throat, I thought, well this is a good acid test. If he slits my throat, then the Occupation won't be a success. (Laughter)

Jacob Van Staaveren. I just want to comment on Professor Christopher's statement that during, I think, during the first week he saw no young girls anywhere in Japan. They stayed off the streets. This is partly true. I can tell you partially where all the young girls went. They went to Yamanashi-ken which is a predominantly rural prefecture and after I had been in Kofu, the capital of Yamanashi, a while, my interpreter told me that as the war was ending, thousands of families in and around Tokyo had sent their unmarried girls to Yamanashi as well as to other prefectures. The numbers, the estimates varied from 7,000 to 12,000 who came to Yamanashi--went to Kofu and then traveled further out to the mountainous villages to be safe from the ravishing Americans that were expected to arrive. And there they stayed until the war ended and then, of course, nothing happened and then gradually they returned to their homes. So, there was apparently quite an exodus of young ladies from the, not only Tokyo, but I suspect from other urban centers that were sent far away, not only to escape the bombing, but to escape from the ravishing GI who was about to land.

Carmen Johnson. First impressions in a big city and first impressions in a rural area are very different. I went all over Shikoku many times with an interpreter in a jeep. There was never a question of treatment except the finest. The one incident that I can tell you was when we went, I went with a Nisei who was another woman, on our bicycles to Ritsurin Park to pick up some photographs that had been developed. This was cherry blossom time and there were many, many people in the park. We went into the little shop to look at things and as we were standing there, there was a crash. And behind us a young man, I thought obviously drunk, and the kimono loose, had pushed over a display case. And, of course, I said to my companion who was younger than I was and I wasn't very old then--I said, "Let's get out of here." So, we hopped on our bicycles and we started out. And Stella said, "It's because of us that that happened." She could understand a little bit of Japanese and she said that the young man had come in and he had berated the shopkeeper because of what he had done. So, I said, "Well, we should report this." So I called the Officer of the Day--and he said, "Get the Japanese policeman to take care of this." So, we found a Japanese policeman and we went back. We on our bicycles and the policeman trotting along beside us. I thought, now that was kind of brave of us to do that. We went back and assembled under the tree with the drunkard with all his friends and as we watched, he pushed a young man off his bicycle. So, I thought he had just been drinking. We went inside with the policeman and they had great conversations--bowing, you know. And I said, I told them who I was, I gave them my name and what I did and I didn't mention my friend who was Nisei because there was resentment sometimes by the Japanese people to the American born Japanese. So, we settled that and I asked, "Will he be punished when he reported to the police?" Yes, he would. So we left. In the morning, I went down to the headquarters to talk to the Colonel who was the head of the military government--you may remember I mentioned yesterday, we had no troops on the island. Nobody had reported to the Colonel that this had happened. So, he immediately got in touch with the police station and the man who was the go-between, who *sumimasen'd* (apologized to) all over the place, said they had been given a wrong name and wrong address. That's the only time that I ever had any fear of anything and I don't think I had any reason ever to be fearing any action that would take place, although we were often all by ourselves out in the countryside with nobody there except two women and a jeep driver.

Helen Hosp Seamans. Maybe I'm the odd note, but when I saw the title

"Fraternization" on the program, I thought it meant socialization. So far fraternization seems to be involved with sex. Well, I'm not talking about that at all. I thought that it meant socialization and I was eager to comment on the fact that at the very beginning, we did not fraternize with the Japanese in the sense of enjoying the same social occasions, but later, of course, we did. We were allowed to fraternize with them and I love all the many memories I have of occasions when the Japanese and Americans socialized in each other's homes. I love remembering the Japanese coming even to a social occasion with notebook and pen or pencil eager to write everything down. If we told a joke and they didn't understand the joke, they nevertheless had written it down. I'm tempted to tell you a joke, but I know time doesn't permit. But I will later when I see you individually. I want to say that I thought fraternization also meant the many instances in which Japanese women and American women got together to exchange recipes and how even one friend of mine sent an angel cake which she had baked to the Emperor and the Empress on the occasion of one of their wedding anniversaries and the Empress was so taken with the angel cake that she wanted to know how to make an angel cake. So my friend supplied her with an angel cake pan and the Empress sent her daughter to this friend's home to learn how to make the angel cake. That was what I thought fraternization meant. So on "Innocents Abroad," let me express my thanks anyway for your patience. (Laughter and applause)

Margaret Carlini. We are going to be showing a tape during the lunch hour. It is an interview that was done with Carmen Johnson on Japanese television. The topic is--Carmen Johnson is a pioneer in the democratization of women's rights in Japan during the Occupation and that's about a 25-minute tape. Then we have been asked by a number of people if we could show the MacArthur film after the conference is over and we will do that at the end of the day.

THE GRASS ROOTS IN TOKYO:
A LANGUAGE OFFICER REMEMBERS

Grant K. Goodman

GRANT K. GOODMAN is Professor Emeritus of History at the University of Kansas. He served in the Allied Occupation of Japan in 1945-46 as a Translator, Interpreter, and Chief, Production Section of the Allied Translator and Interpreter Service, GHQ, SCAP. Grant Goodman received the Bachelor of Arts degree from Princeton University in 1948. His graduate study was conducted at the University of Michigan where he was awarded the Ph.D. in History in 1955. He is the author of numerous articles and books, including *The Dutch Impact on Japan, 1640-1853* (Leiden: E.J. Brill, 1967); *Four Aspects of Philippine-Japanese Relations, 1930-40* (New Haven: Yale University Southeast Asia Program, 1967); *Japan: The Dutch Experience* (London and Dover, New Hampshire: The Athlone Press, 1986); and, *Amerika no Nippon Gannen* (America's Japan: The First Year, 1945-1946) (Tokyo: Otsuki Shoten, 1986).

I would like to begin this personal memoir of "The Grassroots in Tokyo" with a statement of my deepest gratitude to the MacArthur Memorial for their great kindness and courtesy in including my contribution in this important symposium. And I would also like to take this opportunity to assure our hosts that, while my dotage has certainly begun and my decrepitude is probably evident to all of you, I am not yet totally gaga, at least in my own opinion! I say this because much of what I will recount here does come from memory, but over the interceding 45 years that memory has been refreshed frequently by reference to archival materials and to renewed contacts with contemporaries of that era. Most helpful, of course, in this renewal process was the writing in Japanese together with Professor Hideo Kobayashi, of my memoirs of my Occupation experience published in 1986 in Tokyo by Otsuki Shoten, *Amerika no Nippon Gannen (America's Japan: The First Year)*. Many of my comments today will draw on that source.

As many of you already know, I arrived in Japan on 1 October 1945 as a Second Lieutenant in the Military Intelligence Service after nearly two and a half years of training as a Japanese Language Officer. I was a member of the Allied Translator and Interpreter Service (ATIS), GHQ, SCAP to which I had been assigned in Manila in July 1945. On arrival in Yokohama, I, together with several of my fellows, was transported to Tokyo to our temporary quarters in the Ochanomizu YWCA, one of the very few prewar structures left standing in an utterly devastated metropolis. Indeed, the "grassroots" were literally about the only thing left in that bombed out shell of a once great city. My shock and horror at the seeming total destruction of Tokyo, on the one hand, and at the apparent insensitivity of a government which could permit its society to be so decimated, on the other hand, were as profound as any feelings then possible for a 20 year old could be. Seeing at first hand the prostration of the Japanese people, my admiration for their remarkable endurance was more than tempered by my disgust with a government which could so heedlessly impose such suffering on its populace. Accordingly, my innate American "missionary spirit" was aroused to fever pitch, and my image of myself as an unabashed advocate for "democracy" was firmer than ever. If the Japanese were to be "saved" from the terrible depredations of totalitarianism, surely MacArthur, SCAP and I could do the job!

In this sense, my grassroots contacts in Tokyo began with conversations in both Japanese and English on the nature of democracy American-style, and my fervent "preaching" on the subject did not diminish throughout my entire twenty-first year which I spent in Japan. Like almost all of my fellow Occupationnaires, especially in the seminal first year, my belief in the potential of the Japanese for "salvation" never wavered, and my "evangelical" efforts in its behalf were continuous. In retrospect, I have tried to understand why I/we were like that, and several possible explanations come to mind. One explanation was very simply that we Americans had won the war, and more than ever we believed in our own superiority as well as in our obligation to "lift" the defeated and poverty-stricken Japanese out of the morass into which "authoritarianism," "militarism" and "Emperorism" had submerged them. According to the American rationale, it was not the Japanese people we had been fighting. It was their bestial government dominated by "militarists." Therefore, we felt that we could and, indeed, must help these downtrodden victims of that regime while simultaneously eliminating those evil men who had led their trusting citizens to the slaughter.

Another explanation was, of course, our patriotic commitment. This was what the war had been about: to make Japan more like the United States so that Japan would never threaten the United States again. And we were young GIs, especially we young officers, were thoroughly socialized "Candides." American democracy was the best of all possible systems and, if only others could adopt it and adapt to it, the world really would at long last realize Woodrow Wilson's dream. Further, we were all children of the New Deal. America had, in our lifetimes, faced its most rigorous test and had not been found wanting thanks to the New Deal which had preserved and extended our way of life. Moreover, in Japan itself General Douglas MacArthur, despite all the negative rumors about his presumed anti-democratic tendencies, was for his men at GHQ-SCAP the essential progenitor of the reforms Japan was being forced to accept one after another at breakneck speed. While of course we never knew which reforms, if any, MacArthur himself engendered, we certainly did know that no one of them was possible without his approval, and all of them were issued in his name.

After a relatively short stay at the YWCA, I was moved to the Marunouchi NYK Building where ATIS was established and where I lived and worked for the remainder of my year in Japan. My own peculiar missionary work did not flag throughout the rest of my stay, and it seemed that at every opportunity, I tried both to be responsive to Japanese inquiries about democracy, which incidentally were endless, or to use whatever "bully pulpit" might be available to further the cause of democracy.

Almost immediately after arrival in Japan, I joined the faculty of the Nichi-Bei Kaiwa Gakuin where I taught evening classes in English conversation. I used no textbooks but rather set topics for free conversation for each class meeting. You may rest assured that some phase of an American-style democratic society was discussed at each session: voting, equality, free speech, freedom of religion, etc. My memories of those encounters with my Japanese students of whom were adults, have, I am afraid, faded with the passing years. However, I can never forget one woman of very mature years who reported to the class that during the war a Japanese officer had boarded a crowded streetcar on which she was riding. That officer, she said, had noisily harangued the passengers, who had unfortunately failed to offer him a seat, to the effect that they were not only discourteous to an officer of His Imperial Majesty's military service, but that they lacked patriotism in failing properly to acknowledge his presence in the car and to act accordingly. That woman said that it was that moment when she knew that the old system in Japan had to go and that democracy was its necessary replacement. Happily for me as an apostle of democracy, the response by the class to such narratives was uniformly positive. In this way at least, Goodman's civics lessons seemed to be remarkably successful, and I truly felt that the "grassroots" were very hopeful indeed.

Nevertheless, I would like to explain that my view of the intensity of the Japanese interest in democracy in 1945-46 was that it was certainly real but perhaps somewhat misdirected. As I discovered in my classes in the Nichi-Bei Kaiwa Gakuin, the Japanese were obsessed by the mechanics of democracy, especially as it was practiced in America. They asked myriad questions about numbers, functions, mechanics etc. but asked almost nothing about the historical or philosophical basis of democracy as it had evolved in Europe and America. In short, my impression was that the Japanese poplar reaction at that time was simply that the prewar Japanese political system had been a failure since Japan lost the war and that the American system must be better because America won the war. In that peculiar sense MacArthur, in his desire to change the constitution, was very much in line with popular Japanese thinking. And a constitution like America's would be welcomed because it would be "democratic" both for MacArthur and for the Japanese. As Professor Robert Ward has explained so many times, there is a profound difference between institutional democracy and psychological democracy. Both MacArthur and the Japanese people believed that once the institutional democracy, as in the constitution, were put into place, psychological democracy would follow. Certainly in 1945-46 there was minimal psychological democracy in the American sense, and the Japanese people had almost no sense of the complex history of the evolution of the concepts of democracy in the West. Luckily for the survival of Japan's American-written institutional democracy, Japan had over fifty years of experience of governance under the Meiji Constitution, a literate and well educated populace and subsequently a post-Occupation economic boom, all of which have sustained the postwar Constitution. Yet, one may still ask whether or not Japanese culture and society have assimilated psychological democracy.

In ATIS itself my assigned tasks were varied and did not always directly involve my supposed Japanese language competence. One of my earliest assignments was to recruit Japanese and foreign nationals in order to staff our translation, editing and production activities and to assist in the broad scope of work which GHQ-SCAP would assign to us. For example, the largest single task we undertook was the so-called daily press translations which meant that each morning, when General MacArthur arrived at his office on the fifth floor of the Dai-Ichi Building, on his desk would be a full English version of all editorials and of a wide selection of articles from the previous evening's and that same morning's Japanese press. Such a project, as you might well imagine, entailed around the clock translation and, in those bad old days, mimeographing. Clearly ATIS's own personnel could do little more than supervise well over one hundred locally hired civilian employees who did the actual work. My particular assignment in this undertaking was to interview and select these individuals from among the horde of applicants who responded to our help wanted advertisements. Since knowledge of English was obviously a *sine qua non* for such employment, in this case I conducted the interviews in English, and I learned a great deal from my interviewees, many of whom were prewar graduates of the best English and American universities. I heard a series of harrowing first hand accounts of wartime hardship and survival as well as repetitive declarations of gratitude to the Americans for both their military victory and their generous Occupation. The sheer delight of these men and women (who incidentally worked together and on equal employment terms perhaps for the first time) at being able freely to use their English again made their desire for the job that much greater. What was also interesting to me was that, although I was a mere 2nd lieutenant, all of the people whom I hired seemed to evidence singular appreciation of and loyalty to me personally. I was showered with gifts from them, and I received numerous invitations to their homes, all of which I sadly refused since we were under strict orders not to diminish the meager Japanese food supply. Whether or not it was again my missionary spirit at work, I cannot say. However, my impression at the time certainly was that these good souls who were, in effect, my flock would be part of the "new Japanese" who would surely make democracy work.

A very different kind of work in which I was directly involved also seemed to reinforce my unshakable belief in the basic Jeffersonianism that was to be ensconced in the depths of the Japanese soul. This was my work at ATIS on the translation of the letters to MacArthur from the Japanese public. It is hard, perhaps, in this age of computers and faxes to envision the veritable flood of lengthy, hand-written letters which poured into GHQ-SCAP, letters addressed directly to *Ma Gensui* or Marshal MacArthur. These letters which arrived daily from the beginning of the Occupation were, as well as I can remember, uniformly supportive, indeed often congratulatory. Such an outpouring of welcome, affection and encouragement for MacArthur and his Occupationnaires was, I believe, genuine, for at SCAP there was certainly neither any expectation, that such letters would be received and, in any event, surely not in such volume. And in order to assure MacArthur's staff that these letters were being translated and sent to the Dai-Ichi Building as quickly as possible, a special translation group under Major John Shelton of the Australian Army, and of which I was a part, was organized just for the letters to MacArthur.

The contents of these letters, as I indicated, were mostly expressions of gratitude for the Allied victory, for the orderly Occupation and for the anticipated future democracy of Japan under MacArthur's guidance. Some letters from women proposed marriage to MacArthur, and many expressed their desire to sire his children without regard to marital status. A number of letters contained intelligence of various kinds, i.e., information on "war criminals" and their nefarious activities and/or their whereabouts, data on hidden arms caches, reports of ultranationalist political activities which the writers saw as inimical to Japan's nascent democracy etc. One such letter with which I was personally involved led us to the discovery of Ba Maw, Burma's Prime Minister under Japanese occupation, who was hiding disguised as a Buddhist priest in the snow country of Niigata. All of us working with and reading these letters saw them as very positive evidence of grassroots democracy evolving in Japan. Many of these letters are here in the MacArthur Archives, but they are only a small fraction of the total number received.

Two additional efforts by the Occupation to nurture Jeffersonian democracy in Japan might be noted here. In neither case was I directly involved, but in both instances I had close colleagues who were, and I certainly was sensitive to the purports of both. One was, of course, the establishment of the International Military Tribunal for the Far East (IMTFE) to try Class A accused Japanese War Criminals, the so-called Nuremberg East. I will not here even attempt to give the history of this remarkable and complete undertaking and its varied vicissitudes and ramifications. What I do wish to stress, however, was that beyond the obvious level of "crime and punishment," which has been termed by some critics as "victors' justice," was another level which for the grassroots was intended to be educative. In this context the trial was seen by the Occupationnaires as providing the Japanese public with eye-opening revelations which would convince it that its leaders had misguided, misled and indeed duped the Japanese people into going down a "road to ruin." Once that objective lesson had been learned by the Japanese, of course as a result of the IMTFE proceedings, it was seemingly believed that the long repressed nascent democratic spirit in the hearts and minds of the Japanese would come to the fore, and Japan would forever after be a quasi-American just and peace-loving nation. Unfortunately this noble goal was never realized for two unanticipated reasons: 1) the Japanese economy was so precarious that the overwhelming majority of the Japanese people were totally preoccupied with the hardscrabble necessity to survive from one day to the next and could hardly be interested in endlessly detailed legal proceedings in the old War Ministry Building, and 2) those who did pay any attention to the IMTFE were from the very outset convinced that this was simply another cost of Japan's defeat and therefore had no interest in a lengthy process whose conclusion was clearly foregone. Yet one more interesting facet of the failure of the IMTFE to contribute to the generation of a democratic spirit is suggested in the *New York Times Magazine* on Sunday, 3 November 1991. In an article entitled "Pearl Harbor in the Mind of Japan" in trying to explain the contemporary apparent failure of the Japanese to assume any feeling of responsibility for the outbreak of the Pacific War, Stephen Weisman writes:

> Many Japanese legitimately point out that the idea of exonerating the Japanese people was established by the United States itself. According to the Allied-sponsored Tokyo War Crimes Tribunal, a handful of leaders conspired to make war, ignoring the wishes of the people. Thus the trials and conviction of twenty-eight leaders (seven of whom were hanged in December 1948) served American interests in isolating the main culprits and placating the Japanese people in order to enlist them as an ally against Communism.

A very different kind of intended stimulus to democratization was the decision of the United States armed forces to sponsor a production of Gilbert and Sullivan's operetta "The Mikado" in central Tokyo at the Ernie Pyle Theater, the former Takarazuka Gekijo. As far as could be determined, this was the first time that charming and amusing British musical chestnut had been seen in Japan. Whoever thought up this theatrical "bombshell" apparently believed that bringing this clever spoof of Victorian England to a Japanese audience would encourage the development in Japan of the kind of modest irreverence with which the British have generally viewed their monarchy and that this in turn would reenforce the new Japanese democracy. However, even though we were told that the costumes had been borrowed from the Imperial Household, "The Mikado," sung in English for an almost exclusively GI audience at almost the very moment when the Occupation had decided to retain the Imperial institution practically intact, passed unnoticed by the Japanese public.

There are, of course, many other memories of Tokyo and of the Izu Peninsula, Nikko, Kofu and other nearby places which it was my privilege to visit nearly half a century ago. However, as I said at the outset of this presentation, many of those memories have already been committed to paper in *Amerika no Nippon Gannen*. It is not my purpose here to bore you with my nostalgic reminiscences. Rather, I want to stress that in those heady immediate postwar days, the grassroots were truly bi-national. We evangelists of democracy wanted very much to reach their grassroots, and the

Japanese, in turn, with their slates wiped clean by war and defeat wanted to reach up from their grassroots to us. This is, I think, a very important way to look at the Occupation generally. Reforms, no matter how brilliantly devised, are only, in the beginning, pieces of paper. Even with all the power of MacArthur and SCAP, without some degree of receptivity on the part of the Japanese, the implementation of those reforms would not have been possible. My view in retrospect is that in 1945-46 that receptivity was literally limitless, including, I would argue, the abolition of the Emperor system. The grassroots, theirs and ours, were ready for a total societal transformation.

In the end, however, it was we Americans who held back. We decided to retain the Emperor. We based our entire reform program on Constitutional revision. We were no more social revolutionaries abroad than we were at home. The real Japanese potential, if it existed, for true economic and social democracy was never realized nor should we probably have ever thought that it would be. Americans, in their peculiar fascination for foreign royals, could not have been the instrumentalities of "regicide" so to speak. Nor did we ultimately have the stomach for disestablishmentarianism. Thus, while I hold that the grassroots as I understand the term, were open to radical change, the inherent American aversion to seemingly extreme solutions led us to moderate eventually even those reforms which were decreed in the Occupation's first year.

Since that time the congenital American "fear of Communism," the "security" of the Occupation, the clever machinations of Japan's conservative politicians, the Cold War and the like have all been blamed for the particular kind of reform program which the Occupation instituted. While all of these reasons probably contributed to some extent, I would argue that American democracy, while always paying lip service to "grassroots democracy," has by its historical character and traditions always been limited to political democracy of a specifically constitutional nature. "Political science" is an American invention, and it is after all the so-called science of politics, i.e., voting. In postwar Japan, then, the very nexus of the constitution was the franchise. That we never intended to go further is no surprise, but the "grassroots" were surely ready for much more.

SUCCESS IN JAPAN--
DESPITE SOME HUMAN FOIBLES
AND CULTURAL PROBLEMS

Robert B. Textor

ROBERT B. TEXTOR is Professor Emeritus of Anthropology at Stanford University. During the Allied Occupation of Japan he served as an Information and Education Officer at Hq First Corps, Kyoto (1946-47) and in the Wakayama Military Government Team (1947-48). His undergraduate studies were conducted at the University of Michigan in the 1940s while simultaneously preparing for duty as a Language Officer (Japanese) with the U.S. Army. He received the Ph.D. in Cultural Anthropology from Cornell University in 1960, specializing in studies of Thailand. Robert Textor is the author of *Failure in Japan: With Keystones for a Positive Policy* (New York: John Day, 1951), published in Japanese as *Nippon ni Okeru Shippai in Bungei Shunju*, 1952; and *A Cross-Policy Survey* (with Arthur S. Banks) (Cambridge, MA: The M.I.T. Press, 1963).

DEDICATION

RONALD STONE ANDERSON
1908-1985

This paper is dedicated to the memory of a scholar and man of action who devoted his entire professional career to building creative bridges between Japanese and American education. Prior to World War II, and shortly after graduating from Stanford University, Anderson spent six years in Japan, teaching at Aoyama Gakuin and at the higher schools in Kanazawa and Fukuoka. He then returned to Stanford for a master's degree, and taught in California secondary schools. From 1946 to 1950 Anderson served as the first and only regular Chief of the Civil Information and Education Division, Military Government Section, Headquarters, First Corps and Kinki Region, in Kyoto. In this key role, his humanity, his energy, and his deep understanding of Japanese and American education became important factors in the promotion of education for democracy in Western Japan. Ronald Anderson was one of the true unsung heroes of the Occupation.

Thereafter Ron earned his doctorate in history at the University of California, Berkeley, and taught at the Universities of Michigan and Hawaii, where he continued his lifelong involvement with education in Japan and America.

Ron's friends among the Japanese and the Americans were legion. It is an honor to have been one of them.[1]

The last time I was in Tokyo I paid a sentimental visit to the Dai Ichi Building. I took the elevator to the fifth floor, there to find the inevitable *uketsuke* (receptionist). I asked the old man if I could see *Maakaasaa Gensui no jimusho* (General MacArthur's office), and promptly--as though long accustomed to receiving nostalgic *gaijin* (foreign) visitors like me--he slipped on his sandals and led me down the hallway.

There it was: a pleasant room with paneled walls. I looked everywhere for some kind of marker or plaque. There was none. Yet, out of respect for its history, the company that owned the building kept the room clean and tidy but unused, except for an occasional company reception. For this room, from 1945 to 1951, had been the office of General of the Army Douglas MacArthur.[2]

Here, I mused, was where a thousand vital decisions had been made--decisions that would impact upon the entirety of Japanese politics and economics, and indeed on the very fabric of everyday Japanese life. Here was where policies were developed that freed up liberal Japanese to initiate sociocultural change processes that might not otherwise have taken place as quickly--or at all.

I stood there alone quietly for several minutes, thinking a thousand thoughts. Then I left the building and strolled across to the plaza in front of the Imperial Palace. Thousands of school children were there on *ensoku* (school trips). They were smiling, relaxed, spontaneous. I started a conversation with some of them, and was struck by how much easier I found it to speak with these kids in 1983, than with those I had met back in 1946-48. Back then, as an Occupation official, I had made scores of school inspections, during which I had always tried to include conversations with students--but had usually found them stiff and almost ritualistic in their responses. But on this bright day 35 years later, I said to myself, "Hey, these look like the kinds of kids we hoped Japan would some day have, back in the Forties when we were working with Japanese educators." Here in front of me, I ruminated, stood convincing exemplars of the "New Japan" that we in Military Government had talked about with our Japanese colleagues more than a generation earlier. The future had become the present. It was a good feeling.

This article deals with one person's experience in working with Japanese educators and media communicators to help build that New Japan. It deals principally with my "grass roots" work during the first half of 1948 as a civilian official of Military Government (MG) in Wakayama Prefecture. I shall illustrate my experiences by quoting selected excerpts from my monthly reports to higher headquarters.[3]

Ironically, this article reports on events and phenomena of a nature doubtless quite foreign to Douglas MacArthur's own experience in Japan--for he defined his role from the start as that of a sort of latter-day *shogun*, aloof from the masses of ordinary Japanese. He played that role to perfection. In my view, his aloof stance was not only one that came to him naturally, but one that he should have taken even if it had not come naturally. Given the Japanese political culture at the time, his very unreachability gave him maximal charisma, and hence tremendous influence over political, economic, and sociocultural change processes. It did, though, have the disadvantage that it permitted him no direct opportunity to observe events at the grass roots.[4]

ENTER THE OCCUPATIONNAIRE

In 1943 I was a 20-year-old student at Antioch College when the Army of the United States finally decided that it wanted me, on the double, and promptly proceeded to transmogrify me into an infantry heavy weapons gunner. Then, in its wisdom, the military personnel system assigned me to the Army Japanese Language School at the University of Michigan. As the fates willed it, I spent the rest of the war either at Ann Arbor or waiting to go there.

Like millions of young Americans at that time, I believed deeply in America's war aims. When V-J Day arrived, I felt an irresistible urge to get to Japan as quickly as possible and do what I could to promote a democratic new order. I reported to my separation center three days early, hurried to Washington, and took the first War Department civilian job offered me in Japan.

On a sunny April morning in 1946, I arrived in Yokohama aboard an army troop transport ship. Our group was immediately loaded onto busses for the trip to Tokyo. I was shocked beyond forgetting at the sight of this totally flattened city. Little else besides scattered chimneys, steel safes, and stone *kura* (storehouses) had survived the holocaust of American fire bombs. This shock, and others like it which followed, only strengthened my resolve to do what I could to promote democracy in Japan--on the assumption, of course, that a democratic Japan would less likely be an aggressive Japan.

I had been assigned as a civilian interpreter to the Allied Translator and Interpreter Service, Supreme Commander for the Allied Powers (ATIS/SCAP). However, it was immediately clear that if I stayed at ATIS, the odds were strong that my duties would be routine and technical--precisely what I did not want. What I did want was direct contact with those Japanese who were actively working at the intercultural synapse across which Americans and Japanese were attempting to communicate and cooperate in the process of fashioning a New Japan.

Fortunately for me there was at that time a severe shortage of trained Americans on hand to run the Occupation. Tens of thousands of military personnel chafed impatiently to return home for discharge, and only a relative handful of civilians were available to take their places and staff a rapidly expanding Occupation bureaucracy. Given this fluid situation, and the grace of the Almighty, I managed to get myself released from ATIS, and to convince the Military Government Civil Information and Education (MG CIE) Division at Eighth Army Headquarters that my qualifications as a specialist on Japanese language and culture somehow made up for my very limited experience as a teacher.

Thus, unbelievably, at the age of 23 I found myself Assistant CIE Officer, MG Section, Headquarters First Corps, Kyoto. There, my supervisor, the late Ronald S. Anderson, and I were responsible for overseeing the implementation of Occupation policy for the democratic reorientation of all schools and public media in three MG regions embracing one-third of the population of Japan. Similarly, we implemented Occupation policy with respect to religion and the preservation of arts and monuments. Given the priceless artistic and historic treasures of unbombed Kyoto and Nara, this last responsibility was considerable. In pursuit of all these duties, I traveled frequently throughout the three regions.

Anderson and I were also directly involved in the hiring of numerous civilian CIE officers to work in the three regions under our charge. This experience gave us a first-hand awareness of the kinds of Americans who were being posted to 20 of Japan's 46 prefectures--their widely varying competencies, their cultural sensitivity, values, goals, world view--and the extent of their knowledge of Japan.[5]

After a year and a half in Kyoto, I was given the opportunity to conduct my own operation, as CIE Officer in Wakayama Prefecture, near Osaka. During the following eight months, I gave guidance, assistance, and encouragement to a hard-working group of local educators who, with stunning speed and skill, succeeded in achieving a comprehensive restructuring of Wakayama's entire public school system, aimed at achieving gender and class equality of access to elementary and secondary education. This was in effect a bloodless revolution, and will serve as the center-piece for much of the analysis that follows. I also worked with a small group of college professors in designing what is today Wakayama University.[6]

During those heady days I was well aware that I enjoyed a level of responsibility far higher than I deserved, especially in terms of my "paper" qualifications. However, as one who helped hire and supervise numerous CIE officers for First Corps' 20 prefectures, I soon saw how ethnocentric and culturally naive some Occupationnaires were, who did have impressive paper qualifications--e.g., 15 years as a superintendent in an isolated monolingual rural district in the American heartland--I felt less inadequate. "We're all unqualified," I told myself, "so why not just do your best, and hope it's good enough?"

Moreover, my enthusiasm for activism rose as I discovered how many key Japanese leaders, officials, and intellectuals were ready for change. Japan had suffered cataclysmic losses in a brutal war, had experienced the utter horror of nuclear attack, and, for the first time ever, had been occupied by foreign troops. All this trauma had certainly rendered many Japanese wide open to new ideas about how to conduct social life. And the fact that the Emperor had instructed them to lay down their arms gave a powerful legitimacy to Occupation efforts to effectuate or catalyze change.

I was also struck by what can only be termed a cultural characteristic of the Japanese: a tendency to search relentlessly for the best way to do something. This tendency had been in manifest operation throughout Japan's modern period since at least the 1870s, when the Japanese government started sending missions to the West to find out what was the best legal system, the best military system, the best education system, etc., for Japan. And now, due to the exigencies of war and surrender, I found myself besieged daily with questions about the best way to run an organization, a school system, a newspaper, or, indeed, a country. It was a unique and humbling historic opportunity.

So, in the two years that followed, I learned to consider eleven-hour days and six- or seven-day weeks to be a reasonable, and deeply satisfying, work routine. Throughout this entire period, I was in direct daily contact with Japanese educators, writers, journalists, labor leaders, intellectuals, politicians, and reform-minded citizens. I made scores of school inspections, gave countless lectures to teachers' groups, youth clubs, civic associations, PTAs, etc., and held numerous press conferences. Frequently, this contact was through the medium of the Japanese language.

Incidentally, Japan reoriented my entire life. When I returned to the States in 1948 I switched career plans and became a cultural anthropologist. In reflecting today on the grass-roots aspects of the Occupation of Japan, therefore, I do so primarily as an anthropologist--though secondarily through the prisms of history and political science.[7]

HUMAN FOIBLES ON THE AMERICAN SIDE

The pace and profundity of daily life in MG at the grass roots readily revealed numerous human foibles on both sides, as well as the patterned ways in which each side defined the other side's foibles. I will not dwell on these human foibles very long, but a quick summary of a few of them (or more precisely, my imperfect perceptions of them) will serve to create the context for the analysis to follow.

154

Unprepared Personnel

In the early months of the Occupation, almost all MG officers were military -- I being, as I recall, the first civilian of officer rank in First Corps Headquarters' MG section.[8] Gradually, more and more civilians were hired, though the top jobs remained in military hands.

In terms of their fitness for cross-cultural work, MG's officers, military and civilian, varied from excellent to poor. At the positive end of the continuum one found, among others, a number of officers who had been trained for MG duties at various Civil Administration Training Schools (CAT Schools) in the U.S. during the war.[9] Many were citizen-soldiers who could draw upon successful administrative or leadership careers in their civilian past. Some of these officers took discharges in Japan and continued their duties as civilians.

As I recall, all of these CATS alumni that I met were male. Indeed, during the first year or so, MG in the First Corps area was almost exclusively staffed by males. It was only gradually that any appreciable number of women MG officers were hired-- a fact that certainly rendered prefectural and regional teams less sensitive to the needs and problems of Japanese women than would otherwise have been the case.

At the negative end of the preparedness continuum were many officers--especially career military--who often had exemplary war records, but sometimes were hopelessly unprepared by education or experience, and perhaps temperament, for anything like MG work. They lacked previous cross-cultural experience or knowledge of any foreign language, and were further handicapped by a certain narrowness that hardly fitted them to function effectively in Japan, let alone to supervise or to lead in Occupation affairs.[10] I have described this situation elsewhere (Textor 1951: 186-96), and will not belabor it here.

Looking back on all this, I sometimes find myself marveling that MG didn't do more harm. I believe that what saved the organization, in part, was that, for many domains of responsibility, MG officers were formally expected merely to "observe and report" compliance with Occupation directives. This often made it possible for an officer to satisfy higher headquarters while in fact remaining fairly passive--after all, one could always ask for some statistics from the *kencho* (prefectural government office), and put them into a plausible monthly report that would probably satisfy higher headquarters. Many, perhaps most, MG officers, especially military ones, (and most especially career military ones) were inclined to take this route--and then relax and enjoy life.[11] This is not to say that many such officers were not conscientious, but it is to say that many were scarcely inclined to go out of their way looking for problems.

By contrast, some military, and more civilian, MG officers did go farther, and became quite ardent activists. I include myself in this category. Instead of simply "observing and reporting," my philosophy--shared widely in MG CIE--was that we should assertively try to encourage positive change processes by "guiding and assisting" relevant Japanese in a consistent and persistent manner.[12]

Inefficient Structure

The MG structure was a part of the Eighth Army, with headquarters in Yokohama. Under Eighth Army were two corps: the Ninth, headquartered in Sendai, and the First, headquartered in Kyoto. Under the First Corps were three MG regions: Kinki, Tokai-Hokuriku, and Kyushu, headquartered respectively in Kyoto, Nagoya, and Fukuoka.[13] Under each region in the First Corps area were six or seven prefectures, each with its prefectural MG team. At all levels--army, corps, region, and team--the commanding and executive officers were invariably military, as were, typically, the holders of many other key posts.

Note that here was a situation of extreme shortage of qualified personnel, yet the military saw fit to maintain five levels of administration for military governance purposes, where three would not only have done the job faster, but saved manpower for other purposes.[14]. The only justification for such redundancy was, I suppose, the unspoken one that it provided niches for military officers who might otherwise have been difficult to place![15]

Vagueness of Mission

Especially in the early days of the Occupation, prefectural MG teams were plagued by the vagueness of their mission, and the difficulty of securing urgently needed policy decisions, due in part to the three layers of bureaucracy between themselves and SCAP in Tokyo. And it was SCAP alone which, in theory, made all policy decisions.

Perhaps this theoretical administrative model could have worked, but only in a situation in which the structure was highly efficient and the mission clearly defined and widely understood. In reality, however, such was not the situation. Only in some cases would a prefectural MG officer refer a problem to higher headquarters--and be prepared to wait weeks for an authoritative decision. In other cases the officer would simply demur, and assume that the problem at hand would somehow solve itself without MG intervention.[16]

In still other and numerous cases, however, referral or demurral were not appropriate. Such cases were those in which Japanese officials and citizens would ask MG for clarification as to whether this or that option was permitted by Occupation policy, where not to have given an immediate and clear response would have created more problems, or even danger, than to have referred the matter to higher headquarters. In such cases, MG officers would simply, in effect, make interim *ad hoc* policy. Technically, however, such officers might well have been exceeding their authority.[17]

In short, MG CIE officers often found the rigid "observe and report" approach grossly inadequate, and often felt that they had no choice but to invoke the more flexible and positive "guide and assist" approach--and to stretch it considerably.

Paranoia in the Counter Intelligence Corps

Another problem standing in the way of a fully successful Occupation was a certain negativism that pervaded both MG and the Counter Intelligence Corps (CIC), but especially the latter.[18] There was an almost paranoid concern, on the part of numerous military officers, over possible subversion among American civil servants working in Japan. Heading the entire surveillance effort was SCAP's G-2, Chief of Civil Intelligence Section Major General Charles A. Willoughby, a man who had been close to General MacArthur for many years, and who was probably the second most powerful American in Japan. It is said that General MacArthur once described Willoughby as "my lovable fascist".[19] This sobriquet is consistent with my own findings. In 1951 I wrote:

> Not long before Mussolini marched into France, Willoughby wrote a book that was generally sympathetic with Generalissimo Franco and with Japanese military activities in China, and said: "historical judgement, freed from the emotional haze of the moment, will credit Mussolini with wiping out a memory of defeat by re-establishing the traditional military supremacy of the white race, for generations to come." Had a Japanese written this sort of opinion about the Japanese "race," he would have been purged by the Occupation (Textor 1951: 191).

While the Communist threat was certainly real, and assuredly deserved to be taken seriously, General Willoughby and his sprawling national intelligence network sometimes went to absurd extremes that did serious harm to some of the basic positive goals of the Occupation itself (Textor 1951: 120-3). For example, during much of my time in Kyoto, the CIC would send representatives to "monitor" my speeches to teachers' groups, civic organizations, and the like. At one point the CIC even decided, for reasons never explained, that I could not go on a routine field trip into upcountry Kyoto Prefecture--to speak to teachers' groups, inspect schools and historic monuments, and so on--unless a CIC officer accompanied me. This decision was especially mysterious because I had been doing just such work routinely for many months. In any case, my assistant and I, along with our driver, obligingly fitted a fourth person into our jeep-- a CIC lieutenant who proceeded to attend every speech I gave, and otherwise to accompany me night and day throughout a three-day trip through back country villages so remote as to have been virtually unaware of (urban-based) Japanese Communism. Lieutenant P had actually been a class-mate of mine at Ann Arbor, and must have known that I had no reputation for being a Communist or fellow traveler. I knew him as a positive person and nice guy and it did not surprise me that he was visibly embarrassed by his assignment. At the end of the trip he apologized: "Bob, I've felt bad all during this trip, especially since it is so clear that you are contributing a lot more to the aims of the Occupation than people like me are." He later sent me a copy of his report to his superior; it not only cleared me, but was actually laudatory (Textor 1951: 154-5). Surely the Occupation could have found ways of harnessing the talents of this Japan specialist--and numerous other, similarly well-trained and -motivated officers who found themselves in the CIC--in a more positive and socially useful way.[20]

HUMAN FOIBLES ON THE JAPANESE SIDE

Especially during the first year and a half of the Occupation, Americans at the local level held great *de facto* power, and often all that was needed to get something done was to say, directly or otherwise, that "the *Shinchugun* (Occupation forces) want this..." --and it would be done. Such informal edicts were gradually supplanted by more formal ones, such as the formal written "procurement demands" that were used to obtain resources to provide all sorts of facilities for Occupationnaires and their families--to build or refurbish office space, to hire musicians to entertain Americans in the billet dining room, or to make life more efficient, convenient, or pleasant for the Americans in a hundred other ways.

Democratically oriented change, however, cannot be obtained by procurement demand. If the Occupation was to produce positive results in its more complex, substantive goals for the Japanese future, it had to gain a more complex, more consensual kind of cooperation from key Japanese officials who were credible to both the Occupation and to the local Japanese power structure. In retrospect, what amazes me is not that there were so few such willing and credible Japanese, but that there were so many.

This is not to say, however, that those on the Japanese side were without their "foibles," at least as I viewed (and oversimplified) them in my American cultural terms. Many educational officials I found myself dealing with were not really educators at all, but general administrators who possessed administrative efficiency, no doubt, but who had no vision of alternative futures for Japanese education--indeed, in some cases, no apparent vision at all, other than that of a vague maintenance of the *status quo*.

What heartened me, however, was to discover many Japanese educators, often quite junior in status, who actively hungered for change, and were prepared to take risks with their own careers in order to help achieve it.[21] The challenge for the reform-minded Occupationnaire was to identify these liberal, change-oriented Japanese, and to work with and through them.

This is exemplified by an excerpt from one of my monthly CIE reports from Wakayama to higher headquarters.

The new chief of the Education Department, a man in his forties, appears progressive;[22] his new chief of the School Education Section, a man in his thirties, has apparently been the prime mover and planner in educational reorganization throughout the Ken. Top personnel in the Ken Social Education Section and in the education departments of Wakayama, Tanabe and Shingu cities appear hopelessly unimaginative and ill-equipped for their jobs. A new crop of "inspectors" has been appointed, including a few women. A few women have been appointed as principals, including one to a new lower secondary school. The Kencho is believed deliberately but humanely making merit promotions and gradually cleaning out dead wood. (Apr 1948).

LIBERALS VERSUS CONSERVATIVES

As a means of bridging from human foibles to the more complex matter of cultural problems, it is first worth taking a brief look at the matter of liberalism versus conservatism among MG Occupationnaires--which translates, to some extent, to relative activism versus inactivism in promoting the progressive sociocultural change programs of the Occupation.

The "liberals" in MG, as in SCAP,[23] tended to be people who had matured politically during the Roosevelt period, and who endorsed the broad humanitarian and equity goals of the New Deal. They were comfortable with the general notion that government must intervene when non-governmental institutions leave important problems unresolved. In the MG context, they were not comfortable with merely "observing and reporting," and were more inclined to "guide and assist." The liberals were keenly aware of the need (as they saw it) of actively implementing in peace the very aims for which the war had been fought. Hence, they were more likely to "go the extra mile" to contain various Japanese tendencies to revert toward authoritarianism, racism, and ultranationalism--and then to follow this with positive programs aimed at democracy and peace. The more conservative Occupationnaires were more inclined to regard pro-change Japanese as Communist or pro-Communist, and to try to build up conservative elements in the prefecture, so that (as they saw it) the Japanese government and society would serve as a bulwark against the spread of Communism in Asia. Building up conservative elements often meant simply doing little to actively promote many of the reforms called for by Occupation policies. And unsurprisingly, many officers and enlisted men in the Counter Intelligence Corps epitomized this extreme conservative position.

We come now to an important historical fact, namely that in the early months and years of the Occupation, its overall policy orientation was basically liberal in many respects, and frequently offered considerable latitude for Occupation officials to pursue quite liberal goals. This fact is a striking paradox, in view of the generally conservative outlook of most high-ranking military officers of the time. It is even more of a paradox in the case of General MacArthur himself, whose political views, in the U.S. domestic context, were widely known to have been staunchly conservative.[24]

At the prefectural and regional levels of MG in the First Corps area, my impression was that officers who could broadly be characterized as liberal were more likely to be civilian than military, and more likely temporary military than regular. Conversely, officers who were civilian were more likely to be liberal than those who were military. These characterizations are, though, very rough and approximate; there were many exceptional and ambiguous cases.

The MG officers I knew varied widely in how hard they worked. In general, civilian officers tended to work harder than military officers,[25] and liberals harder than conservatives. Conservatives were more likely to rely on the local Japanese prefectural officials, and to assume that reports from these officials were true and accurate, or at least satisfactory. Liberals were more likely to follow up on aspects of these reports that seemed unpersuasive or unsatisfactory. Many relatively liberal Occupationnaires were workaholics, and the majority of workaholics were relatively liberal. I classify myself as having been a liberal workaholic.

Though there was a good deal of genuine camaraderie in MG life at the prefectural level, it was not always easy for workaholic liberal civilian MG officers to work effectively with their non-workaholic conservative military colleagues. To the former, the latter sometimes seemed unconcerned with pursuing many of the announced positive goals of the Occupation. To the latter, the former seemed unreasonably, even suspiciously active.

CULTURAL PROBLEMS

It is a truism to say that when we come into contact with people from another culture, the experience makes strikingly clear to us many features of our own culture about which we had previously not been explicitly aware. The truth of this is all the more compelling when we are officially charged with promoting change in the other culture. In occupied Japan, even where American and Japanese foibles were not too great a problem, and even where there was good faith and some degree of consensus between the American and Japanese sides, there still remained many problems of a cultural nature. That is, there were many respects in which the two sides would consistently meet with difficulty in communicating or cooperating, because they viewed the world from different cultural stances.[26] This section will list some of these cultural problems, and illustrate them by quotations, where available, from my monthly reports.

First, however, some background. When I arrived in Wakayama in November 1947, I had an active interest in all the areas within the CIE purview. These areas ranged from fostering democratic education, and education for democracy; to promoting responsible investigative journalism; to encouraging democratic civic associations; to fostering research by faculty in tertiary institutions; to administering SCAP policy concerning religion; to preserving Wakayama's precious arts and monuments--and on and on. While I dealt actively with all these areas, it was clear to me from the beginning that I had to set priorities in order to maximize my overall effectiveness. I determined to give top priority to structural reform, following guidelines from Tokyo calling for a new 6-3-3-4 ladder system--six years of primary education, three years of lower secondary, three of upper secondary, and four of tertiary--to take the place of an older system. Therefore, as a matter of priority, I worked with selected Japanese officials and citizens to reform the total system of public elementary and secondary education at one fell swoop, which would take place at the beginning of the 1948-49 academic year in April, 1948. In short, all at once, my Japanese colleagues and I undertook to equalize access to educational opportunity across gender and class lines throughout the prefecture. Doing it all at once, I felt, would cause less net dislocation than doing it piecemeal--and, equally important, would promote irreversibility.

In the case of gender, I undertook to promote coeducation at every level--a goal that official Occupation policy broadly and loosely favored, but did not insist upon.

In the case of class, also, my efforts were broadly consistent with, but not mandated by, SCAP policy. Specifically, I undertook to:

♦ promote districting of public schools, with every child in a particular district attending the school in her or his district.

♦ promote "comprehensive" secondary schools, each to contain both a general (academic) and a vocational curriculum--as a means of democratizing the total learning atmosphere within a school, and moving away from elite bias.

The above two structural innovations were intended to replace an older system of privilege in which the education of girls was less valued and hence less emphasized, and in which certain secondary schools were widely assumed to be more or less reserved for elite children. For example, the prefecture's most prestigious secondary school, the *Dai Ichi Chu Gakko* (First Middle School), located in Wakayama City, was the school to which senior bureaucrats and wealthy people would "of course" send their sons--to receive academic rather than vocational education. Some of these boys commuted daily on overcrowded trains from as far away as Tanabe, some seventy miles distant, to attend

159

this elite school.

I realized, of course, that the democratic re-drawing of school district boundaries would not bring about changes in educational practice immediately--but, I reasoned, it would help to do so in the longer run:

◆ by causing better-educated and socio-politically more influential parents to give their genuine interest and support to the local school--rather than to a school for the privileged, located in another community; and

◆ by necessitating that school administrators and teachers actually confront the need to teach all students together: male and female, academically- and vocationally-oriented.

My monthly reports illustrate the changes:

Entire ken (prefecture) has been districted for senior high school purposes. All senior high schools will be coeducational. Out of a total of twenty senior high schools, two will be vocational, all former old system secondary vocational schools will offer general and vocational courses, and former general education old system secondary schools will have a general course with a vocational course or two planned for the near future....Particular attention has been given to securing best possible teachers for junior high schools. Principals of old system secondary schools which became new senior high schools will be transferred. (Mar 1948).

According to the Kencho, structural change in Wakayama's school system is as thorough-going as any in Japan. Advising the Kencho, the city hall and civic groups re these structural changes was CE's biggest job this month. Governor and those whom he appears to represent are patently cool toward re-organization; young teachers, college-graduated citizens and others generally to be categorized as "progressive" are warmly supporting reorganization. (Apr 1948).

This description of the situation Wakayama MG CIE faced will serve to set the context within which we may now examine a number of key cultural problems in which American and Japanese cultural stances were often in opposition.[27]

Open Criticism Versus Harmonious Silence

While most adult Japanese were doubtless shocked by their nation's defeat into feeling that some basic changes in their sociocultural system were needed, many nonetheless manifested a general proclivity NOT to offer overt, public criticism of the *status quo*. By contrast, the American proclivity was much more supportive of active public criticism of the *status quo*.

Perhaps the most thoroughly democratic and profitable discussion series ever held in Wakayama Ken (Prefecture) occurred this month in the Social Education Study Conference. Wakayama Military Government (WMG) and the Kencho wrote a provocative list of questions for each program item. Almost all program items were handled by panels. The list of questions provoked the audience into very wide participation. Some of the attitudes and remarks were caustic and in bad taste, the kind usually associated with enthusiasm mixed with immaturity. For example, one youth group member told a local judge who was serving as panel leader that he thought somebody else should immediately be selected to replace the judge who, he felt, was doing an incompetent job as panel leader. Few youth leaders in the past have ever so addressed a member of the bench. The audience developed the habit of indicating aloud that they could not hear a given speaker, or that a given speaker was long-winded or dilatory in his tactics. One enthusiastic conference participant even attempted to take control of the meeting away from the chairman. This member, who, as far as is known, does not have radical political tendencies,[28] wanted the audience to join him in his enthusiasm to form a new movement aimed at the abolition of the present marriage system and the creation of a free marriage system. WMG at this point suggested that, whatever the merits of the participant's ideas, he should not try to gain acceptance for those ideas through usurpation of the authority of the conference leader. (May 1948).

Action Versus Inaction

Japanese officials in the *kencho* were less likely to come up with plans for sweeping action, than were their opposite numbers in MG. In part, the American position reflected a culturally typical value in favor of change-oriented activity in general. And in part, too, it reflected the fact that the American knew that his or her presence in Japan was temporary, and that the malleable situation in Japan, favorable to change, would exist for only a few more short years or even months. Therefore, if action was going to be taken, it had to be taken soon.[29]

Initiatory Versus Maintenance Action

Although MG was officially expected, at most, to offer "guidance and assistance," in some cases MG's inclination to initiate action, and to support Japanese initiators, went further, as the following excerpt indicates.

Continued firm but gentle pressure was exerted on Japanese authorities to get consolidated junior high schools [established] wherever geographical conditions permit. Great resistance has been met from local bosses, who pander to local superstition and prejudices. (Mar 1948).

Individual Versus Group Expressiveness

Americans are a nation of individuals, or at least our mythology tells us we are. In expressing themselves and their views, Occupationnaires tended, relative to the Japanese, to do so as autonomous individuals.[30] Our opposite numbers among the Japanese were, in sharp contrast, not likely to express autonomous opinions that diverged from those of their colleagues, and highly likely to consult their group first, and to work out a group position with which all members of the group could be comfortable.

Rightness Versus Appropriateness

Americans, imbued with the notion of "inalienable rights," were culturally inclined to stress the need for this or that change because it was seen as the right thing to do. Japanese, to the extent that they were inclined to stress the need for change, were somewhat more likely, in my perception, to justify change as *tekitoo*, or proper. This, as I see it, is consistent with a deep tendency in the Confucian tradition to equate politics with ethics, and to preserve harmony at almost any cost.

One problem with the American cultural emphasis is that rightness can merge into righteousness, which in turn can merge into self-righteousness. I am aware that I was not immune to this problem. In my case, the problem was deftly epitomized in the delightful inscription to a copy of *Fuzambo's Japanese-English Dictionary*, that Wakayama's newspaper reporters gave me as a farewell gift when I completed my service there:

> Present to Mr. Textor
> From the M.G. Beat Men
> Hope you much idealism,
> with a little realism.

I still prize this gift, and take to heart its implied constructive advice concerning rigid idealism and self-righteousness. *Mea culpa*.

Participatory Versus Hierarchical Action

In advocating action to produce change, Americans tended to favor a grass roots approach in which many individuals, of varying wealth and status, would participate. To the extent that Japanese officials and politicians favored action designed to produce sociocultural change of any kind, they tended to prefer the kind that let the government and the established power structure manage the action. This way, they doubtless felt, that very structure would more likely persist through time.

Principal [Civil Information] activities [for this month] centered on the case of Mr. [KW], a well known local businessman who failed to file an income tax return despite an obviously large income. CI backed up the team's Legal and Government Section with publicity on the progress of the [K] Case. [K's] agents attempted to lure some of the newspapers off the case with bribes. Military Government backed these newspapers up in their refusal to "do business" with [K]. It is felt that the giving of publicity to the [K] Case will help restore the confidence of small tax payers in their government. (June 1948).[31]

Civic Versus Governmental Action

Since at least the time of Jefferson, Americans have been suspicious of too much government. During his celebrated visit to the U.S. in the Nineteenth Century, DeToqueville was astounded to note the rich variety of American voluntary civic associations. This cultural tradition was readily evident in MG work; Americans, liberal and conservative alike, were far more inclined to look to civic associations to initiate or carry out change, while Japanese were more inclined to leave the initiation, and much of the execution, to governmental officials.

The principal barrier to desired development of organizations in this Ken is believed to be the officials concerned with women's activities. WMG continued to emphasize the need for separation of government and civil organizations; some of the greatest opposition to this came from the women's organizations themselves, which generally are unaccustomed to shifting for themselves. (Feb 1948).[32]

Equality Versus Special Privilege

Fundamental to the American political culture is the notion that all people have been created equal in their basic rights. On the Japanese side, the degree to which people subscribed to this value varied widely. In general, however, the then-extant polity and economy were far from emphasizing equality.

WMG encouraged the Teachers' Union to contact the Governor in an effort to receive an extra appropriation of approximately six million yen as soon as possible for the realization of the "Equal pay for equal work regardless of sex" principle. The principle already has been achieved, the Union says, in about ten of Japan's prefectures. Since the Governor is generally in opposition to equal treatment for women, some delay and trouble are expected (Feb 1948).

Gender Equality Versus Inequality

Many activist Occupationnaires--female and male--initiated action to promote gender equality. For example, in Wakayama, I stressed that women should have an equal opportunity to enter higher levels of training in the normal schools. In our attempts to incorporate this principle into serious policy, my Wakayaman colleagues and I found ourselves producing action of the type that, twenty years later, came to be called "affirmative" action in the U.S. Our efforts were, though, hardly free of problems.

The Governor of Wakayama is opposed to co-education, and has publicly said so. The Governor and "old line" interests throughout the prefecture are these days opposing, by all sorts of spurious arguments: co-education, new senior high schools, and equality of educational opportunity. Progressive citizens throughout the Ken have been encouraged by CIE to oppose these interests. (Feb 1948).

The entrance examination for the current school year at the Wakayama Economics College will give maximum permitted weight to intelligence testing and minimum permitted weight to scholastic achievement testing, in an effort to admit as many female candidates as possible. (Feb 1948).

Rote Versus Critical Approach to Learning

Japanese educators were wedded to pedagogical approaches that emphasized rote learning.[33] By the time of the Occupation, American educators had long since been emphasizing independent critical thinking and reasoning.

WMG has encouraged the teachers of one county to enter into an essay contest on the subject: "Workable Methods for Encouraging Spontaneous Participation, and Eliminating Memorized Answers in the Class-room." The winning essay or essays will be submitted to various education magazines for publication. (Feb. 1948).

Individual Happiness Versus Social Duty

In my perception, the "ultimate" cultural difference that separated Americans from Japanese was this one. The Americans in the Occupation were culturally committed to the fundamental importance of the "pursuit of happiness," principally on an individual basis, and to the Jeffersonian notion that the duty of government is to permit and foster such pursuit. To the American, duty was also important--but not, I would argue, more important.

My Japanese colleagues, by contrast, seemed to me to emphasize duty, and the precise, persistent, and consistent fulfillment of obligation, vastly more than individual happiness. Individual fulfillment, to them, was a goal to be realized through pursuing one's duty in the context of one's group--and of the higher groups to which one's group owed fealty. The task of government was to require and facilitate the carrying out of social duty.

LOOKING BACKWARD: GIVING TO JAPAN

Today, as I re-read the musty pages of my MG CIE reports of 43 years ago, I am reminded that in 1948 I was constantly asking myself whether this or that specific MG intervention was truly justified--especially changes of the type that, I suspected, the voters of Wakayama, if given the opportunity of a referendum, would not have supported. (I was quite sure at the time, for example, that Wakayamans would not have voted consistently to support the radical, "one fell swoop" re-structuring of their schools that in fact did occur in that year--and without incident.) Under what conditions, I would ask myself, should an Occupationnaire go ahead anyway, on the assumption simply that he or she was right--and that, in the future, the Japanese would come to agree, even if they did not agree now? Asking this question immediately places one on tricky moral ground, for rationalizations of this sort have, after all, been used by dictators and brutal rulers since time immemorial.

I countered my suspicions of excessive ego- or ethnocentrism by reminding myself that soon the Japanese would once again be in control of their own country--and then free, if they chose, to revert to older forms and practices.

I have no systematic data on the extent to which the reforms I helped to catalyze have endured or not. Thirty-five years after I left, however, I was assured by two Japanese educators with whom I had worked closely, that the structural reforms described above have indeed endured and sunk deep roots. I like to believe that this is because, at least to some extent, people have come to value the new institutions and practices, and are now prepared to defend them.[34]

LOOKING FORWARD: LEARNING FROM JAPAN

In approaching my closing, I cannot resist a brief commentary on the fact that in recent years thoughtful Americans have become at least as convinced that America must learn from Japan, as they were 45 years ago that Japan must learn from America. I emphatically include myself among them:

Forty-odd years ago Japan did indeed learn a lot from America, and much of what it learned was, I believe, useful. Today, surprising though it may seem to some, those very elementary and secondary schools that American Occupationnaires helped make democratic and modern, are turning out graduates whose mean achievement scores, especially in math and science, are seriously higher than the American. Today, those same schools are turning out workers who, in many instances, are appreciably more adaptable and efficient at manufacturing than American workers. And today, many Japanese industrial workers labor under conditions that are fairer than those of their American counterparts--a reversal of the situation 45 years ago when we in the Occupation fostered democratic unionism--and indeed a partial explanation for the Japanese industrial miracle.

And a miracle it is. I, for one, am frank to admit that if someone in Wakayama in 1948 had prophesied that within 40 years I would be driving a Japanese-manufactured automobile by choice, I would have doubted his mental stability. Yet today I do drive a Japanese car.

Japanese productive success in the automobile and many other industries has complex implications, and will force Americans to adjust to many new economic and political realities. Making this total adjustment, and making it quickly and adroitly, will certainly not be easy. But adjust we must.

Adjustment can be facilitated by understanding. In seeking understanding, I would argue that the principal reasons why the Japanese are scoring high in scholastic achievement, and in manufacturing, are rooted in Japanese culture. I would further argue that the freeing up of various proclivities that in 1945 were already deeply rooted in that culture, for which the American Occupation was in a primary sense responsible, contributed significantly to various processes of change which in turn help to explain Japan's excellence in many fields today.

Be that as it may, I regard the present widespread tendency among thoughtful Americans to try to learn from Japanese culture, as wise indeed. Any such efforts bring one quickly, of course, to the obvious conclusion that many elements of Japanese culture cannot be borrowed into American culture straightaway, because such borrowing would do damage to too many other aspects of our sociocultural system. Thus, to suggest but one of many possible examples, there is no way that several million American married women, even if they wanted to, could suddenly become stay-at-home *"Kyoiku mamas"* (education mothers)--because most of them have jobs that they cannot afford to give up. And so forth.

Nonetheless, even though direct cultural borrowing is not possible in a given instance, a thorough awareness of how the Japanese have been successful in some particular respect can often inspire creative thinking and innovation: if the American mother cannot perform the monitoring, stimulating, and nurturing role, then perhaps American society can find someone else who can. And so forth.

Today, then, it is literally true that America cannot afford not to learn from Japan. At the same time, it is also arguable that Japan still has much to learn from America. Above all, I consider it a matter of the highest priority that we search vigorously, affirmatively, and creatively for new avenues toward positive Japanese-American cooperation in an increasingly interdependent and borderless world.

THE BOTTOM LINE: SUCCESS IN JAPAN

I conclude as follows. The allied Occupation of Japan, which was really an American Occupation, was, in my view, the most ambitious Occupation the world has seen since the emergence of the nation-state. It was an Occupation that demonstrated that American leaders had learned several vital lessons from the post-World War I experience. Far from being an Occupation of revenge or reciprocated plunder, it was positive in intent and relatively benign and helpful in effect.

A word is here in order concerning my 1951 book about the Occupation, which was widely reviewed, often favorably. The *New York Times*, for example, selected the book for its list of "Outstanding Books of 1951." A Japanese language version was published by Bungei Shunju and immediately became a best-seller.

Forty years later, as I re-read my book, I see many things that I would change--which is hardly surprising, considering that the book was the first scholarly publication I had ever written.

First off, I would change the ill-chosen title: *Failure in Japan*, which is only somewhat redeemed by the sub-title, *With Keystones for a Positive Policy*.[35]

However, I am still glad I wrote that book. It said some things about the Occupation that I still believe needed to be said at that point in history. And Yes, it did criticize General MacArthur, who, I believed and still believe, needed to be criticized on some scores. And it did criticize U.S. foreign policy, which had reversed our policy of deconcentrating the *zaibatsu's* (moneyed clique's) economic holdings,[36] and vitiated other policies in ways that I still think were not appropriate.[37]

But now that a post-Occupation history has accumulated, now that a more tempered judgment can be rendered, let me speak as an anthropologist and say that, in an overall sense, I think the Occupation was--as Occupations go--anthropologically well conducted. Let me speak as a philosophical democrat and say that the Occupation was an epochal contribution to world democracy. And let me speak as a member of the human species and say that the Occupation was, on the whole, humane. Yes, the Occupation was a success!

Finally: however much I may have disagreed with him at the time, let me add my conviction that the record of General of the Army Douglas MacArthur as Supreme Commander for the Allied Occupied Powers serves well to remind us of the social truth that situations do from time to time arise in which a single individual can significantly influence history. General MacArthur showed far greater wisdom and effectiveness than most other American leaders, civilian or military, of the sort that might have been given his assignment, probably would or could have shown. He achieved clear and definite success in an unprecedented undertaking. He holds a high place in Japanese history, indeed, a unique one. He deserves that place.

And he deserves honor in our memory.

NOTES

1.   I wish to thank Dr. Anderson's widow, Mrs. Lucille Anderson, and Dr. David Kornhauser and Ms. Michiko Kornhauser for reviewing this article in manuscript form. Responsibility for all errors is, of course, mine.

2.   Since my visit in 1983, I am told, a Japanese group has begun efforts to restore the office to the way it looked when General MacArthur occupied it, and to preserve it as a memorial.

3.   Each month the Wakayama MG Team submitted a report of activities to higher headquarters. I was responsible for the Civil Information (CI) and Civil Education (CE) sections of each such report. I have obtained xerox copies of my reports from the U.S. National Archives for January through June, 1948. These reports were originally classified as "Restricted," but were declassified on April 12, 1974.

4.   I have no direct information as to how accurate General MacArthur's knowledge of local grass roots conditions was. If I had to guess, I would speculate that his grasp of such conditions was probably greater than I thought at the time, but still considerably less than I (or he) would have preferred.

5.   Perhaps equally important, for the first year or more Anderson and I, and for a while the late Warner I. ("Bud") Weil, were also in *de facto* in charge of MG CIE activities for Kyoto Prefecture. This gave us a direct window on the rapidly changing scene at the local level, ranging from that at the major universities in Kyoto city to that in isolated village schools in Oku-Tango.

6.   The establishment of Wakayama University out of an economics college and two normal colleges was a fascinating experience, but space does not permit its adequate treatment here.

7.   I should add that my primary anthropological specialty is Thailand, not Japan. I do not consider myself a Japan expert.

8.   My civil service rank was that of Clerical-Administrative-Fiscal (CAF) 9, with the simulated rank of first lieutenant or captain.

9.   These officers, many of whom spoke at least some Japanese and understood at least something about Japanese society and culture, included some highly qualified men. However, they constituted only a minority of the total officer personnel in MG, and most of them left Japan within a year or so.

10.   For example, one regular army colonel, with authority over many MG teams, made it clear in staff meetings that he would do all in his bureaucratic power to resist the granting of permission for any Caucasian MG man to marry any Japanese woman, because such a man would thereby be "lowering" himself. However, in the case of a *Nisei* (Japanese-American) MG man, he would not resist, because such a man would be marrying "above" himself. Racist biases of this general sort were by no means rare, though the harshness of this particular stance was not typical.

11.   And life could indeed be enjoyable. Virtually all Occupationnaires enjoyed a level of physical comfort and convenience far beyond their previous experience. There were Japanese servants to take care of all menial tasks. There were plenty of Japanese women available on one basis or another. There were ample black market opportunities for those who were interested--and many were. In some areas, there was extremely comfortable housing. For virtually all Occupationnaires, there were ample sports and recreational facilities, luxurious rest hotels, and the like. Usually, Occupationnaires had fairly ready access to post exchanges or PX trains, where they could buy all sorts of necessities and luxuries, from liquor to wrist watches to Japanese silks or cloisonne. These amenities and luxuries, as well as room and board, were usually available at low prices, and many Occupationnaires could manage to bank most of their monthly salary.

12.   At some point in the Occupation--just when I do not remember--MG CIE officers were officially authorized to go beyond "observing and reporting," to "guiding and assisting." In fact, many of us had already been doing just that, in response to situations that arose which required some kind of immediate constructive response.

13.   At that time the Shikoku and Chugoku MG regions were staffed by Americans for MG purposes, but the tactical occupying troops were those of the British Commonwealth Occupation Force.

14.   As soon as it became obvious that there would be no military or physical resistance to the Occupation by the Japanese, there was really no justification for such a complex table of organization for MG activities. A suitable number of tactical troops could have been maintained to insure domestic tranquility and serve whatever other tactical or strategic purposes were considered necessary, but there was no need for MG to be under the command of tactical units.

    Of the five levels, the Eighth Army and corps levels were obviously redundant, and often served simply to slow the process of communication between the team level and the SCAP policy level. MG affairs would have run much more efficiently and professionally if team had reported to region, and region directly to SCAP.

15.   On January 1, 1950, a change did occur. Military government, re-named "Civil Affairs," was restructured. The total number of personnel was reduced drastically, especially on the military side. Only two levels were retained: the regional teams and the MG Section at Eighth Army Headquarters. The prefectural teams were abolished, thereby depriving MG of true influence at the grass roots. But by this time it hardly mattered, since the Occupation had long since run out of reforming steam (Textor 1951: 192-3).

16.   With respect to the First Corps area, it was my impression that in general junior officers would demur more than senior, military more than civilian, and career military more than non-career military.

17.   During the middle and later months of 1946 Ronald Anderson and I frequently made interim policy in this manner, with respect to Kyoto Prefecture, and, more provisionally, with respect to the entire First Corps area.

18.   The CIC had its own structure, separate from MG, with branches down to prefectural level and below. At least at its lower levels, the CIC was, as far as I know, composed entirely of military personnel.

19.   It is difficult for me to understand why General MacArthur, a leader dedicated to fundamental human rights, kept an individual like Willoughby as a key staff officer for many years. Schaller (1989: 121) describes Willoughby thus:

A German-born immigrant with pretensions of noble birth, Willoughby brought a Prussian demeanor and extremely right-wing views to his intelligence post. MacArthur hit the mark when he once called his aide "my lovable fascist." Willoughby saw Communist and Jewish conspiracies at home, abroad, and especially in SCAP's ranks. His Counter Intelligence Corps (CIC) spied on Americans and cultivated former members of Japan's secret police and armed forces.

20. Lieutenant P was a well educated man. Many of the personnel assigned to isolated CIC posts, however, were not. Often they were the only American personnel in the city to which they were assigned. They operated in secrecy, a fact that gave them considerable *de facto* power, and ample opportunity to assume prerogatives well beyond those officially assigned to them.

21. After the Occupation, some Japanese officials who had cooperated actively with Occupation officials suffered setbacks in their careers. In other cases, however, such cooperation actually resulted in career advancement to a degree greater than probably would have occurred otherwise--though they may not have been particularly concerned about, or aware of, this possibility at the time that they offered their cooperation.

22. The official I found in charge of education when I arrived in Wakayama in November 1947 had previously been associated with ultranationalistic activities, even including the administration of "thought control." It was soon clear that there was utterly no way in which he could have been expected to promote democratic education policies. I made it clear to the appropriate officials that he and I could not work together, and before long he was transferred to other duties. I was, in this sense, responsible for his transfer. I was not, however, responsible for the selection of his successor. It was simply my good luck that his successor was so excellent.

23. For a description of a quintessential liberal Occupationnaire in action, see Chapter 3 of Williams (1979), on Charles L. Kades, of Government Section, SCAP, who played a key role in drafting the present constitution of Japan.

24. For a thorough examination of just how conservative General MacArthur had earlier been, see Schaller (1989).

It remains to explain just why a person so conservative on American domestic issues would turn out to be so liberal when placed in the role of Supreme Commander in Japan. Two reasons seem plausible.

First, MacArthur quickly discovered, if he had not earlier known, that leading conservatives in Japan tended, unlike most of their American counterparts, to be fundamentally anti-democratic. They were what I called, for lack of a better term, the "Old Guard" (Textor 1951: 15-20). MacArthur characterized them thus:

> Control was exercised by a feudalistic overlordship of a mere fraction of the population, while the remaining millions, with a few enlightened exceptions, were abject slaves to tradition, legend, mythology, and regimentation (MacArthur 1964: 310).

Second, MacArthur's liberal policies reflected the influence of liberals in the Roosevelt and Truman Administrations, during which considerable planning for the U.S.'s post-surrender Japan policy took place. This planning was embodied in two documents:

♦ "Initial Post-Surrender Policy for Japan," SWNCC [State-War-Navy Coordinating Committee] 150/4/A, signed by President Truman on September 6, 1945; and

168

♦	"Basic Directive for Post-Surrender Military Government in Japan Proper," JCS [Joint Chiefs of Staff] 1380/5, dated November 3, 1945.

Schaller contends that MacArthur knew the substance of both documents before he landed in Japan on August 30, 1945, and argues that credit for conceptualizing the Occupation's reforms should go primarily to such officials in Washington.

Interestingly, however, in his *Reminiscences*, MacArthur gives the credit to himself. He makes no mention of either Washington document. Instead, he contends:

> From the moment of my appointment as supreme commander, I had formulated the policies I intended to follow, implementing them through the Emperor and the machinery of the imperial government. I was thoroughly familiar with Japanese administration, its weaknesses and its strengths, and felt the reforms I contemplated were those which would bring Japan abreast of modern progressive thought and action. First destroy the military power. Punish war criminals. Build the structure of representative government. Modernize the constitution. Hold free elections. Enfranchise the women. Release the political prisoners. Liberate the farmers. Establish a free labor movement. Encourage a free economy. Abolish police oppression. Develop a free and responsible press. Liberalize education. Decentralize political power. Separate church from state (1964: 282-3).

Schaller disputes this. He contends that the two directives from Washington "outlined virtually the entire reform agenda..." Schaller contends, therefore, that MacArthur took personal credit for conceptualizing reforms that in fact were conceptualized by planners in Washington (Schaller 1989: 123).

I find Schaller's argument convincing. In judging General MacArthur on this apparently excessive claim, however, I think one should bear in mind two points:

♦	He was a very old man when he wrote his book, and died shortly after finishing his manuscript.

♦	Regardless of who conceptualized these reforms (and allowing for the possibility of a considerable amount of independent conceptualization) it was MacArthur whose leadership succeeded in implementing them. This, alone, was an achievement of major historical significance.

25.	Informally, the standard developed that the civilian officers should be expected to do the really hard work of MG, since civilian salaries were higher. There was some resentment over these salary differentials.

26.	My analysis will be somewhat confounded by the fact that it was not just two cultures that confronted each other, but also two situations, that of prosperous victorious nation and that of prostrate defeated nation. Consequently, there is, in this section, always the danger that I will attribute to cultural factors phenomena that can better be explained by invoking situational phenomena. On the other hand, it is sometimes true that in situations of extreme stress, the fundamental values of a culture become more evident than would otherwise be the case. Suffice to say here that I am aware of these problems and have tried to deal with them in the presentation.

27.	The word "often" is important. The differences in cultural stance here outlined represent what I consider to be statistical tendencies only. The listing of these issues in this rough form is intended to indicate general types of situation in which American Occupationnaires tended to take one broad stance, and Japanese officials and leaders tended to take a different, and more or less opposing, stance. Usually there would be exceptions to these tendencies, and these exceptions sometimes provided useful common ground for negotiation. One of the key tasks of the change-oriented C.I.E. officer was to find and utilize these areas of common ground.

28.   In the MG subculture, it was always prudent, especially for a civilian liberal activist officer such as myself, to bend over backwards to make clear to one's superiors that the Japanese with whom one was dealing were not "radical" (in the sense of being Communist or pro-Communist). Otherwise, one risked incurring the suspicion of one's military superiors, and losing their support.

29.   Furthermore, the American knew that his or her future career would not be disadvantaged by changes in the Japanese situation, while the Japanese official was keenly aware that he, his group, and his family would have to live with such changes for the indefinite future -- perhaps at a significant disadvantage. This factor was, then, more a situational than a cultural one.

30.   Riesman (1950), writing of American characterological types, classified many Americans prior to about World War II as "inner-directed." The implication here was that the American searches his or her soul, and then decides quite autonomously what to do. Clearly, Americans working in Japan in 1946-48 varied as to the extent to their inner-directedness, but I would judge that most civilian liberals were inclined to be inner-directed, and would so categorize myself. I and other civilian liberal activist MG officers sometimes resented the military officers who were our bosses, because they tended more to be, again in Riesman's terms, "other-directed"--the "others" being, of course, other (and higher ranking) Americans--and certainly not Japanese. Riesman broadly classified the Japanese as "tradition-directed" (p. 10).

31.   "K," by the way, owned a commodious home in Wakayama City which the local CIC had procured to serve as their residence and office. The chief CIC officer for Wakayama Prefecture once casually informed me that he relied heavily on K for intelligence information--so much so that he was considering inviting K to move in with the CIC contingent in K's old home, so as to facilitate closer "cooperation."

32.   Of course it was true in 1946-48 that due to the dislocation of infrastructure, and the widespread economic hardship, it was often only the government that had the economic or physical resources to carry out a change. My point is, though, that even where such constraints did not exist, this Japanese cultural proclivity was still in evidence. A women's organization, for example, might see nothing particularly strange about receiving advice from a government official or non-governmental "advisor" -- typically an elderly, culturally conservative male.

33.   In part, this tradition clearly stems from the simple facts that the Japanese writing system is a character system, and that fully one-third of an elementary school student's time is devoted to memorizing, using, and appreciating characters.

34.   Wray (1991: 473) looking at the history of Japanese education over the forty years since the Occupation, concludes as follows with respect to the nation as a whole: "The introduction of the 6-3-3-4 educational ladder system achieved...equal educational opportunity and the vested interests of teachers and administrators who bettered their social position has prevented any retreat from the 6-3-3-4 system. [Note that Wray is here explaining permanence by referring to vested interests, rather than to ideological commitment.]   Coeducation was strongly resisted by the *Monbusho* [Ministry of Education], but it is complete at the elementary level and generally characteristic of urban public junior and senior high schools."
    With respect to the comprehensive school, Wray notes: "Before the reforms had a chance to work, the Occupation ended. The Americans really never achieved the

essence of the 6-3-3-4 system, the comprehensive curriculum, or many other changes because there were not enough teachers, appropriate educational materials and funds, or enough time to ensure adequate follow-through."

35.   Other problems with the book, viewed in retrospect, include the following:

♦   The book demanded too much, and was too rigid in its standards.

♦   Although the Japanese "Old Guard" were hardly a savory group by the standards most Americans would use, the book treated them as considerably more diabolical than they subsequently proved to be.

♦   The decision to de-emphasize reform and increasingly emphasize the building up of Japan as a Cold War strategic resource came primarily from Washington. The book did not give MacArthur credit for resisting some of these decisions, simply because at that time I did not have access to adequate information that would have enabled me to do so.

♦   Perhaps most important, the book was delayed in publication, due in part to the fact that I was at the time a full-time graduate student. By the time it came out, many of its policy recommendations were out of date.

36.   I have not researched this point, but I suspect that it could be argued with some cogency that the current difficulties some American firms are experiencing in competing with Japanese industry are traceable to the failure of the Occupation to carry through most of its originally announced *zaibatsu* deconcentration policy.
    Incidentally, in General MacArthur's *Reminiscences*, he does not mention the fact that the Occupation's original program for *zaibatsu* deconcentration was drastically reduced, in fact almost totally scuttled (Textor 1951: 50-60 and Appendix Two). He simply states that "these great trusts were partially dissolved and a truly competitive free enterprise system inaugurated....The main thing was that their influence was broken."

37.   I think it can be argued that some aspects of U.S. political policy toward occupied Japan contributed to a situation in which, ever since the end of the Occupation, the nation has essentially been ruled by just one political party. I do not consider this to be a healthy political condition. In my view, Japan will be more convincing as a democracy when it experiences a peaceful, responsible turnover of its ruling party at the national level.

BIBLIOGRAPHY

MacArthur, Douglas. *Reminiscences*. New York: McGraw-Hill, 1964.

Riesman, David.   *The Lonely Crowd: A Study of Changing American Character*. New Haven: Yale University Press. 1950.

Schaller, Michael.   *Douglas MacArthur: The Far Eastern General*. New York: Oxford University Press, 1989.

U.S. Education Mission to Japan.   *Report of the United States Education Mission to Japan*. Tokyo. Submitted to Supreme Commander for the Allied Powers, 1946.

Textor, Robert B.   *Failure in Japan: With Keystones for a Positive Policy*. New York: John Day. Japanese version published as *Nippon ni Okeru Shippai*, in four editions, by Bungei Shunju, Tokyo, 1952, and included on Yomiuri Best Seller List. English version reprinted by Greenwood Press, Westport CT, 1972.

Williams, Justin, Sr. *Japan's Political Revolution under MacArthur: A Participant's Account.* Athens: University of Georgia Press, 1979.

Wray, Harry. "Change and Continuity in Modern Japanese Educational History: Allied Occupational Reforms Forty Years Later," *Comparative Educational Review,* Vol. 35, No. 3, pp. 447-475. Note: I here use this informative article as an authoritative general summary of the fate, positive or negative, of various Occupation efforts at educational reform. Wray bases his assessments on a wide range of professional literature in both Japanese and English. I find his long "Conclusions" section convincing and valuable, in particular because he relates the relative persistence of various Occupation-sponsored reforms to Japanese culture, institutions, and history, 1991.

GENERAL DISCUSSION

Paul Carlson. I enjoyed your paper, Dr. Textor. I am a history teacher out in the Chicago suburbs. You mentioned that General Willoughby's policy--and I believe you were 22 at the time--that he wanted to have you followed there. I wondered if you perhaps had considered the fact that a thorough check had been done on your past and that some of the professors that perhaps you had at Antioch or some place else may have been listed and, therefore, since you were a student at one time may have picked up some things which the General felt, wisely perhaps, would be reflected in reports that you would give. As a member of the next generation of students, I frankly applaud General Willoughby for that type of feeling and feel that that whole period between 1946 and 1956 will eventually prove to be justified in what some of these so-called "right wing anti-communists" have done.

Robert Textor. Well, there's no rule governing this meeting that two people can't disagree. I have always been a liberal. I'm very proud to be a liberal; I've never been a person to favor any totalitarian system. To me, my basic political credo is to preserve freedom and fairness. In the context of the 1940s, that orientation was normally referred to as liberal. There is a section on General Willoughby in my book, *Failure in Japan*. Mr. Carlson, you don't mention whether you've read that section or not, but it does suggest that too much effort, valuable effort, scarce linguistic talent and the like, by my values at least, was dedicated to snooping on other Americans. This is not to say that there was no threat from communism from Russia or from China in that day. I'm not here to suggest that. The general level of training and sophistication among the CIC officers that I happened to know--that's a small haphazard sample--was not particularly high, in my judgment, when it came to issues like this. I do suggest, though, that we probably have an area here where you and I could talk for a couple of hours and we would not agree. And that, of course, is our right as Americans. That's, I think, the best short answer I can give.

Theodore McNelly. I'm with the University of Maryland. I was wondering about whether Professor Textor felt that the thrust of his book when he wrote it, *Failure in Japan*, was quite similar to the thrust of the comments of Professor Goodman?

Robert Textor. Yes, I had not read Grant's paper and I was thrilled to hear it. He says a lot of things better than I could which I do agree with. I do feel, as I felt when I wrote the book in 1951, that the Occupation did not go deeply enough in the general direction of discouraging what I call "old guard" political forces and did not go deeply enough in the deconcentration of the Zaibatsu. Now, clearly, we have here a question of judgment. We have a question of optima rather than maxima. But the record, I think, Van Staaveren has actually done an unpublished monograph on this subject. The record of deconcentration that was actually achieved is far, far more modest--almost trifling--as compared with the original goal. And that, again, is described in the 1951 book and one of the appendices of that book actually lists the companies that were supposed to be deconcentrated and never were.

Jacob Van Staaveren. Well, Bob and I have talked about the deconcentration of economic power and how he felt it hadn't gone far enough. I do understand his position very well on that. With regard to removing the "old guard"--as I recall about 400,000 Japanese were purged. Is it your belief that this purge should have--we should have had a third major purge? There were two major purges under MacArthur and-- 400,000 is quite a number and keep in mind that when the first election was held right after the war, April 1946, 306 members of the new Japanese Diet were members for the first time. There had been a tremendous housecleaning. Even by April 1946. So is it--as you saw it from Wakayama--should the purge have gone far deeper than it had? Or been more selective?

Robert Textor. Whether the purge went far enough or not, I can't offer any informed opinion about now that 45 years have passed and that many of the specific legal and procedural details are hazy in my memory. I do feel that I would have been happier to have left Japan with a greater assurance that new and fundamentally more modern and more democratic leadership would take over. Let me illustrate this way, looking more at results than at means. In 1963, I believe it was, I was at Harvard University and one day Ambassador Reischauer suddenly returned to Cambridge and a meeting was hurriedly called and we had him for about an hour, off the record, on what was going on in Japan. I asked him--I said, "Sir, it has now been 12 years since the Occupation has concluded and the Democratic Liberals [Liberal Democratic Party] have been uninterruptedly in power. I, for one, would feel better about the solidity of the democratization of Japan if you could reassure me that within the next few years there will be a peaceful transfer of power to some other party. I would just feel more assured that democracy had been institutionalized, that psychological democracy had set it as well as institutional, if you could assure me of that." He said, "I can assure you of that. It's going to happen in a couple of years in all probability." Well, that was 1963--it's now 1991. Something to think about. [The Liberal Democratic Party has been in power continuously since 1955.]

Grant Goodman. Just to reassure the audience, I had never seen Professor Textor's paper before and I don't think the two papers really do cover quite the same thing or take quite the same view, because I was not in the grassroots in a prefecture, but rather in Tokyo. Also, I tried to speak from the viewpoint of the first year of the Occupation; I stressed that. Whereas, I noticed that Bob's references were to 1948 and so much had happened between 1945/1946 and 1948 which changed the situation and thus we can't speak comparably. But 1945 and 1946 were so crucial and remarkable in my experience and, also, I think it's very hard at this late juncture, when this is the last conference we can have because we're all so doddering, that to recapture the--I don't know how to say it really--the incredible optimism that we younger people had about our potential role of the United States in literally reshaping Japan and the Japanese. It was--I didn't use the word in my paper purposely, I suppose (it's a bit strong, but maybe in informal conversation I can say)--there was an incredible naivete about it in retrospect. But that naivete, of course, is part of the enthusiasm and the utter--the naivete of imagining that we Americans from this part of the world could somehow create a little America in Japan. That was really what I was trying to suggest--that was the ultimate--if only they could be more like us--you know that song from the Rex Harrison musical "Why Can't a Woman Be More Like a Man?"--I mean why can't the Japanese be like us? I think in many cases, we haven't given up on that. There are some of us dopes who still feel that way because we started out in that context and if we can throw our--cast our collective psyches back into that milieu, then I think you can get some understanding of the kind of really evangelism--that's the only kind of word I can think of in a secular sense--that we felt at that time. So, my good friend, Mr. Miura was kind enough today to interview me for some poor Japanese readers somewhere who won't understand a word of this--ultimately not because he won't write it brilliantly, but because the psychological context will simply be lacking for the readers of today. But there is that kind of mindset that we had then that hoped for so much--was so optimistic--and to which the Japanese at the grassroots were really responding. And we saw them not only as future little Americans--and by little I don't mean to minimize them, but, they were in those days tiny--I was only 5'6" and I looked down on Japanese. Today when I go to Japan, I have to look up all the time because there have been such radical transformations of their physical beings in the last four decades. But that hope was--and seemed to us to be saying, "We want to be little Americans." And that was that remarkable concatenation for that brief moment in time which made us so hopeful.

W. Soren Egekvist. I understand your concern about the LDP being in control that many years in Japan. What do we do about the Democratic party in our Congress? How do we get them out? (Laughter and applause)

Craig Cameron. That perhaps is a good note to leave on, too. It's now half past and I think we would like to try to get the panel discussion under way on time at quarter of four. I would like to thank our panelists once again for two very nice papers.

PANEL DISCUSSION

(Second Day)

Moderator: **Grant K. Goodman**
                  University of Kansas

Panelists: **Allen H. Meyer**
                  Chicago, Illinois

                  William F. Nimmo
                  Old Dominion University

                  Robert C. Christopher
                  Columbia University

                  Edwin L. Neville, Jr.
                  Canisius College

                  Robert B. Textor
                  Stanford University

Grant Goodman. This is the time when one of the panelists becomes a chairperson. And some of the panelists from this morning and this afternoon gather together for what, in the program, is called a panel discussion. We would like to begin with some comments from some of you who have not had a chance to speak earlier on any of the panels of the day or any of the previous speakers. I know Dr. Helen Seamans has something she would like to say and I would like to begin with her if you will permit her to make her comments.

Helen Hosp Seamans. I want to express my gratitude to Grant Goodman for having mentioned "The Mikado"--it gives me a chance to come back to my subject of fraternization. You remember how I felt about it. I said it's more than sex; it's socialization and the production of "The Mikado" was an example of my socialization-- it meant that the Occupationnaires and the Japanese could go to the theater together to see "The Mikado." I had just a very brief moment with Grant Goodman in between these moments here--I wondered what production he saw of "The Mikado" because he said in the audience there were a few Japanese and I thought there were many. How can he say that? So, I learned that he saw the production in 1946; I saw it in 1948. You see how things change? Through the socialization, the Americans, or the Occupationnaires and the Japanese socialized by going to the theater together. I just loved that production of "The Mikado" and I have to say that, again, we had a little point of difference--because I said to him in that private moment, "The Japanese took some liberties with The Mikado." He said, "No, it was the Occupation production. They did not." Well, I have to explain that I know "The Mikado" very well. You won't believe it from my voice now, but I once was a singer and I sang in "The Mikado" on Broadway in New York, so I know "The Mikado." I know, therefore, the wonderful little changes that the Japanese who produced "The Mikado" made. They made spoofs of some of the very prominent Occupation military high ranking officers and it was delicious. My point is that the Occupationnaires and the Japanese could laugh together and I think that that laughter, that socialization, is very very important to account for the success of the Occupation. This humanization--I'm all for rules and laws and regulations--I wasn't a Dean of Women for many years for nothing--in my days, when I was a Dean of Women, rules were rules. So, I've got that side, too. But I know the importance of laughter and sharing social occasions and I want to say that socialization in the Occupation was one of the most important aspects leading to what, I think we all agree, the success of the Occupation democratization. Thank you.

Grant Goodman. If I may be permitted a footnote to this footnote. I mentioned to Dr. Seamans that "The Mikado" has never been produced in Japan since the Occupation.

Frank Sackton. The whole session has been of enormous interest to me because it is one of the things that I did lack in information when I was in Tokyo for three years and that is, what was going on at the grassroots? There were several reasons for that. Number 1: I was in the Dai-Ichi building about 15 hours a day, seven days a week. This wasn't unusual. I had to do it to stay up with the Old Man. So, the view of the grassroots has been of particular interest to me. One of the things I've learned is that apparently at the grassroots there was an interest in going further faster than the country was moving or we were able to move the country from GHQ. I've been thinking about--well, where is the disconnect? What were the limiting factors? And I would like to mention a few limiting factors that might explain this differential. One, at GHQ I remember General MacArthur saying several times to his staff, "We have only five years." General MacArthur gave himself a five year limitation and he said, "We have to move quickly and we want to move on the right things." So, there was a time limitation--what would you concentrate on? Actually, as you know, it took seven years.

The target was five years from the General's point of view. Now, a big limitation goes back to the Potsdam Declaration and subsequent directives which gave General MacArthur the option of imposing direct military government on the people or to govern the people through the Japanese mechanisms. The General decided he would do it the latter way. Now, had we imposed military government directly and taken over the courts, taken over the currency, taken over everything--then I think there probably could have been a greater responsiveness to the grassroots rather than through the very inflexible machinery of the Japanese government to get things done. I want to give you a few examples. Let's take the constitution. The people were ready for reform, were ready for liberty, were ready for freedom and the independence that the constitution finally gave them. But let me tell you, it was a tough go getting it through. In the first place, the Japanese cabinet wouldn't hear of it. It was so foreign to them from the Meiji constitution under which they were operating and it wasn't possible to get it through. General MacArthur tried a group of scholars--he brought scholars from all over Japan to work on the constitution. They couldn't get anything done. Finally, General MacArthur, in effect, through his staff wrote it himself. I don't know if you are familiar with the fact that Col. Kades in General Whitney's office actually put that thing together. General MacArthur tooled on it a little bit. Still he couldn't get it through and finally appealed to the Emperor who thought it was the right thing to do. That's typical of the terrible obstacles in Tokyo--getting things done--which apparently could have been done more quickly had the grassroots been able to do it, you know, at that level. It was impossible under the form of government that we were exercising.

Now, let me tell you a little bit about a difficulty with land reform. Ninety-eight percent of the land was owned by 2% of the population and the General thought "this is wrong--we must give the land to the peasants who till the soil." Which is exactly what happened--but it wasn't easy. Moving this thing through the cabinet--moving it through the Department of Agriculture--moving it through the Department of the Treasury to get the money to pay the landlords. The General had the authority to confiscate the land and give it to the peasants. He didn't want to do that. He didn't want to punish the landlords, so he had to figure a way of financing it through the Department of the Treasury and the Department of Agriculture. It took months and months and months and finally the peasants got what they would have wanted the first day if they could have had it, you see. But there were these obstacles always--I could go into the same thing on education reform, labor reform--it was a tough fight from the beginning to the end. But finally they were pushed through. In retrospect, I think the General did it the right way. He did it in what we called today participative management rather than control of a dictator. He could have been a dictator, but he elected not to. And by not being a dictator, he had a much, much tougher job. The fact that it turned out so well is a great tribute that everybody put their shoulder to the wheel to make it work. You do things much more quickly if you are a dictator. You do them quick and fast and you can respond to the people, but in the end General MacArthur thought that was not the way to do it and he did not. Thank you.

Rinjiro Sodei. With due respect to General Sackton, I have to really disagree with you about this land reform. It's been known that there had been a plan for land reform by the Japanese bureaucrats during the wartime already and I think that the land reform is one of the very few examples that the Japanese side initiated. Plus the fact that there was a very strong agrarian movement since 1910 for seeking the ownership of the land. These two forces merged and, you know, at least it became a kind of force to bring about this land reform. Of course it took democratic and strong leadership on this reform. The point I am trying to make is that there was grass roots support for this land reform.

Grant Goodman. While you have the microphone, Professor Sodei, would you like to comment on any of the papers or any of the other things that have come up today?

Rinjiro Sodei. Oh, I have been overwhelmed by your paper and Bob Textor's and some other gentlemen's papers and throughout yesterday, I was kind of afraid that the train might be going to Philadelphia after all, but it looks like we have arrived at Norfolk today safely. Thank you.

Grant Goodman. Thank you very much. One of the things that's evoked by General Sackton's comments is that something is obviously lacking from this symposium--the comparative aspect between the German and the Japanese Occupations. This is evoked by the direct/indirect and why one was direct and the other was indirect, and so on. And, of course, in the Japanese, I think by this time to date, it's quite obvious to many of us that the United States simply didn't have the personnel to administer a direct Occupation to Japan. Even had it been determined, and it might have been at some point, that that would be a good idea, we didn't have the Japan expertise or the Japan competence. Whereas, in the German case, of course, we felt we did and could, therefore, initiate a direct Occupation. So, there was some rather realistic logistical factors at work in the determination to have an indirect Occupation and to utilize the Japanese government. There was also throughout the planning for the Occupation of Japan, as I recall, a very strong group in the State Department in particular, and in the State, War, Navy Coordinating Committee (SWNCC) that somehow believed that the Japanese government wasn't really a bad government. There were some bad folks, but that the government was viable and could be used and certainly Ambassador Grew and others like that continued to have a certain level of confidence, if that's the right term, in the existing Japanese hierarchy with the exception of the militarists who were identified as the bad guys. If those people could be eliminated, then the Japanese government could, in their view, operate. In contrast, I think, there was complete agreement in the government that the Nazi regime was not a viable regime with which to work. And that contrast, also, I believe, has some significance in the direct vs. indirect Occupation decision.

Peter Bates. There is another part that occurs to me in your comparison of the German Occupation to the Japanese Occupation and that, of course, is that Germany was divided between four occupying powers. I think that the United States' intention to keep the Occupation of Japan as a unitary Occupation, denying the British and others any part in the military government as it happens, I think it was a wise decision--in comparison to what happened in Germany.

Grant Goodman. Well, of course, that's right. But, still, even so, the Americans theoretically, as sole authority which they assumed quite as you describe it, could theoretically have disestablished the existing regime and made a direct Occupation. In fact, it would have been easier for them to do it because, as it proved, they didn't have to clear with all of these other parties. In fact, they were rather cavalier as I'm sure you know at first hand, toward the other participating powers in the Occupation. I attended a conference--I forget how many years ago--on the British and British Commonwealth role in the Occupation of Japan and it was a cry in the wilderness--so to speak--because even these many years later, the Australian, New Zealand, Indian, BCOF, etc. people are saying, "We really were given no responsibility. We really had little or nothing to do and we had little or no authority." There was, I think, an interesting exception which was in ATIS where in fact we had allied language personnel with whom we worked on a completely equal basis and I, myself, had a series of three different Australian officers who were in charge of me. Each of them was an extremely interesting individual--very competent and had very fascinating personal backgrounds. I was "wowed" by each of them in turn being a very wet-behind-the-ears boy from Ohio, and seeing the sophistication and international experience which these gentlemen had had in the prewar years and the way in which each of them respectively had come to the Japanese language competence which they had. They were very much in authority and in that sense the ATIS really was an Allied translator/interpreter section.

Helen Hosp Seamans. I just want to say that I was also in Germany during after the war and I want to say that I think an Occupation as we had in Japan would not have worked in Germany because the attitude was so totally different. The Germans had the attitude that you had nothing to teach us. Whereas in Japan, they were so receptive to what you had to say. You had to be careful what you said, because they took it at face value as being of great importance. They thought--you won the war, therefore you have a blueprint for everything. But the Germans did not have that feeling. They felt they were on an equal level, educationally and so on. It was a totally different situation and I think the Occupation in Germany would not have had the success, not had the chance that it had in Japan. I won't ask again.

William Nimmo. Let me just say one word on that. I think a key word here, a key phrase that you use, Grant, was existing government in Japan. There was an existing government in Japan because Japan did, in the final analysis, surrender before it was invaded. In Germany there wasn't much of anything existing. Germany was simply militarily conquered by the Western Allies, Britain and United States, from the West and the Soviet Army from the East and simply overran the whole place without much of any existing machinery left--at least at the time of surrender, I think.

Allen Meyer. The indication that this was not an Allied operation--there's no question but that SCAP ran it. I think I referred to all that at one point the Far Eastern Council--we were so far removed at the grassroots from that activity that it was all alien to us. But, Grant may remember that in the early days of ATIS, at least in early 1946, we were Allied translators/interpreters to the extent of having a couple of Russian translators and interpreters there. There were two of them as well as British people to whom I referred to Mr. Bates. They were there--when the Cold War began to accelerate, they were no longer there. But they were there for a few months while I was there. What they were doing exactly--I know one of them was doing translations. He knew some English. The other knew no English--the only way to converse with him was in Japanese.

Grant Goodman. I didn't know that, Al, but your last remark reminds me of the situation in a number of international academic meetings currently that the Soviets-Soviet Japanologists are excellent in Japanese in many cases and that's the common language that we use now in much of our academic interaction with Soviet scholars.

John Arthur. I served in the Headquarters in Tokyo in the Civil Intelligence section and later in the military intelligence under Willoughby. I would like to point out that the Allied Translator and Interpreter Service began in Australia and it was a major base in Australia for the correlation of all the information which was flowing from the various islands where a number of intelligence outposts had been established primarily by the Australians. That particular activity came up in the campaigns and was in the Philippines preparing for the invasion of Japan. The activity was really international in scope because it also included members from the Netherlands East Indies who were Dutch, a number of very excellent translators--women. It also included Australians, as you indicated, and other individuals whose background was rather mixed. We would call it hyphenated backgrounds. When the activity arrived in Tokyo, it became homogenized generally along the line of the U.S. services because our training had been, in our various military schools, directed to activities in Japan.

Grant Goodman. Well, I just might add to what Col. Arthur says that the Australians, the New Zealanders and the UK military all had Japanese language schools at the same time that some of us were going to American Japanese language schools and the generation of post-war Japan specialists in England, Australia and New Zealand, just as in the United States, has largely been made up of graduates of those schools who have continued professionally in the field of Japanese studies subsequently. I think many of you know names like Ronald Dore and Bill Beasley, Pat O'Neil, and others who are all products of the wartime Japanese language schools in the British Commonwealth.

Crawford Millen. I'll try to put this together. I was trying to get it written down so I wouldn't ramble on--it may be a little confusing. But, as a youngster growing up at the time, my dad was British--a naturalized American citizen--so we were very sensitive to what was going on in Europe at the time and most of the people around us, I think, were too--even as a child. And it seemed to me that the people saw Nazism unfold--we listened to the news regularly, etc. In the people's mind, I believe and I am generalizing--I didn't run any studies on this--it was an evil ideology unfolding in Germany. Hitler was seen as a devil incarnate type thing--his ranting and raving--the whole thing. Just the very antithesis of democracy. And we viewed this and then when the Holocaust occurred and became apparent to us, it just terribly reinforced this conception of Germany. Now, on the other hand, we looked at the Japanese

179

situation--the attack on Pearl Harbor, the Death March and all of this--we tended to view this as a cruel action. But there wasn't this identification of Japan as an evil ideological structure that I think we felt in relation to the Germans. And, consequently, when the Occupation occurred, perhaps, the American people were much more sympathetic to the idea of an Occupation being run through the Japanese people who were not seen as evil in the same sense that Germany was seen. Germany being seen as this evil structure, this demonic structure, was certainly something that necessitated a direct government, whereas Japan didn't.

Grant Goodman. Sounds like one of my lines from one of my lectures to my students. Somebody must have had an "evilometer" and read--seen how other people registered on the "evilometer." (Laughter)... and made decisions accordingly, if that were the case. To some extent I think it would be interesting to pursue this, in another conference, in terms of these comparative concepts. It is always useful for people who are deeply involved in a particular concern such as the people here in the Occupation of Japan--to get together with people who are equally deeply involved in another area of the world with some comparability such as the Occupation of Germany. So maybe we can encourage that there will be another conference. This might not be the last. And there might be a new generation of scholars who could evoke some exciting new ideas comparing the Occupations of Japan and Germany. This has been done already in scholarly conferences but not for some time it seems to me and certainly is a possible topic for future research and study.

Betty Lanham. I do think that there was a lot of hostility toward Japan. You know, this moderation of hostility in the comparison toward Germany--I don't think is accurate, because at that time, I didn't personally have that hostility. I would get disturbed when I would go into the post office and see pictures of Japanese with pointed teeth to make them look like animals. But it was amazing--that it was about a week or a month's time [after the war's end]--and I think this was General MacArthur again because the high prestige which he held--radically changed overnight in the reaction toward Japan. So, I don't see it as a difference in the reaction to the Nazism and the reaction to Japan. I think it was hostile in both camps--or in both directions. There was some mechanism afoot in the United States whereby it was changed. In retrospect, of course, the German situation was worse because of the Holocaust, but not that... And I want to add something to what was said here just a moment ago--because, I think as Ms. Seamans was saying--because this was what I was trying to get at just a moment ago--is that one of the reasons we were successful in Japan is because of the receptivity of the Japanese. That's what we have got to investigate and know thoroughly in order to appreciate and that's the other side of the story. Because, for instance, and it's hard to go back to that period now, but I can remember this sort of thing. It's strange. Americans, for instance, were sure, positive that the Japanese really didn't feel apologetic toward the world--because this is what Americans, you know, Americans resist this sort of thing. And the Japanese didn't--it is appropriate and proper. Also, it is appropriate and proper [in Japan], if you are defeated, you accept that and you do what the person over you says. And remember something else, when the Americans went in, they said to the Japanese, "We are not conquerors. We are helping you move toward democracy. We are your big brother." Now, Americans frequently didn't think that, but said, "let's go to work and get with it." And the Japanese accepted that and they expected it and every once in a while when the Americans would do something that didn't indicate that we were big brothers, they would say, "Now, wait a minute, what's going on here?" and they'd back off. It was that kind of attitude that was established that, I think, was part of the reason for our success--in addition to some other psychological ramifications that I was referring to earlier.

Grant Goodman. Thank you very much. With regard to what Betty is saying. You might want to, those of you who haven't read it--read John Dower's book, *War Without Mercy*. I think that'll help you with a lot of the questions that have just come up.

Cornelius Iida. If I may, I would just like to offer a comment. I'm teaching in the southern part of Japan, Yamaguchi. I'm beginning to look at the Meiji restoration--one of the factors that led to the Meiji Restoration is Wan Shinsaku Takasugi's trip to Shanghai shortly after the Opium War. There was a bridge in Shanghai in which the natives had to pay the toll to pass it, to cross over it and the conquerors, of course, the victors, the free traders like they were, the Japanese later, the British then, the free-traders who brought in opium freely to that land had the free passage over the bridge and that alerted Shinsaku Takasugi to no end. This led to the toppling of the one party system then known as the Shogunate. In the perspective of these some 140 years of history there was this threat from the British, from the Dutch, from the Americans, to an extent, and even from the Germans for that matter, towards Japan and the Japanese had the bloodless coup d'etat [1868] in which the ruling government was toppled, but Japan learned too well from the British examples. It went overseas--it went to China. Any of these acts of aggression--colonizing, to my mind, is evil. So when you register on the "evilometer"--or whatever--I would like you to take into consideration not just the past 50 or 60 years, but also 140 years. Thank you very much.

William Nimmo. I have a comment to make concerning the legacy of the Occupation in connection with something going on in Japan right now. A new prime minister, Kiichi Miyazawa, just elected within the last week or ten days or so and an article in *The New York Times* of October 28 [1991] regarding that. These are friends of Prime Minister Miyazawa speaking of him and saying "others note that he has never shaken the bad memories of American behavior after the war, when as a junior aide in the finance ministry he had to listen to imperious lectures from MacArthur and other Occupation leaders." In his recently published memoirs, Mr. Miyazawa wrote that "It may be hard for young people today to understand how unpleasant it was to live under the Occupation." So, that is something from a totally different perspective than we have been seeing. Miyazawa was only about 28 years or so at that time and I don't know if he would have been hearing lectures from General MacArthur personally. General MacArthur spent most of the time on the fifth floor of the Daiichi Building.

W. Soren Egekvist. I want to comment on Miyazawa-san. He was a classmate of mine when I was in Japan before the war and during the Occupation he was very active at helping. He brought his father who was a member of the Diet from Hiroshima, I believe, he came in to see me on the food problems. He was very pro-American, very excellent English speaker and I think he will be a good prime Minister.

REFLECTIONS ON THE OCCUPATION'S GRASSROOTS AND THE EIGHT SYMPOSIA

Thomas W. Burkman

THOMAS W. BURKMAN is Associate Professor of History at Hamilton College, Clinton, New York. Previous positions have been on the faculties of State University of New York-Buffalo, and Old Dominion University, Norfolk, Virginia, where he was founder and director of the Institute of Asian Studies from 1987-90. He also has taught at Colby College, Waterville, Maine, and at Kwansei Gakuin University in Japan. Thomas Burkman was editor of three previous proceedings of MacArthur symposia: *Education and Social Reform*, *The International Context*, and *Arts and Culture*. He is a graduate of Asbury College and received the Ph.D., in Japanese history from the University of Michigan in 1975.

The "grassroots" is a fitting theme for the culmination of this series of eight symposia on the Allied Occupation of Japan. The entire enterprise of biennial, international conferences since 1976 has been a grassroots phenomenon in itself. Norfolk, Virginia is neither Washington nor Tokyo; the MacArthur Memorial and Old Dominion University, the co-sponsors of the meetings, are neither Harvard nor Tokyo University. In all of the symposia, pedigree was never posited as a measure for the significance of memories recalled or opinions expressed. Yet, over the years of the symposia, grassroots voices have called repeatedly for purposeful attention to the implementation level of the Occupation activity. To Occupation scholars, this summons made a great deal of sense. We have gathered here to investigate the grassroots echelons of the Occupation.

As we have listened to grassroots Occupationnaires the last two days, I must say that I am deeply impressed with the apparent youthfulness and vitality of these persons who performed their tasks in Japan forty-five years ago. Some of them have less gray hair than I; the "voice from Yamanashi" cracks less than mine. Their vigor might be attributed to the zest for life and the strong sense of values that energized their work in the Occupation. Or, might their sustained spark be due to the health-giving properties of K-rations and postwar pleasure quarters?

THE GRASSROOTS AND HISTORY

Activity at the grassroots level is of utmost importance in any military occupation. In the case of postwar Germany, thorough de-Nazification could be achieved only by the conduct of governmental functions at all levels--from municipalities up to central government--by the occupying forces. This required that a very intensive Occupation structure be established at the grassroots level.

Another relevant historical case--more ambitious than any on our lifetime, took place in the 13th and 14th centuries. This is the Mongol rule in China. There are some remarkable comparative features. In the Mongol horde we see a foreign conqueror, representing an alien culture, entering and occupying and seeking to remake an entity as large and culturally established as China. The Mongolian khans faced the need to carry out demilitarization and pacification programs and to administer government at the local level. The Mongols had to do this with a relatively small number of Occupation personnel relative to the large population of China. Mongol officials used their native Mongolian as the language of administration in China. The development of an interpreter corps was an extremely important feature of the Mongol administration. (I will leave to your imagination any comparison between Genghis Khan and General MacArthur!) In her recent and highly acclaimed study of Mongol rule in China,[1] Elizabeth Endicott-West focuses on the office of *ta-lu-hua-ch'ih*, which was the local level administrator. Initially, all the *ta-lu-hua-ch'ih* were Mongols and, therefore, foreigners. According to Dr. Endicott-West, the key to the success or failure of Mongol cultural penetration and hegemony in China was the activity of this lower level, grassroots Mongol official. The historical record of military occupations establishes beyond question the key role of grassroots-level personnel.

Our present probe of the grassroots in the Allied Occupation of Japan is also in line with new currents of social history. Recent historical enterprise highlights the importance of what happens in "lowly" places--be it the village, the work place, the kitchen, or the nursery. The new social history stresses the influence of lower echelons of institutions. The stuff of history is at the bottom, says this new history. The top, which we used to think was in charge, responds to the bottom. Decision makers receive, consciously or unconsciously, pulses emanating from below. In turn, the effectiveness of policy articulated at the top is judged by how it is ingested and applied at the local level. In short, in the new social history the grassroots is the generator of human experience and the final court in which history is judged.

We are not here to claim that what happened in GHQ or SCAP or in Washington was without consequence. But we certainly are partaking in the new social history in the claim enunciated here at the Eighth Symposium that the grassroots needs new attention and deserves more emphasis than it has received in the past.

WHAT HAVE WE LEARNED?

As we have probed the grassroots of the Occupation we have confronted some of the distinct problems in observing, analyzing, and evaluating the grassroots of any phenomenon. The evidence with which one works in gathering information is selective. It is anecdotal, and often self-congratulatory. The record of the grassroots is often not a written record--at least not in published form. Survey data, which might tell us whether the experience of one Occupationnaire was the common experience of many, is nonexistent. And those Japanese who were the object of policies and activities at the grassroots level have not spoken out as audibly or written as voluminously as those who were the direct recipients of directives from the top. Moreover, apprehension of the grassroots phenomenon is impeded by the prejudice that history is moved by laws, by top-level policies and political decisions, and by high-profile leaders. So, as Professor Sodei stressed in his keynote address, the enterprise of grassroots historiography encounters many obstacles from the start.

Then there is that problem, of which Carmen Johnson reminded us, of the varied perceptions of the elephant. At the grassroots level, it is very difficult to get a comprehensive picture of the elephant. For some Japanese as individuals, the Occupation was all about new roles for women and new definitions of family. Accordingly, for Occupationnaires who were involved with *fujinkai* [women's associations], women's emancipation was indeed the stuff of the Occupation. For other Japanese who spoke at the symposium the stuff of the Occupation was the communicating of the Christian Gospel. Indeed, it is a fact that in 1945 there were deep hurts and needs in the Japanese psyche, some of which were religious in nature. Overt evangelistic activities by Occupation soldiers helped meet real needs in the hearts of some Japanese. And for those Japanese, the audacity of those GIs who passed out New Testaments and tracts and preached on street corners through student interpreters was the most important grassroots contribution of the Occupation.

For other Japanese, Occupationnaires are remembered as exemplars of character. We were treated to an anecdote about Yamashita Ganji, a Japanese official whose impression of the non-retaliatory personal character of an Occupationnaire helped mold his enduring friendship toward America. (Such positive imprints perhaps counterbalance the recently reported bitter recollections of Prime Minister Miyazawa Kiichi.) On the other hand, the negative image of some arbitrary, despotic "Benjo-min" Austin dominates the perception of the Occupation for other Japanese.

So, at the grassroots level it is impossible to get a comprehensive view of something so multi-faceted as the Occupation. The elephant is never defined, and some minor appendage is likely to be misconstrued as *the* Occupation.

On the positive side, grassroots analysis puts us in touch with the real sentiments felt by the occupiers in their daily chores. Former language officer Grant Goodman spoke of the Japanese in his classes in 1946 as "my flock," "my students,"--reminding me of a dean I once knew who always referred to the professors in his college as "my faculty." Recalling his crusade mentality of the time, Goodman asserts, "If the Japanese were to be saved from the terrible depredations of totalitarianism, surely SCAP and I could do the job." This sense of personal mission is a significant key to the Occupation. Its very arrogance in large part accounts for success at the grassroots. The Japanese, as all humankind, were deeply impressed with convictions so deeply embraced that they seemed to be personified by the propagators. The War Department, the State Department, and SCAP possessed a parallel sense of mission. But the sense of personal mission at the grassroots level in Japan is distinct in its impact. At the grassroots, personality was transparent. Personality and ideology were conjoined.

We have learned of the fear of Japanese violence which Occupationnaires felt on their arrival in Japan in 1945. We see that in the process of repatriating millions of Japanese soldiers and civilians to their homeland there was real unrest and that Occupation personnel feared for their physical safety into 1947. From Ed Neville and Robert Christopher we hear these fears, but at the same time we see how experience taught them this apprehension was often unfounded. Mark Orr was speaking for grassroots Occupationnaires when he reminded the audience of the 1980 symposium, "Remember that in the first small group that went into Japan, everyone had on a uniform. Everyone had been involved in some way in the war that was just over."[2]

Through grassroots analysis we obtain a graphic picture of the Japanese environment of physical deprivation in the fall of 1945. Robert Walker, an educational specialist in Shizuoka Prefecture in 1945 and 1946, told the same 1980 symposium, "I never saw a child with a free nose during the winter I was in Japan."[3] Ed Neville now reminds us of the stench of Sasebo.

From grassroots analysis we acquire a broader understanding of fraternization. Thank you, Helen Hosp Seamans, for telling of the exchange of recipes and jokes and of the sharing of laughter.

The grassroots window gives a realistic view of how the Occupation functioned at the lower level. At the local level Occupationnaires were obliged to perform a variety of roles even though formal assignments were more specific. Grassroots personnel not only gave orders and monitored compliance with policies originating in Washington and Tokyo, but also served as advocates of the interests of Japanese locales. Many instances have been cited where Japanese would go around their officials and appeal directly to military government teams. In creating manuals in the field for *fujinkai* or for *seinindan* [youth associations], grassroots military government officials were in effect creating policy in the field. They had latitude in the implementation of directives because of light supervision.

The grassroots perspective also reveals some of the foibles of the Occupation. There was disharmony between the many layers of Allied administration. Again, quoting Robert Walker, "Since I was 'in the field', . . . I assumed, with everybody else in the field, that everything that came down from Tokyo--from SCAP, from CIE--was wrong. . . . I was right only about half the time."[4]

Walker goes on to talk about his role in teacher screening, a topic of Professor Yamamoto's paper. I found this quotation very suggestive of the misgivings held by local-level Occupationnaires as they applied SCAP policy.

> From the top we had quotas coming down requiring us to expel from teaching anybody who showed super-patriotic or hyper-nationalistic tendencies. . . . I remember the gloomy room in which the hearings were held. I remember that the people screened out were given no retirement benefits. I remember that my office was crowded with informers, nasty little people who wanted to vent their grievances on those who were their betters. I always thought we were perhaps screening out the best people in the Japanese education system. . . .[5]

OCCUPATIONNAIRES LOOK BACK AT THEMSELVES

When grassroots Occupationnaires speak of their accomplishments, I am impressed that, generally, they do not proffer grandiose estimates of what they did. As one former school inspector recorded in a published proceedings,

> We didn't do anything except waste a half a day for these people, but it showed them that we were interested and we asked questions about their welfare. . . . I had the opportunity to be offered the central seat at the table and the opportunity to decline and to make sure the principal sat there; and the opportunity to do some things to promote women to attention, . . .[6]

186

Rather than gloating over striking achievements, grassroots Occupationnaires generally speak in terms of opening new doors or displaying alternative models; raising questions; giving vent to long-suppressed doubts, resentments and aspirations; initiating or accelerating a process of incremental and gradual, long-term change.

Much has been said in the conference about the attempt by Occupation personnel to inculcate American values in Japan. One feature of the malaise of the 1980s and 1990s is the inability to assert anything non-material with finality. Value judgments which posit one system superior to another are viewed as dogmatic and intolerant. Well, as we all know, Occupationnaires in Japan made and applied value judgments with gleeful abandon. Perhaps they were the last of their breed. It would have been impossible for this country to undertake such a mission of social and cultural reform in any war subsequent to the Pacific War--be it Korea, Granada, Panama, or the Persian Gulf. Think how ill-equipped and unmotivated most Americans today would be to carry out such a democratizing mission. Consider the young people you know in their late teens and early twenties--the age of the grassroots Occupationnaires. Can you imagine them in the role of teaching democracy in some non-Western setting? Grant Goodman used the term "naivete", and I think it's appropriate. The perception of democracy of American military and civilian personnel at the grassroots level was naive, ethnocentric, and dogmatic. American models and institutions, be it Protestant Christianity, the 6-3-3-4 system, or co-education, were perceived as media for the inculcation of democracy. Japanese society was "feudal." One has to exaggerate to make a point, and the Occupationnaires' message of democracy was communicated in unmistakable terms.

In view of this dogmatism, it is remarkable that values transferred as well as they did. It is not surprising that those elements of Japanese society out of power were the most receptive. By this I mean teachers, women, tenant farmers, wage laborers, students. They were the greatest beneficiaries of reform. But those in power, be they school principals, Monbusho [Education Ministry] officials, bureaucrats like Miyazawa, gang leaders, land owners--they bristled in the face of Occupationnaire audacity and embraced the GHQ--"Go Home Quickly" view of the Occupation.

THE UNFINISHED TASK

A multitude of grassroots topics remain to be mined by students of the Occupation of Japan. Let me list a few of the items that need further research:

- ♦ Language interpreters--both Japanese and foreign--at the local level.

- ♦ The Japanese at the local level--school principals, election officials, regional and local newspaper editors, etc.--who encountered local military government teams and were subjected to SCAP orders.

- ♦ The Japanese who served on the staffs of prefectural Occupation units.

- ♦ Fraternization, broadly construed.

- ♦ Relief activities--both official and non-official--carried out by Occupationnaires.

- ♦ The transfer of popular culture. Grassroots Occupationnaires were the conveyors of music, dance, dress, dating practices, sports, and recipes.

- ♦ The role of American Nisei in the Occupation, including their treatment by Caucasian Allied GIs.

While foreign scholars can contribute in this research, the task of probing the

Japanese context can be most effectively carried out by Japanese students of the Occupation. There is still time--but not much time--for interview research.

TWO OCCUPATIONS?

Could we say, on the basis of this symposium, that there were two Occupations, one Occupation of GHQ and another at the grassroots level? To pursue this issue, we could raise a series of questions: What were the lines of command and feedback between Tokyo and the prefectures? How effective and binding was the communication of policies from GHQ? What measures were taken to insure compliance with central directives? Was situational deviation encouraged?

The scenario of a monolithic Occupation would have common goals at the top and the bottom. Allied governments would decide goals and tactics and issue decrees through SCAP, which decrees would be followed by the grassroots. GHQ would assist the grassroots in implementing policies. Reports would flow upward from the local level, to be read and analyzed. Such reports would be taken seriously in the process of fine-tuning the Occupation agenda.

A contrasting scenario would be a bifurcated Occupation. While goals would be shared initially, they would diverge as the months passed. GHQ would become preoccupied with the anti-leftist campaign and economic development while the grassroots would go on with democratization. GHQ would collect but ignore reports from below. Tokyo would not monitor activities at the local level and let the grassroots go its own way.

Undoubtedly, the truth lies somewhere in between these two scenarios. There were two distinct, yet intertwined, Occupations. The distinctiveness was a function of the differing environments of Tokyo versus the prefectures, of theory and policy versus people's everyday lives. At least initially there was a common ideology, but this unity deteriorated as the Occupation progressed. The grassroots was formally charged with implementing policies forged above; in reality, the grassroots bent those directives and created policy in the field.

THE LEGACY OF THE MacARTHUR SYMPOSIA

The MacArthur Memorial symposia over their course of fifteen years have played a major role in creating the historical record of the Allied Occupation of Japan. With the MacArthur Memorial as a gathering place, they have fostered an international community for the study of postwar policy toward Japan and life in Japan under the Occupation. From their inception, the MacArthur symposia have broadly defined the field of Occupation studies. Peruse the seven published *Proceedings*, and you will find papers on economics, fisheries, trade, education, welfare , theater, radio, cinema--an almost exhaustive variety of approaches to the Occupation experience. Indeed, the study of the Occupation cannot be divorced from the study of early postwar Japan in all its facets. All the context must be mined; all aspects of its impact explored. More than any other scholarly enterprise, the MacArthur symposia have led the way in enlarging the concept of Occupation studies.

The symposia have been a stimulus for individual and collective recollection, for the writing of memoirs, and for critique of scholarship. They have served to encourage the utilization of documentary collections at the MacArthur Memorial, the University of Maryland, the National Archives, and the National Diet Library. The biennial meetings have brought together Japanese and North American scholars, as well as Occupationnaires and scholars from Allied nations in Europe and Australia. Throughout, there was freedom to praise and criticize any aspect of the Occupation and its leadership. While the Memorial is--as it should be--a shrine to General Douglas MacArthur, the symposia have not been rituals of adulation. After each symposium, the printed *Proceedings* have been placed, without charge, in some 100 scholarly libraries in North America, Japan, and the United Kingdom. Published locally in softcover, these compilations of memoir and scholarship are affordable--a fact which underscores the grassroots nature of the symposia.

Our spirits would be much the poorer were it not for the times of laughter which have enlivened our discussions of the Occupation. Recall Dick Nanto's recollection of his teamwork with Gordon Berger and John Dower in Japan, when the three were tagged by Japanese colleagues as *"Nanto baka dawa"*! Who can forget Bob Booth's depiction of an avant-garde kissing scene in an early postwar movie: "Everything came but the battleships!" And now, from the Eighth Symposium, we have Benjo-min Austin and--in the context of talk of fraternization--reference to the "seminal" effects of the Occupation. The good humor of the symposia keeps us aware that the Occupation is a story of real life and real people.

The unique interface of the Occupationnaire actors of history and scholars of history has been the key to sustained interest in this series. Tom Rimer expressed it beautifully when he dubbed a symposium "a healthy mixture of reality and scholarship." In no other ongoing study of the Occupation has this mix been so successfully implemented.

Many deserve credit for envisioning and carrying out the MacArthur symposia: the supporting institutions and the foundations that contributed funds, the directors and staff of the MacArthur Memorial, editors of the *Proceedings*, and--most of all--the Occupationnaires and scholars who gave of themselves meeting after meeting.

Occupation scholarship, in part stimulated by this series, will go on. With the passage of time we are becoming more aware of how indelibly the critical postwar experience colored life in Japan for the rest of the twentieth century. Private papers and unpublished memoirs--including those of grassroots participants in the Occupation--need to be made accessible through deposit in the Archives of the Memorial and other repositories. Someday--let us hope before the year 2000--some Japanese or Western scholar will compile a comprehensive history of the Allied Occupation of Japan. Such a writing should give due credit to Occupation activities at the grassroots level. And the written and living record of the MacArthur symposia will be an irreplaceable resource for the creation of this major historical work.

NOTES

1.   Elizabeth Endicott-West, *Mongol Rule in China: Local Administration in the Yuan Dynasty* (Cambridge MA, Harvard University Press, 1989).

2.   Mark T. Orr (former chief of the Education Division of CIE), "Discussion," in Thomas W. Burkman, ed., *The Occupation of Japan: Educational and Social Reform* (Norfolk, MacArthur Memorial, 1982, p. 194.

3.   Robert H. Walker, "Discussion," in Burkman, ed., *The Occupation of Japan: Educational and Social Reform*, p. 235.

4.   Ibid., p. 237.

5.   Ibid., pp. 237-238.

6.   Ibid., p. 238.

SYMPOSIUM ROSTER
THE OCCUPATION OF JAPAN: THE GRASS ROOTS

November 7-8, 1991
(These addresses were valid at time of symposium)

PARTICIPANTS

Thomas W. Burkman
800 Kirkwood Drive
Grand Island NY 14072

Robert C. Christopher*
P.O. Box 842
Old Lyme CT 06371
  *Unable to attend; paper
  read by Chris Szpilman

James A. Cogswell
1347 Talcott Place
Decatur GA 30033

Grant K. Goodman
P.O. Box 968
Lawrence KS 66044

Cornelius K. Iida
Isako R. Iida
588-6 Ouchiyata
Yamaguchi Shi 753-02
Japan

Carmen Johnson
2929 Connecticut Ave., NW
Washington DC 20008

Allen H. Meyer
Suite 1025
111 W Washington Street
Chicago IL 60602

Edwin L. Neville, Jr.
Department of History
Canisius College
2001 Main Street
Buffalo NY 14208-1098

William F. Nimmo
222 - 89th Street
Virginia Beach VA 23451

Helen Hosp Seamans
Apartment 1111
90 Edgewater Drive
Coral Gables FL 33133

Rinjiro Sodei
6 Ichigaya-daimachi
Shinjuku-ku
Tokyo 162
Japan

Robert B. Textor
3435 NW Luray Terrace
Portland OR 97210

Jacob Van Staaveren
7115 Burtonwood Drive
Alexandria VA 22307

Reiko Yamamoto
937 Imajukuhigashi-cho
Asahi-ku, Yokohama 241
Japan

ATTENDEES

Yoshinobu Araki
Political Science &
  Economics
Matsusaka University
1846 Kubo-cho
Matsusaka-shi, Mie-ken 515
Japan

John E. Arthur, Jr.
8 Club Terrace
Newport News VA 23606

Mrs. John E. Arthur

Peter Bates
12 Lindisfarne Road
Wimbledon
London SW20 ONW
England

Mrs. Peter Bates

Robert Paul Carlson
Maine Township High
  School East
Dempster and Potter Roads
Park Ridge IL 60068

Chia Ting Chen
U.S. Department of Labor
Room N-3718
200 Constitution Ave., NW
Washington DC 20210

Mrs. James A. Cogswell

Edwin D. Dodd
One Seagate
Toledo OH 43666

Mrs. Edwin D. Dodd

Sakae Edamatsu
Apartment 308
1301 S Scott Street
Arlington VA 22204

W. Soren Egekvist
President
Sorenco, Inc.
5318 Malibu Drive
Minneapolis MN 55436

Joseph Frankoski
838 Chatsworth Drive
Newport News VA 23601

Reginal J. Garrick
Apartment 3
128 Georgetown Road
Charlottesville VA 22901

Kenichi Hoshi
Apartment 301
1101 S Quincy Street
Arlington VA 22204

Mieko Ishibashi
209 Carlisle Way
Norfolk VA 23505

Masashi Izumi
Research Center for
  Postwar Educational
  History of Japan
Meisei University
2-1-1 Hodokubo, Hino-shi
Tokyo 191
Japan

Atsushi Kajiura
23812 Leonardtown
College Park MD 20742

Kanji Katsuoka
Research Center for
  Postwar Educational
  History of Japan
Meisei University
2-1-1 Hodokubo, Hino-shi
Tokyo 191
Japan

James A. Kokoris
2137 N Home Avenue
Park Ridge IL 60068

Masako Kubota
1939 Dai, Kamakura-shi
Kanagawa Prefecture 247
Japan

Ryo Kurosawa
1482-B-206
Higashinakano
Hachioji-shi
Tokyo 192-03
Japan

Betty B. Lanham
2529 Willard Drive
Charlottesville VA 22903

Lewis A. Martin, Jr.
600 Knoll Ridge Drive
Charlottesville VA 22903

Theodore H. McNelly
14800 Cobblestone Drive
Silver Spring MD 20905

Myra M. McNelly

Crawford Millen
4928 Atterbury Street
Norfolk VA   23513

Ann Millen

Junji Miura
Kyoda News Service
400 National Press Building
Washington DC   20045

Bernard L. Muehlbauer
17 Mill Creek Terrace
Hampton VA   23663

Rose Muehlbauer

Yurio Mukai
4210-A Parker Avenue
Norfolk VA   23508

Kaeko Nagasawa
1936 Dai, Kamakura-shi
Kanagawa Prefecture 247
Japan

Mrs. Edwin L. Neville, Jr.

Mark T. Orr
2807 Samara Drive
Tampa FL   33618

Kay Orr

Audrey M. Page
Apartment 1017
90 Edgewater Drive
Coral Gables FL   33133

Frank J. Sackton
Professor of Public Affairs
Arizona State University
Tempe AZ   85287-0603

Chitose Sato
Apartment A
209 Anderson Street
Durham NC   27705

Walker N. Stockburger
7736 Leafwood Drive
Norfolk VA   23518

Fumie Tateoka
Apartment 1215
2311 Pimmit Drive
Falls Church VA   22043-2827

Kazuo Ueyama
Apartment 808
9308 Cherry Hill Road
College Park MD   20740

Constantine N. Vaporis
Department of History
Baltimore County Campus
University of Maryland
Baltimore MD   21228-5398

Yoshiko Yoshimura
Apartment 1215
2311 Pimmit Drive
Falls Church VA   22043-2827

PARTICIPATION INDEX